THE *Seer* OF PALMYRA

REFLECTIONS OF THE FIRST VISION

THE *Seer* OF PALMYRA

REFLECTIONS OF THE FIRST VISION

STEVEN A. WILDEN

CFI
An imprint of Cedar Fort, Inc.
Springville, Utah

This is not an official publication of The Church of Jesus Christ of Latter-day Saints. The opinions and views expressed herein belong solely to the author and do not necessarily represent the opinions or views of Cedar Fort, Inc. Permission for the use of sources, graphics, and photos is also solely the responsibility of the author.

ISBN: 978-1-4621-4431-0

Published by CFI, an imprint of Cedar Fort, Inc.
2373 W. 700 S., Suite 100, Springville, UT 84663
Distributed by Cedar Fort, Inc., www.cedarfort.com

Library of Congress Control Number: 2022949281

Cover design by Courtney Proby

Printed in the United States of America

10 9 8 7 6 5 4 3 2 1

Printed on acid-free paper

For Evelyne

"Blessed are the pure in heart: for they shall see God."

Jesus Christ, from the Sermon on the Mount,
the Holy Bible, Matthew 5:8

"For Joseph [who was sold into Egypt] truly testified, saying: A seer shall the Lord my God raise up, who shall be a choice seer unto the fruit of my loins."

Lehi, from the Book of Mormon, 2 Nephi 3:6

1. "The First Vision" painting by Julie Rogers, 2020. Used with permission.

Contents

Illustrations

Joseph Seer of Latter Day

Listen to the angel's trumpet,
Sounding over every land.
Bringing tidings of Jehovah,
Light and truth restored to man.

Heaven opens to her Prophet,
Joseph Seer of Latter Day,
Born to bring us God's own Gospel,
Lost, yet now restored to stay.

Ancient Joseph, son of Jacob,
Truly saw this coming morn.
When the promise he was given,
Through his loins, a seer was born.

Son of Joseph and of Judah,
Of New England's fairest blood.
"Joseph Smith," his father's namesake,
All the earth this name will flood.

Born in Vermont's woodland verdure,
At sweet Sharon's cabin dale.
Apt to read the sacred scriptures,
One to pray and pierce the veil.

Hear my plea, O Lord, for wisdom,
"Which of all the sects are right?"
Joseph saw the heavens parted,
In the grove he saw the light.

In the light two Men descended,
God the Father and the Son.
To the boy, a declaration,
Truth the vict'ry now has won.

Joseph learned the ancient mystery,
That the Gods have flesh and bone,
He was told the sects corrupted,
Precious truths the saints had known,

Joseph hearkened to God's message,
He now brings a brighter day,
In the darkness, light was planted,
Now mankind may find the way,

This began the dispensation,
To which modern saints embrace.
He was called like unto Moses,
For he saw God face to face. . . .

Foreword

During the past three-hundred-plus years, or from the period known as the Age of Reason, or the Enlightenment, to the present day, the belief that God is actively involved in the lives of His children on earth, in our daily walks, in our families, communities, and nations, has diminished greatly. The idea going back to the creation and placement of Adam and Eve into the Garden of Eden, that living prophets of God actually saw and spoke with Deity, such as Adam, Enoch, Noah, and Abraham, and many others after them, and received divine revelations, performed miracles and opened the windows of heaven to those who would listen to God's voice through them, was swallowed up in the new wisdom and science that developed in the Age of Reason and during the centuries that followed.

The loss of spiritual gifts and signs from heaven coupled with the rise of state-run churches during the Medieval Ages and Reformation period did little to correct the problem for the millions who lived during those times. Those who believed in God and Jesus Christ during these times sought after the gifts of God, but struggled to find them in their churches. Pilgrims and Separatists sought freedom and a new world to practice their faith without persecutions from kings and prelates. The ancient idea of prophets of God who saw visions and performed miracles had all but disappeared from among them. This was the prevailing culture and practice of religion during the life of the young Seer of Palmyra.

Among Christians in the "burned over district" of upstate New York, there rose up a young man named Joseph Smith Jr. (1805–1844) who read the scriptures and believed what his King James Holy Bible said, "If any of you lack wisdom, let him ask of God, that giveth to all men liberally, . . ." (James 1:5). This youth took the ancient apostle's challenge seriously and personally. His life and the lives of millions were changed forever because of the things which God revealed to the young prophet during his tragically shortened, yet divinely inspired life.

How can Joseph Smith's First Vision of 1820 be compared to ancient Biblical epiphanies? How can the story of Joseph Smith's revelation coexist with current religious views of Deity? How can one's personal faith be proven as Galileo proved the earth orbited the sun, or as Newton proved the laws of earthly physics? How can Joseph Smith's vision of the Father and Son be considered true with any degree of assurance?

The Seer of Palmyra, who is the Prophet Joseph Smith, gave the reader the answers to these most important questions in a simple and straight forward way.

Each of us can spend our mortal lives seeking temporary wealth, power, and status, or we can seek eternal truth. We can seek *human knowledge* or *revealed knowledge*. To many the latter seems beyond our reach. Yet, there is a practical and even scientific way to seek and obtain eternal truths. It is the exact same method employed by the young prophet Joseph Smith in 1820 and during the remainder of his life as he restored the ancient truths of the gospel of Jesus Christ. It involves similar efforts that one would apply to any clinical or scientific study, problem, or question. One must study and investigate, develop a hypothesis, conduct an experiment, and follow through until actual results are received.

As in science, so in revelation, a peer may claim to have gotten different results. Usually that's because the two studies and efforts were not identical in their attitude and integrity, or in their assumptions and methodology. The divine truths of God that come by revelation need not be counter to the universal truths of science.

Ultimately, anyone can discover eternal truths regarding God, man, and this earth as easily as one can discover that the earth moves around the sun, which the ancient prophets already knew. *The Seer of Palmyra* brings the message that God our Father and His Son, Jesus

Christ, live and reminds the modern world of the ancient method to discover that truth. The Prophet Joseph Smith witnessed these truths with his own eyes, ears, and feelings, as did his later associates. We, too, by the gifts of the Spirit of God, can see and feel with equal assurance that what God has given to us is true. But we cannot do this without making a similar effort that begins with *faith* (HBKJV Hebrews 11:6; D&C 46:11-26).

Why should seekers of truth and scholars alike read this book entitled *The Seer of Palmyra*?

The Seer of Palmyra will confirm that the Prophet Joseph Smith's first vision of Deity was not only unique among all the revelations of religious history, but of supreme importance to initiate the prophetic mission of the most important religious figure since the birth of Jesus Christ and the establishment of the Early Church in Jerusalem. This book probes the depths of five primary accounts, six contemporary accounts, and fourteen total documents detailing the First Vision and answering important questions about the Godhead and of the Prophet's critics. *The Seer of Palmyra* recounts twenty sacred truths revealed through the Prophet Joseph Smith's First Vision and their relevance to every living soul. This book provides a deep and wide look at the Prophet's First Vision of Deity, his use of the Urim and Thummim and seer stones, and the revelations that followed as he was commanded by the Lord to organize the restored Church of Jesus Christ.

Steven A. Wilden
November 13, 2022

Acknowledgments

WRITING ABOUT THE LIFE AND MISSION OF THE PROPHET JOSEPH Smith is a humbling and marvelous experience. It is humbling as an independent historian and writer trying to keep the standards high, while marvelous to search out the details of such an epochal event as Joseph Smith's First Vision of Deity and its result, the kingdom of God in the latter days. If the story told here aligns with both history and scripture and reflects the spirit and intent of Joseph Smith's own testimony, then the transforming power and eternal importance of Joseph's First Vision may be felt and understood by those willing to study it. Such reflections this book investigates.

The work of nineteenth-century prophets, apostles, and many clerks prepared the early records, journals, and histories that included the First Vision. Joseph Smith Jr., Brigham Young, John Taylor, Wilford Woodruff, Willard Richards, Heber C. Kimball, George A. Smith, and Franklin D. Richards each played key roles in preserving Joseph Smith's First Vision of Deity. Chapter 9 gives the names of many of the clerks who recorded the Prophet Joseph Smith's histories and revelations.

Later, twentieth-century prophets and apostles, including Joseph Fielding Smith Jr. and Bruce R. McConkie, wrote of Joseph Smith's First Vision. Elder B. H. Roberts edited and The Church of Jesus Christ of Latter-day Saints published the first multi-volume *History Of The Church* between 1902 and 1912. B. H. Roberts later edited *The Comprehensive History of The Church* published in 1930 in six volumes.

Mid-to-late twentieth-century and early twenty-first-century modern scholars rediscovered, edited, and, with the help of donors and the Church, published the canonized and non-canonized first-hand and contemporary accounts of the First Vision from Joseph Smith's journals, histories, letters and early Church periodicals. Others wrote about why Joseph Smith's many revelations and use of seer stones should be expected from a true prophet. These scholars among others included Paul R. Cheesman,[1] Dean C. Jesse, Richard Lloyd Anderson, Milton V. Bachman[2], James B. Allen[3], Richard L. Bushman, Donna Hill, Marvin S. Hill, Susan Easton Black, John Welch, Richard E. Turley Jr., Eric A. Eliason, Steven C. Harper, D. Michael Quinn, Larry C. Lefgren, Ronald K. Esplin, Michael H. McKay, and Nicholas J. Frederick.[4]

Matthew B. Brown's well-researched *A Pillar of Light* (2009), Robert L. Millet's doctrinal teachings in *I Saw A Pillar of Light* (2020), and the commemorative papers delivered at the Huntington Library conference and later published in a special issue of *BYU Studies Quarterly* in 2020 (59:2), were recognized and read after this book was written and submitted to the publisher.

For what began in 1965 with the work of these and other modern scholars, I am thankful. Without their research efforts during the past fifty-five years, this book would have far fewer primary and secondary sources to draw upon.

I wish to thank my long-time best friend, physician, and Book of Mormon scholar, Dr. Mark E. Mitchell, who first introduced me to the life of the Prophet Joseph Smith, his First Vision, The Book of Mormon, and The Church of Jesus Christ of Latter-day Saints. Later, Mark would baptize me a member of the Church in 1973. Mark gave encouragement while I worked on this project and also made me aware of one of the rarely remembered accounts of Joseph's First Vision of Deity.

The person most responsible for getting me started on this project, I wish to thank my long-time friend, Scott S. Mitchell, a former deputy district attorney in Clark County, Nevada and a former bishop. My promise to Scott to write an essay about the First Vision during our long correspondence of nearly two-hundred church related letters during 2015–2017 led to this much expanded work. While Scott and

I have very different views of Joseph Smith's First Vision, I am grateful to him for the challenges he presented which led to the research and writing of this book.

Sincere appreciation goes to Rob Gorman, a mechanical engineer, former bishop, and former counselor in the Silverdale, Washington Stake Presidency who taught me, in spite of my reluctance at first, the principle that we have no record of God the Father personally or bodily visiting the earth since appearing with His Son Jesus Christ to Adam and Eve in the Garden of Eden, until the First Vision of Joseph Smith in 1820 (DofS 1:27). This concept will be repeated several times throughout the book.

I wish to express deep appreciation to my dear wife Evelyne M. Wilden to whom this book is dedicated for her constant support throughout this project without which it could not have been finished. I wish to give special thanks to thank Dr. Mark E. Mitchell, MD, and his wife, Dr. Catherine E. F. Mitchell, PNP, Dr. John R. Fry, DDS, a former bishop, and to James M. Green, PT, a former bishop, his mother, Norma Green, and to my wife Evelyne M. Wilden for their willingness to review the manuscript and for their comments and encouragement. I'm very grateful to Cedar Fort Publishing who were willing to take a second look at the manuscript after significant condensing work was completed on the original "Limited First Edition."

Introduction

It is very appropriate that in remembering the 200th year since Joseph Smith's First Vision, or the year 2020, that a literary celebration take place. *The Joseph Smith Papers* alone would satisfy that need in every respect were it not requiring one to read twenty-four thus far published volumes of nineteenth-century religious text with twenty-first-century scholarly commentary. At least three or four volumes of that set of books cover the First Vision accounts. It seems expedient that an easy to read, while fully documented, single volume work, with interpretive reflections of Joseph's youth and First Vision, his later major revelations, and development as the first latter-day prophet and seer, be part of the literary outpouring of this bi-centennial year and beyond.

These spiritual, historical, and doctrinal reflections of Joseph's early life touch upon his family dynamics and his becoming a "seer" in a scriptural sense both Biblically and in Book of Mormon terms, including Joseph's use of seer stones and the Urim and Thummim. This writing will identify each of the major aspects of Joseph's first vision of Deity, relying heavily but not only upon Joseph's canonized account found in The Pearl of Great Price (PofGP, JS-H 1:1–26). Other accounts found in *The Joseph Smith Papers* in his histories, including Joseph Smith's own and contemporary accounts, are each revisited. Discovering the significance and authenticity of the First Vision will be explored from different angles throughout the book.

An early apostle and the Fourth President of the Church, Wilford Woodruff (1807–1898) gives us perhaps the greatest reason why we should learn more about Joseph Smith's First Vision:

> I have never read anywhere, that I know of, of the same power manifested in any dispensation to the children of men, which was manifested to the Prophet of God in the organization of this Church, when the Father and the Son both appeared to the Prophet Joseph in answer to his prayer . . . This was an important revelation, which has never been manifested in the same manner in any dispensation of the world, that God has given concerning His work. So in its organization, the Prophet of God was administered to by the angels of heaven. They were his teachers, they were his instructors, and all that he did, and all that he performed from the commencement, from that day to the day of his martyrdom, was by the revelation of Jesus Christ. (MS 52:258)

It will be discovered by the reader, that what has been generally assumed by the critics of Joseph Smith in relation to their antagonistic historical coverage of his First Vision, or that Joseph imagined or invented his First Vision, that such criticism does not align well with actual history and common sense as pointed out by faithful and documentary scholarship. Until the 1970s, the primary records of Joseph Smith's First Vision, his journals, histories, and letters were not even consulted by most of Joseph's critics, due to availability in part, but mostly due to partisanship. Once these original records became available, the antagonists were forced to use these primary accounts which sometimes differed. After that they tried to make a more scholarly attack upon Joseph's First Vision by comparing them together and pointing out the differences. Critics used local newspaper and Church records to "prove" what did or did not happen in early nineteenth-century Palmyra.

A highly regarded Mormon Historian and noted biographer of Joseph Smith, Professor Richard Lyman Bushman, in his 2001 article in *Brigham Young University Studies* entitled, "A Joseph Smith for the Twenty-First Century," gives us his personal summation of where Joseph Smith fit into the world of religion, rationality and revelation:

> To me, that is Joseph Smith's significance for our time. He stood on the contested ground where the Enlightenment and Christianity confronted one another and his life posed the question, Do you believe God speaks? Joseph was swept aside, of course, in the rush of ensuing intellectual battles and was disregarded by the champions of both great systems, but his mission was to hold out for the reality of divine revelation and establish one small outpost where that principle survived. Joseph's revelatory principle is not a single revelation serving for all time, as the Christians of his day believed regarding the incarnation of Christ, nor a mild sort of inspiration seeping into the minds of all good people, but specific ongoing directions from God to his people. At a time when the origins of Christianity were under assault by the forces of Enlightenment rationality, Joseph Smith returned modern Christianity to its origins in revelation...
>
> . . . Is it possible that Biblical revelation could be renewed? Could the enlightenment have shut up the heavens through its disbelief? Must we foreclose the very possibility of divine communication? Those questions raised by this "modern" prophet, may seem worth pondering by at least a few.[5]

As Professor Bushman alludes, the Age of Enlightenment by Joseph Smith's day had already begun, having started its dismantling of Christianity. By the time Joseph had received his first vision of Deity in 1820, the two movements, Christianity and Rationality had long since agreed to forego new revelation from God as a viable principle for obtaining truth.

The sum total of the literary opposition to Joseph Smith can be best understood when approached with the understanding that this latter-day prophet stood alone in his day in the face of a condemning nineteenth-century Christianity which opposed him solely because he said that God had spoken to him. Critics of Joseph Smith, and of his First Vision in particular, have most often approached him in accordance with their own predetermined beliefs, rather than meeting Joseph on his own ground, the ground of revelation, the same rock that ancient prophets of Biblical Christianity once stood upon.

In this light, it is hoped that those who will read about the First Vision and of Joseph's other major revelations will attempt to meet Joseph Smith on his own terms, as a true prophet and seer. Those who allow this possible outcome, will find a factual reality in history, a spiritual basis from the Holy Ghost, and a practical method through prayer to confirm Joseph's testimony of the First Vision and the many other revelations he received during his shortened life (PofGP, JS-H 1:1–26; BofM, Moroni 10:3–5).

Chapter 1

A Prophet and a Seer for the World

WAS JOSEPH SMITH THE FIRST MAN TO TESTIFY THAT HE HAD SEEN God the Father and Jesus Christ in a heavenly vision? God spoke to Adam and Eve in the Garden of Eden during the sixth day of creation (HBKJV, Genesis 1:26–31). Later on, the Old and New Testaments give us their testimony that prophets have seen the Lord, as Moses saw the Son of God or Jehovah "face to face" (HBKJV, Exodus 33:11). Stephen saw both the Father and the Son before his martyrdom when he declared, "I see the heavens opened, and the Son of man standing on the right hand of God" (HBKJV, Acts 7:56). There was no conversation in that account between Stephen and Deity. We have no record since the fall of Adam and Eve in the Garden of Eden of any mortal man experiencing such a detailed *visitation and communication* from Deity, by both the Father and the Son, as Joseph Smith's First Vision in 1820 (DofS 1:27).

Many prophets since Adam including Enoch, Noah, Abraham, Moses, and Isaiah have had the heavens opened to them and heard the voice of angels or even Jehovah who is the pre-mortal Jesus Christ, yet they did not have the physical presence of Elohim who is God the Father introducing His Son Jesus Christ to them as did the mortal Joseph Smith (PofGP, Moses 6:53–54; HBKVJ, Genesis 5:24; 6:9–13; 17:1; Exodus 24:9–11; 33:11; Isaiah 6:1).

John the Baptist and the prophet Nephi heard the voice of the Father testify of His Son, but the Father did not show Himself in person on those occasions like he did to Joseph Smith. Why is that? It can only be explained by understanding the greatness of the latter-day prophet's divine mission, a mission that Joseph Smith was called to perform before the foundations of the earth were laid, a mission so important it was only to be eclipsed by the Savior Jesus Christ Himself (HBKVJ, Matthew 3:17; BofM, 2 Nephi 31:15; MDoc, 395–396; D&C 135:3).

The Book of Mormon tells us that several prophets living in ancient America saw the Lord Jesus Christ appear to them in person and in glory from heaven during their lifetimes or ministries. They include the brother of Jared, Nephi, Jacob, Mormon, and Moroni (BofM, Ether 3:13–14; 2 Nephi 11:3; Mormon 1:15; Ether 12:39). There may be others not readily spelled out in the ancient American scripture who saw the Lord.

All believers in the God of the Bible look to the One who is called Jehovah, who declared Himself to be "in the beginning with God" and "the first and the last; I am he that liveth, I am he who was slain; I am your advocate with the Father," "I am he that liveth, and was dead; and, behold, I am alive for evermore," (HBKJV, John 1:1–3; 8:58; Revelation 1:18; D&C 110:3–4). Whenever the Father has a work to do on earth, He sends His Son Jehovah to carry out the plan. He is the same whom we know as Jesus Christ, whom every living soul must eventually recognize, for the apostle has spoken it: "That at the name of Jesus every knee should bow, of things in heaven, and things in earth, and things under the earth; And that every tongue should confess that Jesus Christ is Lord, to the glory of God the Father" (HBKJV, Philippians 2:10–11; PofGP, Moses 1:33).

The Jews, the remnant of the Children of Israel, were and are still less than one percent of the world's population. The Christians in the fourth-century Roman Empire numbered only six million, less than one percent. Considering that thirty percent of the human population of the world today believes in Jesus Christ as the Son of God much progress has been made in Christendom. Yet, dozens of denominations and doctrinal divisions exist among this number. In comparison, in similar numbers to the Jews, only two-tenths of one percent have accepted the restored gospel of Jesus Christ and are members of The Church of Jesus Christ of Latter-day Saints. This means that when "a unity of faith" is concerned, the world overall is generally in a state of disbelief in terms of the fullness of the gospel or what is available to God's children. Some may disagree with this statement, yet bear with the thought.

A passage from the Book of Mormon confirms that this minority would exist in the latter days as far as the *Gentile* saints were concerned, those which make up the Church of Jesus Christ that accept the "fullness of my gospel," as the Lord calls it below. While visiting the Nephites the resurrected Savior Jesus Christ said:

> And thus commandeth the Father that I should say unto you: At that day when the Gentiles shall sin against my gospel, and shall reject the fullness of my gospel, and shall be lifted up in the pride of their hearts above all nations, and above all the people of the whole earth, and shall be filled with all manner of lyings, and of deceits, and of mischiefs, and all manner of hypocrisy, and murders, and priestcrafts, and whoredoms, and of secret abominations; and if they shall do all those things, and shall reject the fullness of my gospel, behold, saith the Father, I will bring the fullness of my gospel from among them.
>
> And then will I remember my covenant which I have made unto my people, O house of Israel, and I will bring my gospel unto them.
>
> And I will show unto thee, O house of Israel, that the Gentiles shall not have power over you; but I will remember my covenant unto you, O house of Israel, and ye shall come unto the knowledge of the fullness of my gospel.
>
> But if the Gentiles will repent and return unto me, saith the Father, behold they shall be numbered among my people, O house of Israel. (BofM, 3 Nephi 16:10–13)

Generally, the Gentiles have neither repented nor accepted the fullness of the gospel of Christ, except for a few, which does not bode well for the Gentiles in the latter days. That also means that only this same few, or a small fraction of the Gentiles, two-tenths of one percent of the world's population, believe in the divine role of the current or living prophet and seer. This does not mean that believers outside The Church of Jesus Christ of Latter-day Saints do not believe in the

Savior, feel the Spirit of the Lord, and receive revelations which are true. It does mean that the fullness of eternal life comes only through the Restored Church and the keys of authority held by prophets of God (HBKJV, Ephesians 2:19–22; 4:11–14).

Christians today recognize ancient prophets such as Noah, Abraham, and Moses. Many accept the guidance of faithful pastors and other trained church leaders. Some may recognize men or women with prophetic or spiritual gifts. At the same time, anyone who can see, hear, and feel must recognize the great divergence and contradictions of the many different denominational faiths which exist in the world today. And almost everyone can see the satanic corruptions and evils, murders and wickedness that presently grip the Gentile nations, cities, and their inhabitants. This reality of contradiction and confusion truly justifies the need of a modern prophet of God to lead the modern Saints, to organize, to authorize, and to direct the work of God in the modern world. Such a prophet today presents revelations of Jesus Christ to The Church of Jesus Christ of Latter-day Saints as Moses to the Mosaic Church of Israel and as Peter to the Early Church in the New Testament.

Just as Moses went up to Mount Sinai to speak with God and receive instructions, so also did Jesus take Peter, James, and John up on the Mount of Transfiguration where they received knowledge and priesthood keys from the former prophets Elias or Elijah and Moses who possessed them in heaven. These three apostles not only received the keys of the kingdom but a promise of eternal life. (HBKJV, Matthew 17:1–9; 2 Peter 1:10, 17–19; MDoc, 109–110, 219–224, 571; TPJS, 158).

These three were the prophetic voice of leadership for the ancient or Early Church of Christ, the Apostle Peter being the chief apostle or president of the Church (HBKJV, Matthew 16:19). They also heard the voice of the Father testify, "This is my beloved Son, in whom I am well pleased; hear ye him" (HBKJV, Matthew 17:5).

These words would be repeated nearly verbatim again by the Father to the young Joseph Smith in a grove of woods in Palmyra, New York about eighteen-hundred years later to initiate the last dispensation of the gospel (PofGP, JS-H 1:17).

If such a prophet like Moses or Peter were to arise today, would the world as a whole accept him? Ninety-nine percent of the people would not. Such was and is the case with Joseph Smith and his successors to the current day. That should be a strong warning to anyone putting their eternal safety in a super-majority of religious opinion. If such representatives of God of the stature of Noah or Abraham, Moses or Peter would arise in our modern age of technology and information enlightenment, they would be pushed aside almost universally in favor of the rationalism of our predetermined and calculated world, where the ends often justify the means. The ancient prophets of the Bible and the Book of Mormon were pushed aside in their own day too, save the power of God, which was manifested at their hands individually, and together among the relatively few saints and converts who listened to them. The pharaohs, emperors, and kings, the presidents, governors, and the people in general rejected the prophets, persecuted them and killed them. They tried to kill Abraham but he was saved by an angel of the Lord, while the Savior Himself and the apostles of Jesus Christ each suffered martyrdom as did Joseph Smith (HBKJV, Matthew 24:9; PofGP, Abraham 1:12–17; D&C 134:4–7).

These ancient prophets, as Joseph Smith in the nineteenth century, had relatively few believers at first, they and the saints who believed their testimony were always being persecuted and were part of a small minority during their entire lives and ministry. Abraham left the wicked city of Ur of the Chaldees, after preaching many years and nearly being killed by Nimrod and the priest of Elkenah, to live in the land of Haran. Jehovah visited Abraham when Abraham was sixty-two years old and commanded him to leave Haran. So Abraham took his wife Sarai, their kindred, and three hundred men with their families, their tents, and their herds and departed Haran to the land of Canaan, which the Lord or Jehovah promised to give Abraham and his family forever (HBKJV, Genesis 12:1–5; Genesis 14:14; PofGP, Abraham 2:8–15).

Assuming the reader may be open to taking a significant, if not a giant leap of faith, out of the rational melee of human wisdom, and by so doing turn not only to God the Father and to His Son Jesus Christ, but also to *their* way of doing things, and thereby realize *three* supporting principles set forth in the Holy Scriptures in order to achieve their quest of communing with God.

The *first* principle from the scriptures is predominantly important. As in ancient times, so also in this latter-day generation, the Lord has said, "Surely the Lord God will do nothing, but he revealeth his secret unto his servants the prophets" (HBKJV, Amos 3:7; D&C 21:1–3). This means that everything that is important to know concerning our purpose on earth comes from God through *the prophets*. These men must be called directly by God and ordained originally by divine or angelic ministrations, or by mortal living prophets or apostles holding the keys of authority, not by earthly orders and authorities. One must be able to trace his authority and ordination history back to Jesus Christ or Jehovah in order for it to be valid (HBKJV, Matthew 17:1–9; John 15:16; Hebrews 5:4; D&C 110).

The *second* principle is, "Where there is no vision, the people perish" (Proverbs 29:18). Here, the wise Prophet-King Solomon tells us that visions or revelations from God are required so that we know by whom, what, and when to do what is the Lord's will, or that which is essential in God's eyes for our own good. The Holy Scriptures provide many such visions and revelations from God. Modern revelations given to living prophets can provide specific guidance for the modern saints in their own day and time. Without divine revelation from heaven to guide both the individual Saint and the body of The Church of Jesus Christ of Latter-day Saints, there can be no "perfecting of the saints," no "unity of the faith," and no "knowledge of the Son of God unto a perfect man" (HBKJV, Ephesians 4:12–13).

The *third* principle is given in that same verse, "but he that keepeth the law, happy is he" (Proverbs 29:18). Obedience to the laws and covenants of God or the revelations, commandments, and ordinances of God is paramount in receiving God's blessings. By so doing we can become perfected in Jesus Christ through the Savior's Atonement and the ordinances of the gospel. The Lord told the Prophet Joseph Smith, "And, if you keep my commandments and endure to the end you shall have eternal life, which gift is the greatest of all the gifts of God" (D&C 14:7).

Naturally, the need for a living prophet, once realized, must be coupled with the scriptural definition which answers the question, "What is a prophet?"

Joseph Smith's grandnephew, Joseph Fielding Smith Jr., the Tenth President of The Church of Jesus Christ of Latter-day Saints, gave an excellent definition of a prophet to the Latter-day Saints in general and specifically to the sisters of the Relief Society organization of the Church in the mid-twentieth century. President Smith wrote:

> A prophet is one who teaches by the voice of inspiration the words of eternal life, and who officiates in the saving ordinances of the gospel. Predicting is only one qualification of a prophet . . . "the testimony of Jesus is the spirit of prophecy" (Revelation 19:10) . . . In other words, every person who is baptized and confirmed should have the spirit of inspiration, and should know that Jesus Christ is the Son of God. Every person should live in harmony with the revealed truth; and in doing that, and receiving the testimony through the Holy Spirit that Jesus lives and is the Son of God, he or she becomes a prophet or prophetess, and is entitled to the guidance of and inspiration from the Holy Ghost, which is the spirit of prophecy. (DofS 1:185)

President Smith also reminded, "Every man that holds the priesthood, and magnifies his calling, is a prophet; and he has a right to the inspiration of the Holy Spirit, so far as he is concerned—but not to receive revelation for the Church. There is only one who is appointed to that office" (DofS 1:185; D&C 43:3–6).

Anciently, before Saul was anointed the first King of Israel, the term "seer" was understood among the Hebrew prophets and priests in these words of Samuel, "Beforetime in Israel, when a man went to inquire of God, thus he spake, Come, and let us go to the seer: for he that is now called a Prophet was beforetime called a Seer" (HBKJV, 1 Samuel 9:9).

A Latter-day Saint scholar, Steven C. Walker wrote, "A 'prophet' is one who speaks for GOD; the office of 'seer' extends that divine endowment to a capacity for envisioning future and past." Modern revelation would add to these two roles the appellation "revelator" because as The Book of Mormon teaches, a "seer is greater than a prophet," because a seer is "a revelator and a prophet also" (BofM, Mosiah 8:15–17; EofM 3:1292–1293).[6]

During the years that followed his First Vision, the words of the Book of First Samuel defining a prophet as "a seer" (HBKJV, 1 Samuel 9:9) must have struck a chord when Joseph Smith and Oliver Cowdery as they translated The Book of Mormon and came upon the passage in 2 Nephi 3:6–7. This passage of scripture speaks of a Latter-day Seer, who was a descendant of ancient Joseph who was sold into Egypt, who would have that same name; and again when they read Mosiah 8:13–18 regarding seers and their ability to translate ancient records and to know of things both past, present, and future by the power of God. Joseph must have understood that he was the "choice seer" referred to by ancient Joseph as quoted by Lehi in the Book of Mormon, and that he too after receiving the Urim and Thummim from the angel Moroni was translating the Nephite record by "the gift and power of God" as ancient seers had done with other sacred records.[7]

The heavenly calling of a "prophet" remained absent in modern history until the year 1820 when God the Father introduced His Son Jesus Christ to the young Joseph Smith Jr. at Palmyra, New York. But it wasn't until seven years later, resurrected beings bestowed upon Joseph Smith and Oliver Cowdery the priesthood authority to act in God's name as "apostles" of the Lord.

Assistant Church Historian Richard E. Turley Jr. wrote the following regarding the meaning of the word "seer" to the young Joseph Smith while the latter was living in early nineteenth-century New England:

> What did seer mean to the young prophet and his contemporaries? Joseph was raised in a family that read the Bible, which mentions seers repeatedly (1 Samuel 9:9). The Bible also mentions people receiving spiritual manifestations by means of physical objects such as rods, a brass serpent on a pole (which became a widespread symbol of the medical profession), and ephod (a part of the priestly clothing that included two precious stones), and the Urim and Thummim[8] (HBKJV, Exodus 4:1–5; Numbers 17:1–10; Hebrews 9:4;

Numbers 21:7–9; John 3:14–15; Exodus 28:12; 1 Samuel 23:9–12; 30:7–8).

Richard Turley explained further about the culture of seers in nineteenth-century New England:

> "Seeing" and "seers" were part of the American and family culture in which Joseph Smith grew up. Steeped in the language of the Bible and a mixture of Anglo-European cultures brought over by immigrants to North America, a significant number of Christian people in the early 19th century believed it was possible for gifted individuals to "see," or receive spiritual manifestations, through material objects such as seer stones.[9]

As has been pointed out, there are few modern thinkers today who would allow for things like manifestations of divine beings from heavenly realms and the use of seer stones, yet honest scholarship shows that such events and objects were considered doctrinal and orthodox anciently in Israel, again during the Early Christian Church and also in the days of the young Prophet Joseph Smith in pioneer New England. Joseph lived in the period of religious history known as the Second Great Awaking, a time of great religious revival and proselyting activity. Within that greater movement Joseph Smith's family lived in what was called The Burned Over District of upstate New York.[10]

The center of that regional religious activity was in Rochester, not far from Palmyra where Joseph lived. To the nineteenth-century New Englander, the Bible in its literal form was the singular most important book on the earth. While prevailing Calvinist and Anglican doctors of religion discouraged modern repetitions of the miracles of Jesus and the manifestations given to his apostles and the early saints, the idea that God worked in mysterious and even supernatural ways was acceptable to the greater population, much more than in later centuries, whether controversial or not. This generation of evangelical Protestants believed they were in some ways contributing to the advent of the great Millennium when Jesus Christ would return and rule on earth for a thousand years.[11]

As he stated in his several accounts of his First Vision, while Joseph Smith contemplated the different religious doctrines between 1818 and 1820, the New England Protestant doctors and minsters of religion held to their rigid view that individuals could not receive visions and revelations from God (PofGP, JS-H 1:21).

After Joseph's great First Vision in 1820, and by 1830 or 1831, the religious excitement gradually began to take on a new face, which would consider that mankind was no longer subject to a limited election to grace, the predominant Calvinist notion—rather that all humanity could change and be saved in the kingdom of God according to their own choices. This change would create an environment conducive to the doctrine of agency that future Saints would teach from the Book of Mormon (BofM, 2 Nephi 2:27–30).

This "agency" doctrine would thrive even under persecutions among nineteenth-century "Mormon" converts, so-named for their belief in the book by that name and their conversion to the Church of Christ that Joseph Smith would later organize under the direction of God (D&C 20:2; 21:2).[12] The opening of the heavens to the young Joseph Smith in 1820 started the rolling forth of that stone spoken of by Daniel the Prophet (HBKJV, Daniel 2:44–45) which would introduce God's truth and authority again through a prophet and seer for the world.

Today there are many tribes of faith, so to speak, each having centuries old cultural followings and national and global political associations. When the Lord comes again to receive and reign over his kingdom on earth, true believers in Christ, those in the world who would believe correct principles and receive correct ordinances, will eventually be united under "one Lord, one faith, one baptism," as Paul described the true faith (HBKJV, Ephesians 4:5). This will include one governing prophet or voice from heaven, for "Surely the Lord God will do nothing, but he revealeth his secret unto his servants the prophets" (HBKJV, Amos 3:7; D&C 21:1–3).

Chapter 2

From Plowboy to Prophet

Before his martyrdom in 1536, the English Biblical scholar, translator, and priest, William Tyndale made a complete translation of the New Testament into early modern English which was published the year of his death. That same year, he began a translation of the Old Testament, which was not completed due to his arrest by the Imperial Church authorities and execution by strangling and burning at Brussels. Translating the Latin or original language scriptures into local vernaculars was a heresy which brought the penalty of death. Nonetheless, Tyndale's works remained; his English Bible was the first of its kind translated from the original Hebrew and Greek language texts. Prior to Tyndale's monumental achievement, while debating a learned man, Tyndale said, "If God spare my life, ere many years I will cause a boy that driveth the plough, shall know more of the scripture than thou dost."[13]

The printing of the Bible in the English language was the spiritual fire of the Separatist and Puritan movements, which eventually led the Mayflower pilgrims to the shores of America at Plymouth, Massachusetts in 1620. The availability of the Holy Scriptures in the common vernacular of the American Pilgrims is of transcendent importance not only in the establishment of the American nation but was an essential requirement for the laying of the foundation of the Restoration of the gospel in its fullness, beginning with the faith of a humble farm boy reading his family's Bible while living in Palmyra, upstate New York in the early 1800s.

It is likely that the world and the Latter-day Saints today know the very least about the first twelve years (1805–1817) of the life of the Prophet Joseph Smith Jr. in comparison with later periods of his life. Other than giving a brief family background, this writing will not cover that first period of the Prophet's life. The next five years, or the Prophet's life from age twelve to seventeen (1818–1822) while living in the Township of Palmyra, is the nucleus of this study; because, it was certainly a transformative period in the Prophet's life and the foundation of a new dispensation of eternal truth in the Lord's plan for this world. This second period in the Prophet's life is then the most important as it includes those events of his struggle with contemporary religion, studying and pondering of the Bible, and his decision to ask of God in a humble prayer of faith leading to his glorious First Vision—from which the resulting knowledge, divine direction through future revelations and persecutions would shape the remainder of his relatively short life.

The life of the latter-day Prophet Joseph Smith Jr. (1805–1844) can be described as unparalleled in religious history since the birth and mission of Jesus Christ, the Son of God (D&C 135:3). Joseph's early life has been remembered in history as that of a humble farm boy or "plowboy" becoming a prophet of God, who "was doomed to the necessity of obtaining a scanty maintenance by his daily labor" (PofGP, JS-H 1:23). As a youth he was sometimes hired as a hand to labor for various enterprising men in the vicinity of Palmyra, New York. There he lived with his father's very much Christian yet generally non-sectarian family. Joseph's humble beginnings, reliable manual labor, and goodly Christian family are important in illuminating the purity of his heart, and the great faith and desire the young Joseph would express to God while seeking to find the true Church of Christ on the earth, if there was one to be found (PofGP, JS-H 1:1–4).

Joseph's mother and three of his siblings for a time attended and later joined the Presbyterian Church (1820–1828), while both Joseph Smith Sr. and Joseph Smith Jr. remained very religious yet unchurched, until 1830 when Joseph was commanded by God to organize anew the Church of Christ (D&C 20:1–2). Joseph Smith Sr. attended one meeting with Lucy to a non-denominational church, and Joseph Smith Jr. attended the Methodist Church briefly (PofGP, JS-H 1:8), yet neither joined any of the churches of their day. The Smith Family had moved to upstate New York to the Village of Palmyra south of the Erie Canal in the early winter or November-December of 1816 from Norwich, Vermont.[14]

While both agrarian labors and financial struggles followed Joseph's father, Joseph Smith Sr. (1771–1840), and grandfather Asael Smith (1744–1830), the historical records show that the Prophet Joseph Smith Jr. and his Smith forbearers descended from the gentleman Robert Smith of Topsfield, Massachusetts (1623–1693). Joseph's mother, Lucy Mack Smith (1775–1856), was a devoted and virtuous daughter, the eighth and youngest child of Solomon Mack (1732–1820) of Lyme, New London County, Connecticut. Solomon was a farmer of considerable property, yet after a series of misfortunes he was reduced to penury, in large part due to the perfidy of his fellow men. Solomon Mack is notable as a patriot, and in later years he became a devout Christian. Solomon enlisted and fought in the French and Indian War and in the American Revolution.[15]

Prior to these first ancestors, Joseph Smith's forbearers have been traced by genealogical research and DNA testing to notable, noble and royal lines of Great Britain in both England and Ireland and linked all the way back to the Biblical Patriarchs and to the father of us all, the first man to live on this earth, Adam.[16]

After Joseph Smith Sr.'s family had arrived in Palmyra in the fall of 1816, the family worked hard and saved their money. During the first year and few months while renting in Palmyra, Joseph Smith Jr.'s older brothers Alvin and Hyrum hired out their labor and in 1818 the Smiths purchased 100 acres of farm land in what later became Manchester Township in 1822.[17] While still part of Palmyra Township, Joseph Smith Sr. built and moved into a log cabin on their land in 1818 where Joseph Smith Jr. lived when he received his First Vision of God the Father and the Son Jesus Christ in 1820, in the nearby grove. This log cabin and farm was also the place where several annual visitations of the angel Moroni took place beginning in Joseph's own room from 1823 to 1827 (PofGP, JS-H 1:29–59; DofS 3:241–242).

Like many ancient prophets before him, Joseph Smith Jr. was born of goodly parents (BofM, 1 Nephi 1:1). In the fertile religious soil of New England's "burned over district" Joseph was able to grow and develop his innate abilities and divine potential to their greatest heights. Joseph Fielding Smith Jr., as an apostle in 1931, summarized the role and place of the great latter-day Prophet Joseph Smith Jr. in the great plan of Jehovah:

> Noah was sent to the world to warn it of the flood. If the people had hearkened they would have escaped. Moses was sent to lead Israel into the promised land, to fulfil the promises made to Abraham. John the Baptist was sent to prepare the way for the coming of Christ. In each instance the call came through the opening of the heavens. Isaiah, Jeremiah and other prophets, were sent to warn Israel and Judah before the scattering and captivity came upon them. Had they given heed a different page of history would have been written. They had their chance to hear; they were warned and had the means of escape which they rejected.
>
> The Lord promised to have the same interest in humanity preceding his second coming.
>
> Joseph Smith was sent to prepare the way for this second coming, by the proclamation of the fullness of the Gospel and the granting to all men the means of escape from iniquity and transgression. (DofS 3:3–4)[18]

Joseph Smith's prophetic life as the "choice seer" spoken of by ancient and modern prophets is marked by his performing "great and marvelous things." The Prophet Joseph Smith has done more for the salvation and eternal life of men on earth than any other prophet other than Jesus Christ, the Son of God. Joseph's life culminated in his martyrdom at the age of thirty-eight along with his brother Hyrum in June of 1844 (BofM, 2 Nephi 3:6; Mormon 8:34; D&C 135:3–4).

Chapter 3

Joseph's Grandfather's, Father's, and Mother's Dreams

As one of Joseph Smith's excellent twentieth-century biographers, Donna Hill stated that Joseph's grandfather Asael Smith and father, Joseph Smith Sr., were of the independent or more congregational view, believing at one point in universal salvation, independent interpretation of the scriptures, and that "truth would be granted to the individual through his own efforts and study of the scriptures" (D. Hill, p.24). While daily reading the scriptures and teaching their children in daily devotions, neither of these patriarchs attended an organized church for reasons similar to their young grandson and son, Joseph Smith Jr. After studying the Bible, both Asael Smith and Joseph Smith Sr. were not sure if any of the churches of their day were true[19] (PofGP, JS-H 1:7). Both Joseph's grandfather and his father, while independent of organized religion, were firm believers in the validity of the holy scriptures, as well as in dreams and the efficacy of other divinely inspired manifestations and miracles.

To those both part of and independent of late eighteenth- and early nineteenth- century Protestant orthodoxy, as Joseph's grandfather Asael Smith was, such ancient-like manifestations were acceptable and even applicable in their own lives. Smith family history shows that both paternal and maternal grandfathers of Joseph Smith had significant heavenly dreams or intuitions in their lives which separated them from those who denied the efficacy of such occurrences. In one such inspiration Joseph's grandfather Asael Smith stated:

> It has been borne in upon my soul that one of my descendants will promulgate a work to revolutionize the world of religious faith.[20]

In a letter written by Asael Smith to his friend Jacob Perkins Towne, the clerk of Topsfield, Vermont on January 14, 1796, Joseph Smith's grandfather wrote of his belief in the imminent fulfillment of Daniel's prophecy of the Restoration of Christ's ancient kingdom. Asael eventually shared this belief with his grandson, the young Joseph. Asael believed that the American Revolution was the first event in the great millennium and the soon-to-come rule of God predicted by ancient prophets.

Asael Smith wrote to his friend Jacob Towne on January 14, 1796 the following:

> He has conducted us through a glorious revolution, and has Brought us into the promised Land of peace & Liberty, and I Believe that he is about to Bring all the world in the Same Beatitude in His own time & way . . . And I Believe that the Stone is now cut out of the mountain, without hands, spoken of by Daniel, and has Smitten the image upon his feet, By which the iron, the Clay, the Brass, the Silver and the gold, (viz all monrical and Ecliesaistical Terony) will be Broken to peaces, and Becom[e] as the Chaff of the Summer Thrashing flore, the wind Shall carry them all away that there Shall be no place found for them . . . [Daniel 2:44–45].[21]

After his vision of 1820, when the Lord said that he would eventually receive the fullness of the gospel, Joseph Smith likely remembered his grandfather's words.

Joseph Smith's biographer, Donna Hill, wrote, "The Smiths were like many people of that day who, according to the contemporary revivalist and philosopher Lorenzo Dow, believed that dreams were inspired by God."[22]

Joseph Smith's father, Joseph Smith Sr., was a man of night visions or dreams. Joseph Sr.'s wife Lucy could recall in detail many years later the seven dreams her husband had between 1811 and 1819. These dreams ended the year before Joseph Smith Jr.'s First Vision of 1820.

Lucy tells us this excitement was noticeable sometime after a dream her husband had in 1819. According to Lucy's record, Joseph Smith Sr. received his last of seven dreams in 1819 about "the man with a peddler's budget [or bag] on his back" who had "called upon [Joseph Smith Sr.] seven times" the last or seventh of which he was going to tell the senior Joseph Smith what he "lacked in order to secure salvation." Joseph Sr. asked the visitor if he would write the important message on paper and the messenger said he would, except when Joseph Sr. got up to get some paper, he awoke in his excitement.[23]

Not just Joseph Smith's father and grandfather had prophetic dreams about their family which would ultimately involve the leading role of their son and grandson, so also did Joseph's mother, Lucy Mack Smith. Before Joseph Smith Jr. was born, Lucy went to a grove of trees near her home in Vermont and prayed about her husband's repudiation of evangelical religion. That night she said she had a dream which she interpreted as a prophecy that Joseph Sr. would later accept the "pure and undefiled Gospel of the Son of God."[24]

Chapter 4

Religious Excitement in "that region of country"

It has been established that the Smith family moved from Norwich via Royalton, Vermont to Palmyra, New York in 1816. Nearly thirty years later, the Prophet Joseph's mother, Lucy Mack Smith, dictated to scribes in her history of the religious excitement which was ongoing in the "surrounding country" shortly after her husband's 1819 dream or "vision" summarized earlier.

Regarding this religious excitement, Mother Smith wrote:

> Shortly after my husband received the forgoing vision, there was a great revival in religion, which extended to all the denominations of Christians in the surrounding country in which we resided. Many of the world's people, becoming concerned about the salvation of their souls, came forward and presented themselves as seekers after religion. Most of them were desirous of uniting with some church but were not decided as to the particular faith which they would adopt. When the numerous meetings were about breaking up, and the candidates and the various leading church members began to consult upon the subject of adopting the candidates into some church or churches, as the case may be, a dispute arose, and there was a great contention among them.[25]

The Prophet wrote in his 1838 history of his First Vision, that there was where he lived a great deal of excitement about religion in "that region of country" and the "whole district of country seemed affected by it" (PofGP, JS-H 1:5). Some historians have ignored or missed these two phrases and assumed all the excitement was in Palmyra or the Township of Manchester where Joseph lived at the time he began to consider his condition before God, the various Christian religions around him and ultimately his theophany.

This great regional religious excitement known to historians as the Second Great Awakening, of which Palmyra was a lesser part, was centered in Rochester, New York. The religious excitement started as early as 1815 according to scholars on the subject and revivals moved from town to town like a circus troop with little need of local newspaper advertising. The growth of the evangelical Protestant churches peaked in 1831 as church membership doubled from the year 1800 to 1835. Dr. Paul E. Johnson, Professor of History at the University of South Carolina, tells us, "The awakening began near the turn of the century in the villages of New England and in isolated Yankee colonies in western New York."[26]

The fact that there was during these years "a great excitement on the subject of religion" by predominately the Methodists, Presbyterians, Episcopalians, Baptists, and other evangelical churches of fewer numbers has been established by all the historians of this period. Church records are minimal or not complete until about 1825 and thereafter, yet all historians do agree that the excitement and growth of Protestant churches from Wayne County to Genesee Counties and beyond along the Erie Canal route of upstate New York, including Palmyra, began to increase significantly by 1815 for the next twenty years.26 Records show that membership increased from a few members to as many as 400 to 1,000 souls in each of the Presbyterian and Methodist churches of Rochester, twenty-three miles northwest of Palmyra, the same churches that Joseph Smith and his family had shown early interest in at Palmyra.[27]

Traveling preachers and start-up churches to which settlers were listening to and joining during those revival years (1816–1825) in Wayne County would have avoided newspaper advertising costs. Most revival activities would likely have been self-promoted with the use of cheaply printed posters or by word of mouth. There were few advertised revivals in the *Palmyra Register* and *Palmyra Herald* weekly newspapers in regard to the "religious excitement" period that Joseph Smith wrote of in his 1838 history.

In a 1964 book by Milton W. Hamilton about early nineteenth-century newspapers, the author stated "the editor's definition of his function included neither the purveying of neighborhood gossip nor the describing of outstanding happenings in the immediate vicinity." D. Michael Quinn asks, after quoting this statement by Hamilton, "Why?" Quinn then gives Hamilton's answer that small-town editors in the early 1800s always assumed that local residents would not "pay for information which they could secure by word of mouth from their neighbors." In other words, the local newspapers were not as interested in local revivals as they were about news and happenings out of town. This practice did not start to change until about 1827.[28]

Latter-day Saint Church Historian Milton V. Backman wrote in 1969 that religious outbreaks occurred in 1819–1820 within a fifty-mile radius of Joseph Smith's home:

> Church records, newspapers, religious journals, and other contemporary sources clearly reveal that great awakenings occurred in more than fifty western New York towns or villages during the Genesee Conference of Methodists of 1819–1820. Primary sources also specify that great multitudes joined the Methodist, Presbyterian, and Calvinist Baptist societies in the region of country where Joseph Smith lived.[29]

During an interview in 2005, the bicentennial of Joseph Smith's birth, Dr. Backman said, "I found that probably there were more revivals and more people joining churches in upstate and western New York in 1819 and 1820 than in any other region of the United States."[30]

Regarding regional growth of the Methodist Conference, Dr. Backman reports, "Methodist membership figures for 1820, indicate that during the year of the First Vision there was an increase of 2,256 members in western New York. This was the largest annual increase reported by this group for that region of America."[31]

Undoubtedly, as the Prophet Joseph Smith and contemporary and later historians recorded, there was a great fervor of religious activity in New England and particularly in upstate New York along the Erie Canal towns which led to the western territories. Joseph Smith could not have been in a better place to arouse his spiritual feelings than in this "burned over district." History overwhelmingly confirms that Palmyra, New York and its environs were part of "that region of country" where this "unusual excitement" took place (PofGP, JS-H 1:5).

Chapter 5

Religious Excitement "in the place where we lived"

In 1818 Joseph Smith Sr.'s family moved to Manchester, a township of farms where the Smith family built a log home, then a frame home on their own farmland. The Smith home and farm in Manchester were located a half mile south of Joseph Smith Sr.'s first log home which was about two miles south of the larger village of Palmyra, New York. Manchester is where the young Joseph Smith lived at the time of his most remarkable religious experience, his first vision of God the Father and Jesus Christ (PofGP, JS-H 1:5).

Joseph Smith said in his most comprehensive 1838 account of his First Vision:

> Some time in the second year after our removal to Manchester there was in the place where we lived an unusual excitement on the subject of religion. It commenced with the Methodists, but soon became general among all the sects in that region of country. Indeed, the whole district of country seemed effected by it, and great multitudes united themselves to the different religious parties, which created no small stir or division amongst the people, some crying "Lo, here!" and others crying, "Lo, there!" Some were contending for the Methodist faith, some for the Presbyterian, and some for the Baptist. (JS-H 1:5)[32]

According to Columbia University Professor of History Richard L. Bushman, Joseph Smith "began to be concerned about religion in late 1817 or early 1818, when the aftereffects of the revivals of 1816 and 1817 were still being felt."[33]

Recognizing that from 1818 to 1820 there were only two Methodist revivals in Palmyra, none in tiny Manchester, within the time frame indicated in Joseph's several accounts of his vision, one revival in 1818 and the other two years later in 1820, tells us that Joseph could have attended the 1818 Palmyra religious revival or camp meeting and then spent the next two years studying and pondering what he should do.

Professor Milton V. Backman Jr. commented in 1980, using records from the Brigham Young University Library, "Blakeslee discusses in his [contemporary] manuscript history a camp meeting held near Palmyra in 1818, in which twenty were baptized and forty converted to the Methodist society, and which was not reported in the newspapers and religious journals of that age."[34]

D. Michael Quinn tells us that "the published diary of the Reverend Aurora Seager commented that Palmyra had a revival in June 1818, "I received, on the 18th of June, a letter from Brother [Billy] Hibbard, informing me that I had been received by the [eastern] New York Conference, and, at my request, had been transferred to the Genesee Conference. On [Friday,] the 19th [of June 1818,] I attended a camp-meeting at Palmyra [nearly fourteen miles from Phelps].'"[35]

Dr. Quinn pointed out that the Genesee Conference of Methodists was held in June of 1818 and corresponds better to the same Methodist revival meeting which Joseph Smith attended at age twelve as he indicated in his first 1832 account of his theophany. Critics Reverend Grant H. Palmer and H. Michael Marquardt failed to acknowledge this revival of 1818. Rev. Palmer even claimed there were no revivals in Palmyra from 1817 for six years or until 1823, which when considering what they knew, was a very dishonest statement. Dr. Quinn further pointed out that according to the primary records they had cited from their research, Palmer and Marquardt knew about the 1818 revival, which corresponds to Joseph Smith's first 1832 account of his First Vision.[36]

It appears that the Genesee Conference of the Methodists was held in 1818 rather than 1819. This fits better with Joseph Smith's first 1832 account of his First Vision, which vision then occurred two years after Joseph first became interested in religion. According to Joseph's first account it was when he was "about the age of twelve years" that he began to be impressed with the importance of the state of his own "immortal Soul." That would have been during Joseph's thirteenth year or the "season" of the Methodist "camp meetings" in the summer or fall of the year 1818 of which one was held in Palmyra.[37]

Dr. Quinn continues in a revisionist tone which makes sense, "During this research, I [at first] found no evidence of a great revival in Palmyra in 1819 or 1820." Later Quinn tells us of the June 1820 Methodist revival indirectly referenced in a *Palmyra Register* death notice. Quinn also indicates that Latter-day Saint Church History Professor Milton V. Bachman later said that Joseph Smith had been wrongfully interpreted as saying there was an 1820 revival in the immediate vicinity of Palmyra-Manchester, whereas "I found that probably there were more revivals and more people joining churches in upstate and western New York in 1819 and 1820 than in any other region of the United States." Quinn summarizes, "Thus, the crucial revivalism was strictly regional and allegedly not in Joseph's neighborhood . . .," a slightly revised view from Professor Backman's earlier (1969) emphasis on the Palmyra Register's articles of 1820. Remember, by 1818 Joseph Smith lived in Manchester with his father's family about two miles south of Palmyra where the 1818 and 1820 Methodist revivals did take place.[38]

Professor Richard Lloyd Anderson of Brigham Young University corroborates both Bushman and Quinn by pointing out that there was a Methodist Camp Meeting in Palmyra in 1818, with about 400 in attendance which is verified by a contemporary record, Rev. Seager's journal. This agrees with the three-year time frame of his pondering on religion mentioned in Joseph Smith's 1832 account.[39]

There is solid evidence of a Methodist Camp Meeting in Palmyra in June 1820. Dr. Backman reported in his 1969 article in *BYU Studies*, "Awakenings in the Burned-Over District: New Light on the Historical Setting of the First Vision," that Irishman James Couser died on June 25 at the Methodist Camp meeting in Palmyra as reported by the *Palmyra Register*, June 28, and July 5 1820.[40] It should be noted that the death notice was the theme not the camp meeting in the *Register's* publication. As mentioned earlier, at the time, small town newspapers often covered vitals, legal notices, and out-of-town news rather than local events such as revivals.

For the year of Joseph's First Vision, 1820, only one revival, a Methodist camp meeting, is reported to have been held on Sunday, June 25th in the *Palmyra Register*, as background information in association with a death publication. June 25, 1820 might be past the "early in the spring of eighteen hundred and twenty" (PofGP, JS-H 1:14) and possibly would not have been the revival that Joseph was writing of. There were no direct references in local newspapers to revivals in Palmyra in 1820 other than this anecdotal account. This does not present a problem when Joseph's 1932 account of his vision is considered, telling us that it was in 1818 that Joseph first felt to consider his place before God and began investigating the different religions by attending the religious camp meeting of his choice. Such a revival has been identified for the Genesee Conference of the Methodist Church to have met in Palmyra, New York in June of 1818. Thus, when both the 1832 and 1838 vision accounts are taken as a whole, Joseph's later reference to his being in his "fifteenth" year in the 1838 account obviously refers to Joseph's decision to pray for answers to his questions, about not only the condition of his soul before God, but also, which of all the churches should he join?

Joseph's statement, "there was in the place where we lived an unusual excitement on the subject of religion" in the "second year" or 1818 after his family "removed to Manchester" in 1816 (PofGP, JS-H 1:5) is correct and corresponds to the record of local excitement in Palmyra then. Two years later, when Joseph says, "I was at this time in my fifteenth year" or 1820, some have criticized the Prophet's history for a lack of huge religious excitement that year in Palmyra. Yet, Joseph only says that his "father's family was proselyted to the Presbyterian faith" that year [1820] and that he "attended their [the Methodist's] several meetings as often as occasion would permit" (PofGP, JS-H 1:7).

The lack of any known Methodist revivals in 1819 and no multiple Methodist revivals in 1820 Palmyra in the historical record, notwithstanding Joseph's 1838 account of "unusual excitement" is a minor anachronism which can be attributed to what normal journal writers experience. Such it was in Joseph's case, combining the events two years back to 1818, which culminated in his First Vision in 1820, and Joseph's way of recording the regional quality of the religious excitement felt where he lived, in the greater Palmyra-Manchester area. The region overall as noted underwent huge church growth in 1820. It becomes apparent also when reading all four of the firsthand accounts, that this process of Joseph's soul searching, investigating the churches, studying of the scriptures, his deciding to pray, and his resulting vision took at least two years between 1818 and 1820.

Writing of church growth in the 1820s, Dr. Quinn states, "a local Methodist minister understandably wrote that it was 'most consoling' when 'about a dozen sinners were converted' out of the six hundred persons who attended a camp-meeting in September 1822." The fact that the Ontario Circuit of the Methodist Church lost a net of six members in 1820, according to Reverend Walters's 1969 *Dialogue* article, has nothing to do with Joseph's overall description of religious excitement. Why? Because the overall religious excitement in the place, district, and region where Joseph lived, which lasted all of Joseph's youthful years, was not determined by the number of Methodist converts in one county (Ontario), in one year (1820). As noted above, in 1820 or the year of Joseph's First Vision, there was an increase of 2,256 Methodist members in the region of Western New York where Joseph lived.

Joseph was never chronologically specific about the year he attended his first Methodist camp meetings. When Joseph wrote in his 1838 account, "I was at this time in my fifteenth year," he was referring as noted above to his father's family being "proselyted to the Presbyterian faith," his becoming "somewhat partial to the Methodist sect," and the general "confusion and strife among the different denominations." These were general statements which covered several years. Joseph does not name the year "1820" until he tells the world in his "fifteenth year" that he has determined to ask of God in prayer, which of all the churches was true. This is a key distinction for those concerned about the "religious excitement."[41]

Two former BYU professors, Milton V. Backman and D. Michael Quinn, documented that there were definitely religious excitement and increased church attendance in Palmyra, including a "Methodist Camp" held in 1820, the year of Joseph Smith First Vision. They wrote, "In June 1818, for example, a Methodist camp meeting took place in Palmyra, and the following summer, Methodists assembled again at Vienna (now Phelps), New York, fifteen miles from the Smith family farm. The journals of an itinerant Methodist preacher document much religious excitement in Joseph's geographic area in 1819 and 1820. They report that Reverend George Lane, a revivalist Methodist minister, was in that region in both years, speaking 'on Gods method in bringing about Reformations.'"[42]

To summarize this period of religious excitement where Joseph lived, it has been established that Joseph Smith first became interested in religion, according to his 1832 vision account, at the age of twelve in late 1817 and 1818, the latter year of which saw a large revival of the Methodists in Palmyra. Later, additional religious excitement continued around Palmyra during 1819 and in Palmyra in June of 1820 possibly after Joseph's vision. It has been established that there was at least one Methodist "Camp Meeting" in the late spring, likely June 25 of 1820 in Palmyra, which fits Joseph's naming of that sect when he wrote, which "commenced with the Methodists" (JS-H 1:5). Finally, Joseph Smith, apparently and honestly, writing twelve to eighteen years after the fact may have, as Dr. Quinn states, "conflated" the later revivals and heavy church growth years he also lived through during 1824–1825 with Joseph's own first experiences, which began earlier at age twelve years or during the documented revivals of 1817 to 1820.[43]

This common attribute of Joseph's journal writing is irrelevant except perhaps to those demanding a perfect chronology in order to criticize. Some researchers have based their criticisms upon the most attended revivals, how many revivals took place, and where revivals occurred in the district and country around Palmyra. Attendance totals, proximity disputes, and whether there were more revivals in any given year than another, don't affect Joseph's integrity and are all irrelevant in determining whether God the Father and Jesus Christ actually visited the young Joseph Smith. To those investigators who have prayed and received an answer to the foregoing question, knowing how many revivals might have occurred during Joseph's youth is only a curiosity and an exercise to silence the critics. Historical records prove conclusively what Joseph said was true that, "there was in the place where we lived an unusual excitement on the subject of religion" (PofGP, JS-H 1:5).

Chapter 6

"It was . . . a beautiful, clear day"

Joseph Smith never recorded the exact date of his First Vision other than to say: "it was on the morning of a beautiful, clear day, early in the spring of eighteen hundred and twenty" (JS-H 1:14). To most believers of the First Vision, knowing the exact date is not critical to one's understanding of the importance of Joseph's vision. On the other hand, what follows is a very interesting set of separate but identical conclusions which may further prove that everything is important to God and that He has foreordained all His works to be fulfilled in a very prophetic, orderly, and magnificent fashion. And all this must eventually be of certain and great value to the history of The Church of Jesus Christ of Latter-day Saints.

Economist and researcher Dr. John C. Lefgren and astronomer Dr. John P. Pratt produced a video in 2018 entitled, "How Lovely was the Morning!" titled after the first verse of George Manwaring's 1878 poem and later hymn, "Joseph Smith's First Prayer." This video gives a scientifically determined and precise date for the First Vision of Joseph Smith in 1820. Dr. Lefgren and Dr. Pratt combined their research impressively using US Army weather records, maple syrup sap flow characteristics in upper New York State, and the Enochian Calendar derived from the Book of Enoch to pinpoint a proposed date.

It was noted early in the video by Susan Easton Black, emeritus Professor of Church History and Doctrine at Brigham Young University, that the traditional and historically unrecorded date for the First Vision was given by the apostle Elder Bruce R. McConkie in a "magnificent" General Conference talk in 1978, "The Morning

Breaks; the Shadows Flee," as taking place on April 6th. This traditional date follows the traditional calendar date for the birth of Jesus Christ and the recorded date for the organization of The Church of Jesus Christ of Latter-day Saints.[44]

While researching for his book, *April Sixth*, about the sesquicentennial of the organization of The Church of Jesus Christ of Latter-day Saints, the period from 1830 to 1980, John Lefgren researched early US Army records and discovered that beginning in the year 1820 the 8th Surgeon General of the Army, Dr. Joseph Lovell, first ordered all Army field doctors nationwide to measure and take weather readings for air temperature, precipitation, wind and sky conditions. Prior to 1820, only sketchy weather measurements were taken. These records are preserved on microfilm in the National Archives in Washington DC from military fort locations of the United States, including Sackets Harbor on the shores of Lake Ontario just eighty miles from Palmyra, New York.

Dr. Lefgren reported that the field doctor's weather record for Sackets Harbor, New York on April 6, 1820 at 7 a.m. indicated "cloudy skies, winds: northeast, temperature 32 degrees." Weather reports for the day before April 6th indicated "snow" and for the day after "sleet and rain and strong winds." April 6th was not a good day for the First Vision.

Since Joseph said he had his vision "early in the spring" Dr. Lefgren checked the Army weather records for each day from March 1st to April 15th and determined that Sunday, March 26th was the warmest, clearest, and best weather day of that group. Four other days were possible but they were eliminated when it was determined that the Smith's maple sugar business would have precluded Joseph from leaving his chores on those days except for Sunday, March 26th, the Smith's regular day of rest. Maple sugar farmers say that maple tree sap requires at least one sub-freezing or frost day for every three consecutive days in order for the sap to run. This means, from Army records before March 26th, these four possible warm days mentioned above were each followed by cold days when maple tree sap would run and the Smith Family would have been busy collecting sap from at least five hundred maple trees in order to collect and process the thousand pounds of maple sugar the family produced each year.

Coming from a very different astronomical and ancient scripture viewpoint, Dr. John P. Pratt has shared his research about the Enochian Calendar in several papers as well as in the same "How Lovely was the Morning" video with Dr. Lefgren.

Dr. Pratt shared Enoch's insight into the entire history of the earth and a perspective for the First Vision as the starting point of the great Restoration of the gospel foretold by Enoch according to the Ethiopic version of the Book of Enoch. As noted elsewhere in this writing, many prophets have prophesied of the Restoration in the latter days including Enoch, Moses, Isaiah, Lehi, Daniel, Joel, Peter, Ether, and other prophets of God. Enoch gave us more by prophesying of each major phase of the earth's spiritual history from beginning to end (PSDP, 1 Enoch 92:14–15: HBKJV, Deuteronomy 30:1–6; Isaiah 29:11–14; Daniel 2:44–45).

The Book of Enoch is an apocalypse or heavenly vision and sometimes is labeled by modern scholars as an apocryphal book, having a hidden or private meaning and origin, and a pseudepigraphal text, or written after the time of the named author. The Book of Enoch from the Ethiopic is called 1 Enoch and was translated from the Ethiopic Bible which was carried out to Ethiopia in the fifth century by Syrian monks fleeing from the Byzantine Church. There is a Slavonic version called 2 Enoch and a Hebrew version called 3 Enoch. 1 Enoch is generally referred to most often by modern Christian writers and is referred to in this chapter to discuss the Enochian Calendar.

The authenticity of the Ethiopic version 1 Enoch was confirmed in 1945 when Enoch fragments in the original Aramaic language that compared well to the Ethiopic version were found in Qumran Cave 4. These Dead Sea fragments, identified as 4Q 201 of the Aramaic Enoch, have been dated to 200 BC.

From 1945 until the present, the Book of Enoch has been considered one of the "lost books" of the Bible. The Book of Enoch was highly revered by the Early Christians and quoted in the Book of Jude (HBKJV, Jude 1:14).

The early church fathers of the second century considered The Book of Enoch scripture, including Clement of Alexandria, Irenaeus, and Tertullian. Tertullian wrote that the Jews rejected The Book of Enoch because it prophesied of Christ (ANF 4:16; 1 Enoch 46:1–3;

48:1–6). Later in the fourth century, The Book of Enoch was omitted from the canon of scripture by the Church Councils of Nicaea, Hippo, and Carthage. The Medieval Church condemned the Book of Enoch, at least in part, because it prophesied of their doctrinal corruption (1 Enoch 92:10–12).

Enoch divided the year into four seasons of 13 weeks each. Each of these seasons consisted of two 30-day months followed by one 31-day month, with the 31st day ending the season. In this way, Enoch's Year consisted of exactly 364 days with every quarter year or season starting on Sunday.

Dr. Pratt explained, "The Enoch calendar has been criticized as hopelessly primitive because, with only 364 days, it would get out of sync with the seasons so quickly: in only 25 years the seasons would arrive an entire month early. Such a gross discrepancy, however, merely indicates that the method of intercalation has been omitted." Dr. Pratt "pointed out that by adding an extra week at the end of every seventh year or Sabbatical year, and then adding two extra weeks to every fourth Sabbatical year or every 28 years, the calendar could be as accurate as the Julian calendar."[45]

Enoch's Calendar, described in chapters 71–74 of 1 Enoch, is similar to the later Hebrew Calendar, in that it starts at the beginning of creation and runs until the end of time and its weeks are determined by the phases of the moon.

Enoch divided up the earth's history into ten prophetic weeks that each consisted of 728 years or two of Enoch's great weeks of 364 day-year periods. The prophet Daniel did the same thing but with one prophetic week equaling only seven years (Daniel chapters 9–12).

Enoch prophesied the major events for each of these ten "prophetic week" periods: "first week," Enoch identified his own birth as the "seventh" generation "in the first week;" "second week," Adam dies and Enoch is translated; "third week," "Iniquity shall grow," the Flood and Abraham; "fourth week," Moses restores Israel with "visions of the holy;" "fifth week," "the house of glory erected" at Solomon's Temple, 1,000 B.C.; "sixth week," in a time of "darkened hearts . . . in it a Man shall ascend;"; "seventh week," "a perverse generation shall arise. . . and all its deeds perverse. . . the righteous shall be selected. . . given the sevenfold doctrine[?] of his whole creation;" "eighth week,"

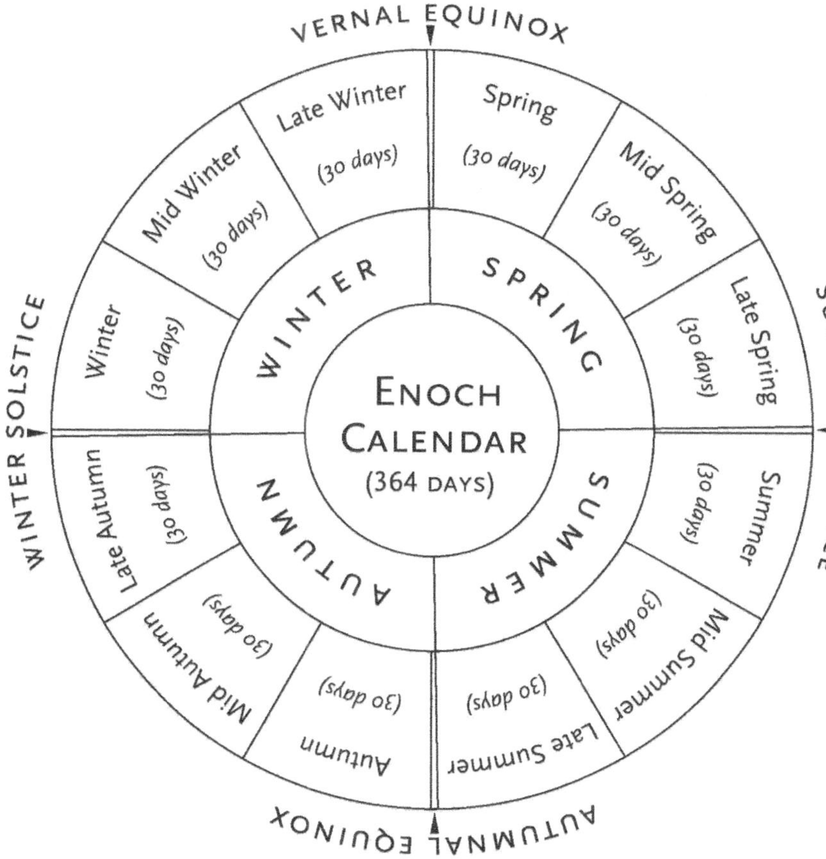

2. The Enochian Calendar prepared by Dr. John P. Pratt based on the descriptions in *The Book of Enoch* (1 Enoch or the Ethiopian version). Accessed June 15, 2020 at: https://www.johnpratt. com/items/docs/2020/enoch_cal_model.html. Image used with permission of Dr. John P. Pratt.

"judgment and justice . . . shall acquire habitations by their righteousness . . . the great king shall be established forever;" "ninth week," the millennial reign of Jesus Christ on earth; "tenth week," final judgment and a new heaven and new earth (PSDP, 1 Enoch 92:4–16).

Dr. Pratt tells us next that during Enoch's prophetic "eighth week" or the rise of the American nation, history would see the day "of righteousness, to which shall be given a sword to execute judgment and justice upon all oppressors. Sinners shall be delivered up into the hands of the righteous" (PSDP, 1 Enoch 92:13). This eighth prophetic week ends, according to Dr. Pratt's calculations, in 1819, the year prior to Joseph's First Vision. This would place the beginning of the eighth week 728 years before or at AD 1092 when archaeological and historical evidence shows that the first Norse explorers began making cultural contact with North America, 400 years before Christopher Columbus (Ancient American, 33:20–25).

Then Dr. Pratt calculated that the first day of spring after the Vernal Equinox, or the first day of the next great year and great prophetic week of Enoch, was Sunday, March 26, 1820, marking the beginning of the "ninth week," when the "judgment of righteousness [would] be revealed to the whole world. Every work of the ungodly shall disappear from the whole earth;" or the First Vision which ushered in the Restoration and fullness of the gospel of Jesus Christ and the Millennium of peace (PSDP, 1 Enoch 92:14–15).

The prophetic "tenth week" follows after the Millennium when Satan is released for a season and goes out to deceive the nations again which culminates in the last great battle of Gog and Magog, like Armageddon prior to the Millennium, which takes place between good and evil at the end of time as described by Ezekiel and the Apostle John in Revelation (HBKJV, Ezekiel 38–39; Revelation 20:7–10). Enoch writes, "And after this, on the seventh day of the tenth week, there shall be an everlasting judgement, which shall be executed upon the Watchers [or fallen ones]; and a spacious eternal heaven shall spring forth in the midst of the angels." Enoch continues, "The former heaven shall depart and pass away; a new heaven shall appear; and all the celestial powers shine with sevenfold splendor for ever" (PSDP, 1 Enoch 92:16–18; D&C 76:43–44).

It is understood that "a new heaven" means the changing of the constellations as the earth moves out of its present location in our solar system into its glorious Millennial location back where the earth was first created. Then, after a thousand years, the earth moves again into its much brighter and far more glorious "celestial" place, nearest to God toward the much brighter center of our galaxy or galactic universe. This is the place of habitation for all righteous resurrected beings, which Paul referred to as having the "glory of the sun" as compared to the respective glory and brightness of the moon and of the stars. Joseph Smith would cast great light upon this subject (HBKJV, 1 Corinthians 15:40–42; D&C 76:70; 88:45).

These remarkable prophecies of Enoch and his unique calendar help us see the orderliness and foreknowledge of God the Father or Elohim, and His Son Jesus Christ or Jehovah, as the latter reveals to holy prophets the great mysteries and eternal destiny of our earth and its inhabitants during each period of its progress.

It should be remembered that both Dr. Lefgren and Dr. Pratt arrived at Sunday, March 26, 1820 as the date for Joseph Smith's First Vision independently, and by using completely different approaches, methods, and subject matter.

Whether it was the traditional date of April 6th or the calculated date of March 26th, the actual day of Joseph's first vision of Deity is important to figure out. However, it is not as important as figuring out by faith, study, and prayer the fact that this tremendous and divine event actually took place as the Prophet said it did. As to when it happened, we can be satisfied to know that Joseph Smith's First Vision took place "on the morning of a beautiful clear day, in the spring of eighteen hundred and twenty" (PofGP, JS-H 1:14).

Chapter 7

Joseph Smith's First Vision

THE PLACE WHERE THE FIRST VISION TOOK PLACE IS A SACRED GROVE, or a significant stand of trees, three-quarters of a mile long and about one-third of mile wide, called by those in Manchester Township the "North Woods" which runs north and south across the Wayne and Ontario County lines, west of Manchester and south of Palmyra, New York. The exact location in the grove where Joseph had his vision is not known, while its proximity to the Smith log home is obvious. The Sacred Grove was directly south and west of the Smith family log house built in 1818 and lived in until 1825 when the Smith family moved into the frame house which Alvin Smith had started before his untimely death in 1823. This grove of trees was less than a few hundred feet from the Smith cabin and just across Hathaway Brook. It was the place naturally selected by the young Joseph Smith to approach God in prayer.[46]

President Russell M. Nelson, President of The Church of Jesus Christ of Latter-day Saints, while visiting recently with Jean B. Bingham, Relief Society General President, discussed the role of women in the latter-day Restoration of the gospel. President Nelson said:

> And then I think of how Joseph went into the woods to pray near their home in Palmyra, New York. Where did he go? He went to the Sacred Grove. Why did he go there? Because that's where Mother [Joseph's Mother Lucy Mack Smith] went when she wanted to pray.[47]

Joseph's mother, Lucy Mack Smith, as noted earlier, prayed in the woods of Vermont before Joseph was born and later had a dream that her husband Joseph Smith Sr. would one day embrace the pure and undefiled gospel of Jesus Christ. Mother Smith also recorded in her history that the Smith family was "in the habit of offering up their secret devotions to God" in the grove of trees near their home in Manchester.[48]

Joseph Smith was a humble agrarian youth with little formal education and was subject to the work ethic and poverty placed upon his father's family. These attributes, combined with a strong and independent faith in God, a belief in the divine inspiration of the scriptures found in the Bible, and belief in inspired dreams running back several generations, created a unique quality of personality that heaven could work with. The religious excitement in the place where he lived was the scenery and not the source of Joseph's inspiration to prayerfully seek the counsel of God as to which of the many churches he should join as the faith or religion acceptable to God. What Joseph Smith would ultimately discover was not what he expected.[49]

What follows are those verses from the most comprehensive account written by the Prophet Joseph Smith in 1838 of his marvelous First Vision of the Father and the Son, taken from Joseph Smith's History in the latter-day scripture, The Pearl of Great Price:

> Owing to the many reports which have been put in circulation by evil-disposed and designing persons, in relation to the rise and progress of The Church of Jesus Christ of Latter-day Saints, all of which have been designed by the authors thereof to militate against its character as a Church and its progress in the world—I have been induced to write this history, to disabuse the public mind, and put all inquirers after truth in possession of the facts, as they have transpired, in relation both to myself and the Church, so far as I have such facts in my possession.
>
> In this history I shall present the various events in relation to this Church, in truth and righteousness, as they have transpired, or as they at present exist, being now [1838] the eighth year since the organization of the said Church.

I was born in the year of our Lord one thousand eight hundred and five, on the twenty-third day of December, in the town of Sharon, Windsor county, State of Vermont. ... My father, Joseph Smith, Sen., left the State of Vermont, and moved to Palmyra, Ontario (now Wayne) county, in the State of New York, when I was in my tenth year, or thereabouts. In about four years after my father's arrival in Palmyra, he moved with his family into Manchester in the same county of Ontario—

His family consisting of eleven souls, namely, my father, Joseph Smith; my mother, Lucy Smith (whose name, previous to her marriage, was Mack, daughter of Solomon Mack); my brothers, Alvin (who died November 19th, 1823, in the 26th year of his age), Hyrum, myself, Samuel Harrison, William, Don Carlos; and my sisters, Sophronia, Catherine, and Lucy.

Some time in the second year after our removal to Manchester, there was in the place where we lived an unusual excitement on the subject of religion. It commenced with the Methodists, but soon became general among all the sects in that region of country. Indeed, the whole district of country seemed affected by it, and great multitudes united themselves to the different religious parties, which created no small stir and division amongst the people, some crying, "Lo, here!" and others, "Lo, there!" Some were contending for the Methodist faith, some for the Presbyterian, and some for the Baptist.

For, notwithstanding the great love which the converts to these different faiths expressed at the time of their conversion, and the great zeal manifested by the respective clergy, who were active in getting up and promoting this extraordinary scene of religious feeling, in order to have everybody converted, as they were pleased to call it, let them join what sect they pleased; yet when the converts began to file off, some to one party and some to another, it was seen that the seemingly good feelings of both the priests and the converts were more pretended than real; for a scene of great confusion and bad feeling ensued—priest contending against priest, and convert against convert; so that all their good feelings one for another, if they ever had any, were entirely lost in a strife of words and a contest about opinions.

I was at this time in my fifteenth year. My father's family was proselyted to the Presbyterian faith, and four of them joined that church, namely, my mother, Lucy; my brothers Hyrum and Samuel Harrison; and my sister Sophronia.

During this time of great excitement my mind was called up to serious reflection and great uneasiness; but though my feelings were deep and often poignant, still I kept myself aloof from all these parties, though I attended their several meetings as often as occasion would permit. In process of time my mind became somewhat partial to the Methodist sect, and I felt some desire to be united with them; but so great were the confusion and strife among the different denominations, that it was impossible for a person young as I was, and so unacquainted with men and things, to come to any certain conclusion who was right and who was wrong.

My mind at times was greatly excited, the cry and tumult were so great and incessant. The Presbyterians were most decided against the Baptists and Methodists, and used all the powers of both reason and sophistry to prove their errors, or, at least, to make the people think they were in error. On the other hand, the Baptists and Methodists in their turn were equally zealous in endeavoring to establish their own tenets and disprove all others.

In the midst of this war of words and tumult of opinions, I often said to myself: What is to be done? Who of all these parties are right; or, are they all wrong together? If any one of them be right, which is it, and how shall I know it?

While I was laboring under the extreme difficulties caused by the contests of these parties of religionists, I was one day reading the Epistle of James, first chapter and fifth verse, which reads: If any of you lack wisdom, let him ask of God, that giveth to all men liberally, and upbraideth not; and it shall be given him.

Never did any passage of scripture come with more power to the heart of man than this did at this time to mine. It seemed to enter with great force into every feeling of my heart. I reflected on it again and again, knowing that if any person needed wisdom from God, I did; for how to act I did not know, and unless I could get more wisdom than I then had, I would never know; for the teachers of religion of the different sects understood the same passages of scripture so differently as to destroy all confidence in settling the question by an appeal to the Bible.

At length I came to the conclusion that I must either remain in darkness and confusion, or else I must do as James directs, that is, ask of God. I at length came to the determination to "ask of God," concluding that if he gave wisdom to them that lacked wisdom, and would give liberally, and not upbraid, I might venture.

So, in accordance with this, my determination to ask of God, I retired to the woods to make the attempt. It was on the morning of a beautiful, clear day, early in the spring of eighteen hundred and twenty. It was the first time in my life that I had made such an attempt, for amidst all my anxieties I had never as yet made the attempt to pray vocally.

After I had retired to the place where I had previously designed to go, having looked around me, and finding myself alone, I kneeled down and began to offer up the desires of my heart to God. I had scarcely done so, when immediately I was seized upon by some power which entirely overcame me, and had such an astonishing influence over me as to bind my tongue so that I could not speak. Thick darkness gathered around me, and it seemed to me for a time as if I were doomed to sudden destruction.

But, exerting all my powers to call upon God to deliver me out of the power of this enemy which had seized upon me, and at the very moment when I was ready to sink into despair and abandon myself to destruction—not to an imaginary ruin, but to the power of some actual being from the unseen world, who had such marvelous power as I had never before felt in any being—just at this moment of great alarm, I saw a pillar of light exactly over my head, above the brightness of the sun, which descended gradually until it fell upon me.

It no sooner appeared than I found myself delivered from the enemy which held me bound. When the light rested upon me I saw two Personages, whose brightness and glory defy all description, standing above me in the air. One of them spake unto me, calling me by name and said, pointing to the other—This is My Beloved Son. Hear Him!

My object in going to inquire of the Lord was to know which of all the sects was right, that I might know which to join. No sooner, therefore, did I get possession of myself, so as to be able to speak, than I asked the Personages who stood above me in the light, which of all the sects was right (for at this time it had never entered into my heart that all were wrong)—and which I should join.

I was answered that I must join none of them, for they were all wrong; and the Personage who addressed me said that all their creeds were an abomination in his sight; that those professors were all corrupt; that: "they draw near to me with their lips, but their hearts are far from me, they teach for doctrines the commandments of men, having a form of godliness, but they deny the power thereof.

He again forbade me to join with any of them; and many other things did he say unto me, which I cannot write at this time. When I came to myself again, I found myself lying on my back, looking up into heaven. When the light had departed, I had no strength; but soon recovering in some degree, I went home. And as I leaned up to the fireplace, mother inquired what the matter was. I replied, "Never mind, all is well—I am well enough off." I then said to my mother, "I have learned for myself that Presbyterianism is not true." It seems as though the adversary was aware, at a very early period of my life, that I was destined to prove a disturber and an annoyer of his kingdom; else why should the powers of darkness combine against me? Why the opposition and persecution that arose against me, almost in my infancy?

Some few days after I had this vision, I happened to be in company with one of the Methodist preachers, who was very active in the before mentioned religious excitement; and, conversing with him on the subject of religion, I took occasion to give him an account of the vision which I had had. I was greatly surprised at his behavior; he treated my communication not only lightly, but with great contempt, saying it was all of the devil, that there were no such things as visions or revelations in these days; that all such things had ceased with the apostles, and that there would never be any more of them.

I soon found, however, that my telling the story had excited a great deal of prejudice against me among professors of religion, and was the cause of great persecution, which continued to increase; and though I was an obscure boy, only between fourteen and fifteen years of age, and my circumstances in life such as to make a boy of no consequence in the world, yet men of high standing would take notice sufficient to excite the public mind against me, and create a bitter persecution; and this was common among all the sects—all united to persecute me.

It caused me serious reflection then, and often has since, how very strange it was that an obscure boy, of a little over fourteen years of age, and one, too, who was doomed to the necessity of obtaining a scanty maintenance by his daily labor, should be thought a character of sufficient importance to attract the attention of the great ones of the most popular sects of the day, and in a manner to create in them a spirit of the most bitter persecution and reviling. But strange or not, so it was, and it was often the cause of great sorrow to myself.

However, it was nevertheless a fact that I had beheld a vision. I have thought since, that I felt much like Paul, when he made his defense before King Agrippa, and related the account of the vision he had when he saw a light, and heard a voice; but still there were but few who believed him; some said he was dishonest, others said he was mad; and he was ridiculed and reviled. But all this did not destroy the reality of

> his vision. He had seen a vision, he knew he had, and all the persecution under heaven could not make it otherwise; and though they should persecute him unto death, yet he knew, and would know to his latest breath, that he had both seen a light and heard a voice speaking unto him, and all the world could not make him think or believe otherwise.
>
> So it was with me. I had actually seen a light, and in the midst of that light I saw two Personages, and they did in reality speak to me; and though I was hated and persecuted for saying that I had seen a vision, yet it was true; and while they were persecuting me, reviling me, and speaking all manner of evil against me falsely for so saying, I was led to say in my heart: Why persecute me for telling the truth? I have actually seen a vision; and who am I that I can withstand God, or why does the world think to make me deny what I have actually seen? For I had seen a vision; I knew it, and I knew that God knew it, and I could not deny it, neither dared I do it; at least I knew that by so doing I would offend God, and come under condemnation (PofGP, JS-H 1:1–25; JSP, H1:208–215).[50]

Orson Pratt's 1840 account of Joseph's First Vision, told to him by Joseph Smith and published in Scotland, gives more details concerning the adversary's attack while Joseph exerted his faith to pray, the appearance of the gradually descending heavenly light and the appearance of two divine personages:

> At first, he was severely tempted by the powers of darkness, which endeavoured to overcome him; but he continued to seek for deliverance, until darkness gave way from his mind; and he was enabled to pray, in fervency of the spirit, and in faith. And, while thus pouring out his soul, anxiously desiring an answer from God, he, at length, saw a very bright and glorious light in the heavens above; which, at first, seemed to be at a considerable distance. He continued praying, while the light appeared to be gradually descending towards him; and, as it drew nearer, it increased in brightness, and magnitude, so that, by the time that it reached the tops of the trees, the whole wilderness, for some distance around, was illuminated

> in a most glorious and brilliant manner. He expected to have seen the leaves and boughs of the trees consumed, as soon as the light came in contact with them; but, perceiving that it did not produce that effect, he was encouraged with the hopes of being able to endure its presence. It continued descending, slowly, until it rested upon the earth, and he was enveloped in the midst of it. When it first came upon him, it produced a peculiar sensation throughout his whole system; and, immediately, his mind was caught away, from the natural objects with which he was surrounded; and he was enwrapped in a heavenly vision, and saw two glorious personages, who exactly resembled each other in their features or likeness. He was informed, that his sins were forgiven. He was also informed upon the subjects, which had for some time previously agitated his mind, viz.—that all the religious denominations were believing in incorrect doctrines; and, consequently, that none of them was acknowledged of God, as his church and kingdom. And he was expressly commanded, to go not after them; and he received a promise that the true doctrine—the fullness of the gospel, should, at some future time, be made known to him; after which, the vision withdrew, leaving his mind in a state of calmness and peace, indescribable (JSP, H1:517–546; original spelling retained.).

When Joseph Smith walked out of the grove in Palmyra, New York in the spring of 1820, following his interview with both God the Father and the Son Jesus Christ, he was the most intelligent man then living on the earth regarding the state of religion. Nobody then living could match his knowledge of the nature and purposes of God. Joseph Smith was from that day forward an apostolic witness of God the Father and of Jesus Christ (MDoc, 46–47). Nor did any man possess a divinely accurate assessment of the condition of the churches in America and the world as he did. Just hours earlier, Joseph was an uneducated and humble farm boy; now, endowed with knowledge from on high, he was a prophet and seer and the wisest man living since the last Biblical apostles laid down their lives as martyrs for the testimony of Jesus Christ.

It is interesting to compare the modern critics of the Prophet Joseph Smith with the ancient critics of the Apostles of Jesus Christ. The Jewish rulers, elders, and scribes of the New Testament era considered the formally uneducated Peter, James, and John "unlearned and ignorant men" and implied they were not able to understand the things of the scriptures and of God (HBKJV, Acts 4:13). Yet great and wonderful things came forth from the mouths and pens of these three great prophets, seers, and revelators, who were apostles of Jesus Christ.

Their most important knowledge was their testimony of Jesus Christ. They received that by numerous divine revelations from heaven: (1) the voice of God the Father on the Mount of Transfiguration; (2) the voice of the *transfigured* Jesus Christ; (3) the former prophets Moses and Elias or Elijah, both translated beings, appearing to the *transfigured* Peter, James, and John; (4) the Holy Ghost while Jesus was still with them during His earthly mission; (5) the Holy Ghost to all eleven apostles and to 3,000 other Jews at Pentecost; (6) and again during Peter's visit to Cornelius the Centurion, the first Gentile to receive the gospel of Jesus Christ, after the angel had appeared to Cornelius in his house and then to Peter (HBKJV, Matthew 17:3–5; John 14:6; Matthew 16:15–17; Acts 2:1–4, 41; 11:15; MDoc, 223).

Modern prophets confirm that during the First Vision, the Holy Spirit had overshadowed Joseph Smith and he was *transfigured* or quickened in order to see God and endure his presence (D&C 67:11). The knowledge of God was restored to a prophet, and the position of Jesus Christ as mediator for all the earth was also confirmed. The young Joseph also learned that a great apostasy had taken place many centuries before and of the apostate condition of the doctrines which were prevalent at the time of his vision (DofS 1:2, 28, 42–43; 3:283–288; EofM 3:1484).

As in ancient times from the Apostles of Jesus Christ, so also in the latter days would wonderful things come forth from the Prophet Joseph Smith's mouth and pen. The fifteenth President of the Church, Gordon B. Hinckley, proclaimed in 1997, "Joseph Smith learned in those minutes, however long or brief, more about the nature of God than all of the learned divines of all time had ever learned."[51]

Chapter 8

Persecutions after the First Vision

Since the 1960s, unbelieving and skeptical writers have questioned the details of the First Vision accounts as compared to historical records of the region and have attempted to challenge Joseph's testimony. They ask, why were there no newspaper accounts in the Palmyra Register in the months just following young Joseph Smith's First Vision of the Father and the Son? Or, why is there no press report of the "vision" itself or the "persecution" Joseph tells us he received in 1820? To the open-minded historian there may be good reasons for this absence of news publications regarding Joseph's earliest vision and persecution. To the closed-minded writer there may be only one conclusion if they assume that an absence of newspaper articles means the events didn't happen. There are good answers to these questions. As noted earlier, local papers in those days did not publish local news, as thrifty New Englanders generally would not pay for what they could obtain freely from neighbors and friends.

The skeptics point out that Joseph's mother Lucy Mack Smith made no mention of this vision in her first draft or "preliminary manuscript" of her history of Joseph Smith written in 1845. It should be pointed out that in regard to Lucy Mack Smith's history, she *did* include the First Vision in the edited, approved, and final version of her manuscript which was first published in England in 1853 by Orson Pratt.[52]

From Joseph's own record we learn that he told "one of the Methodist preachers" about his vision, who rejected it and then said, "it was all of the devil." This minister then told other "professors of religion" who unitedly condemned it and persecuted Joseph Smith with negative gossip in the local community (PofGP, JS-H 1:22). There is no reason for historians to think that all the newspapers in town would jump on the story of a 14-year-old boy telling a minister that he had seen a vision of God. To publish such a story in negative terms against a minor youth would be improper and highly frowned upon. That does not mean that the ministers of religion, when promoting their beliefs, along with other residents in the vicinity of Palmyra, would not verbally assail the boy Joseph in their social and religious settings or when they saw Joseph, to such a degree that he would have haunting memories of this persecution throughout his life.

Joseph's only comment to his mother shortly after his First Vision was, "I have learned that Presbyterianism is not true" (PofGP, JS-H 1:20). After the persecution of the Methodist minister, to whom Joseph had told his vision, there is reason to believe Joseph's mother knew of Joseph's 1820 First Vision and the persecution Joseph received for it. Joseph's older brother Alvin Smith had constructed the wood frame of a new house for his parents by November 1822. Lucy wrote in her history of Joseph Smith, "From this time until the twenty-first of September, 1823, Joseph continued, as usual, to labor with his father, and nothing during this interval occurred of very great importance–though he [Joseph] suffered severe opposition and persecution from the different orders of religionists."[53] In other words, at some time prior to Alvin Smith's death in 1823, Joseph had a tremendous spiritual experience which caused him great "opposition and persecution" from the religious preachers where he lived. These persecutions must have been associated as Joseph tells us with his First Vision and would also be prior to Joseph's later sacred interview with the angel Moroni on September 21, 1823 (PofGP, JS-H 1:22–27).

Historians and critics have asked, what caused Joseph's mother and siblings to leave the Presbyterian Church in 1828? There is no available record indicating that the young Joseph shared his First Vision with his family. Joseph's mother and three siblings didn't leave the Presbyterians because of comments made by the minister at the funeral, following the November 19, 1823 death of Joseph's brother Alvin, who said Alvin Smith would not enter into heaven because he was not baptized into the Presbyterian Church (EofM 3:357).

From 1823 to 1828, Joseph Smith remained independent from all the churches of Palmyra and joined none of them. Lucy and Joseph's siblings, Hyrum, Samuel, and Sophronia continued to attend the Presbyterian Church until 1828. Not until Joseph had obtained the gold plates of the Book of Mormon on September 22, 1827 and thereafter, did it became clear to the Smith family that Joseph Smith Jr. was not only going to translate the ancient American record, the Book of Mormon, but he was going to restore the ancient truths of the Early Church, and only then did Joseph's mother Lucy Smith and Joseph's siblings Hyrum, Samuel, and Sophronia disengage from the Western Presbyterian Church they had been attending since 1820 (PofGP, JS-H 1:7).[54]

Critics have claimed without merit that since there are no public records or newspaper stories about Joseph's First Vision and persecutions in 1820, or soon thereafter, then the whole story must be a fabrication. Nobody currently disputes that the largest revival in Palmyra appears to have occurred in 1824.

Professor Richard L. Bushman confirms that both secular and sectarian history reveals that Joseph could experience religious excitement in Palmyra Village which resulted from revivals in nearby towns in 1820, as well as from revivals which took place in or out of Palmyra during a period from 1818 to 1824 both before and after his First Vision.[55]

The assertion that silence is proof is not only poor historical reasoning, it ignores the fact that adults cannot publicly defame youth in newspaper stories who are not of age, at least not in 1820 Palmyra, New York. It also ignores the family dynamics and the respectful nature of the Smith family for each of its members, including young Joseph Smith Jr.

It appears that, with Joseph's mother and three siblings attending and by 1820 joining the Presbyterian Church, the fourteen-year-old Joseph felt in no position to rock the boat by challenging his mother and two older brothers and sister in their religious freedom after the Lord told him to join none of the churches.

As related above, Joseph's mother Lucy specifically commented that during 1822 and 1823, "he [Joseph] suffered every kind of opposition and persecution from the different orders of religionists." This then must have resulted from Joseph's telling of his marvelous First Vision of the Father and the Son which took place in 1820, compounded by Joseph's refusal to join any of the churches as he had been commanded by the Lord. As for himself, Joseph would remain independent until he received divine direction to do otherwise (PofGP, JS-H 1:19–26; JSP, H1:13).

Joseph's 1838 account of his 1820 vision, with eighteen years of perspective behind him, reveals that he did suffer great persecutions regarding his First Vision and later translation of the Book of Mormon. His earliest persecutions between 1820 and 1823, before he was visited by the angel Moroni, were more of an emotional and verbal nature most likely among neighbors and local ministers, not in the newspapers and journals of the day.

Not until 1830 would the events of the Restoration of the ancient gospel of Jesus Christ put Joseph Smith on the pages of local and national newspapers. Joseph's persecutions began as unreported negative community gossip after his 1820 vision, yet certainly intensified by the time he had obtained the plates from Moroni in late 1827. At that point, Joseph was being physically pursued and attacked by those who wanted to steal the gold plates of the Book of Mormon, that they supposedly didn't believe he had.[56] The angel Moroni prophesied to Joseph that both "good and evil" would be spoken against him "among all people" (JS-H 1:33).

As an adult, Joseph was open game for the ministers of religion, treasure seeking and literary antagonists to attack, verbally and in print, as well as at times physically. Joseph Smith endured dozens of frivolous lawsuits and false arrests during his shortened lifetime. He was beaten nearly unconscious with Sidney Rigdon and tarred and feathered on March 24, 1832 by a mob in Hiram, Ohio, where the young Church had moved from Palmyra, New York ironically to escape persecutions.

Laws against libel would have protected the young Joseph from newspapers publishing stories without the consent of his parents. It was after Joseph Smith had reached maturity, published the Book of Mormon, and organized the Church of Christ in 1830 that the greater powers of wicked men assailed against him and the public record of persecutions began, not in 1820. The early or pre-1830 persecution

Joseph would have remembered emotionally, as much as if he had been hauled into court like "Paul before Agrippa," which he would be many times after 1830 (PofGP, JS-H 1:24–25).

The writing of Eber D. Howe, who authored *Mormonism Unveiled* in 1834, proved that a literary attack upon Joseph Smith, the Book of Mormon, and the Church had begun. Howe's attempt to smear the young prophet Joseph Smith and early Church leaders including Oliver Cowdery and Sydney Rigdon and others are so transparent in *Mormonism Unveiled* that many readers and historians will not give the book much time or credit. The book was republished in Salt Lake City, Utah in 1884 by critics of the Church to a mostly uninterested population other than a small cadre of curious antagonists meting out religious opposition in cities of the east coast. It is this book, with all of its biased and apocryphal storytelling that gets quoted by the later twentieth-century academic historians, who know better but cannot resist quoting from Howe's endless contemporary gossip and fanciful conclusions.

Antagonists and critics have used Howe's *Mormonism Unveiled* to attempt to show that the First Vision never happened. Of course Howe did not mention Joseph's First Vision of 1820 because he didn't know about it. Joseph had not first recorded it until 1832 in his private journal and had not allowed it to be published in America until March 1, 1842 in the *Times And Seasons* in Nauvoo, Illinois. This published 1842 account was based on Joseph Smith's letter of that year to John Wentworth, the editor of the *Chicago Democrat* newspaper. Joseph relates, "Mr. Wentworth says that he wishes to furnish Mr. Bastow [Barstow], a friend of his, who is writing the history of New Hampshire, with this document."[57]

It should be noted that the Wentworth letter tells not only of Joseph's First Vision but also of the translation of the Book of Mormon, its relation to the American Indians, and the organization of The Church of Jesus Christ of Latter-day Saints and its early growth and persecutions. A member of the First Council of the Seventy and a Church Historian, B. H. Roberts, wrote, "The letter is one of the choicest documents in our church literature; as also it is the earliest published document by the Prophet personally, making any pretension to consecutive narrative of those events in which the great Latter-day work had its origin . . ." (DHC, 4:535–41; CHC 1:55).[58]

All this being true, in accordance with Joseph's own accounts, historians should not expect to find public records, newspaper, and private journal accounts in Palmyra or elsewhere referencing the First Vision. Such attacks from the press did not occur in the period of 1820–1827, and published attacks were never described by Joseph Smith in his personal accounts of the First Vision and its aftermath.

Joseph applied pure and undaunted faith. He was nearly overcome yet fought off the devil. As the heavens opened to him he was quickened and saw the Father and the Son in a glorious pillar of celestial light. This made Joseph Smith a prophet in every respect. Not only did he see God and Christ, he was given direction from Christ not to join any of the churches of his day. Joseph recorded what no living being had recorded seeing since Steven, the first martyr of the Early Church, who was one of first seven deacons chosen by the apostles of Jesus Christ, who before he was stoned for his testimony had looked steadfastly up into heaven and "saw the glory of God . . . And said, I see the heavens opened and the Son of man, standing on the right hand of God" (HBKJV, Acts 6:5; 7:55–56). Like Steven, Joseph Smith had seen both the Father and the Son and according to the scriptural definition he was a modern prophet of God.

Chapter 9

Primary Accounts of the First Vision

There are six firsthand accounts of the First Vision which were written in Joseph Smith's lifetime in his own hand or dictated by him and recorded or rerecorded by his clerks between 1830 and 1844. One of the six is a single verse of scripture. All six of these records can be found in Joseph Smith's journals, revelations, and histories now published in *The Joseph Smith Papers* volumes. Two of the 1835 accounts are a rerecording from first person to third person by clerks from Joseph Smith's "Ohio Journal 1835–1836" to his "History 1834–1836." Also similar accounts, the 1842 Wentworth Letter and 1843 Rupp Letter and all others were published by Dean Jessee in The Papers of Joseph Smith, two volumes, 1989-92.

Five other secondary accounts were written by close contemporaries of Joseph who wrote in private and public journals, a book or in pamphlets mostly in the third person of what they heard Joseph tell. They include, Apostle Orson Pratt friend Levi Richards, Apostle Orson Hyde, friend Alexander Neibaur, and publisher David Nye White's article which was written and published in the *Spectator* in first person in 1843.[59]

Church historians have indicated that the 1832 account, four shorter 1835 documents considered as one account, the 1838-39 account, the very similar 1842 Wentworth Letter, the 1843 Rupp Letter, and the five contemporary accounts make up "ten accounts in thirteen documents" (Opening the Heavens, Welch, p.35). With

D&C 20:5 where Joseph refers to receiving "a remission of his sins" there are eleven accounts in fourteen documents recorded during Joseph Smith's lifetime.

Dr. Allen's and Dr. Welch's "ten accounts and thirteen documents" are presented clearly in the first seventy-five pages or the first two chapters of Opening the Heavens (2005) written by Dean C Jessee, James B. Allen, and John W. Welch.

This source also mentions two contemporary letters by William W Phelps to his wife Sally Phelps in 1835, "This is my beloved Son, hear him," and Parley P. Pratt to the Elders of the Church . . . in 1836, "relating many Particulars of the manner of his [Joseph Smith's] first vision & c." (Welch, p.26, 27, 33, notes 32 and 33)

These last two, the Phelps and Pratt letters were not included in the list of accounts by Professors Allen and Welch apparently because they are not first hand from Joseph Smith, were partial, not part of Joseph's journals or histories and never published in Joseph's day (Welch, p.37).

Below, in historical order, are each of the accounts and documents listed with the date they were recorded, their author's name, and original sources including references for the currently available volumes of *The Joseph Smith Papers* (JSP):

FIRSTHAND ACCOUNTS AND DOCUMENTS

1. 1830, Joseph Smith, revelation, third person account by him, April 1830 in the handwriting of John Whitmer, "Articles and Covenants," *Evening and Morning Star*, 1832; *Book of Commandments*, 1833; current *Doctrine and Covenants* 20:5–8, Joseph received "a remission of his sins" (verse 5) prior to the visit of the angel Moroni in agreement with the 1832 account (JSP, R2: 195, 202).[61]

2. 1832, Joseph Smith, first person account, "History" [circa summer 1832], Autobiography and Letterbook, CHL; this "History" is in the handwriting of Joseph Smith and Frederick G. Williams (JSP, H1:10–13).[62]

3. 1835, Joseph Smith, first person document, November 9, 1835, "Ohio Journal 1835-1836," CHL; in the handwriting of Warren Parrish" (JSP, J1:87–88).[63]

   1835, Joseph Smith, third person document, November 9, 1835, "History 1834–1836," CHL; in the handwriting of Warren A. Cowdery" (JSP, H1:115–116).[64]

   1835, Joseph Smith, first person document, November 14, 1835, "Ohio Journal 1835–1836," CHL; in the handwriting of Warren Parrish (JSP, J1:100).[65]

   1835, Joseph Smith, third person document, November 14, 1835, "History 1834–1836," CHL; in the handwriting of Warren Cowdery (JSP, H1:124).[66]

4. 1838, Joseph Smith, first person account, April 30, 1838, Manuscript History of the Church, six large handwritten volumes, 1838–1856, volume A-1, pp. 2–3, dictated by Joseph Smith, CHL; handwriting of George Robinson; Draft 2 copied by James Mulholland in 1841; and a revised Draft 3 copy was made by Howard Coray in 1841 under Joseph Smith's direction; *Times and Seasons*, vol. 3, no. 10, 15 Mar. 1842, pp. 726–28, 748-749; "Extracts from the History of Joseph Smith," Pearl of Great Price, 1851 published by Franklin D. Richards, apostle in England; Pearl of Great Price, 1878 first American edition, canonized 1880; Joseph Smith-History 1:1-26, The Pearl of Great Price, 1981 (JSP, H1:208–215).[67]

5. 1842, Joseph Smith, first person account, Joseph Smith to John Wentworth, letter, no orig.; "Church History," 1 March 1842, *Times and Seasons*, vol. 3, no. 9, March 1, 1842, pp. 706–710, (T&S) signed by JS, CHL (JSP, H1:489–501).[68]

6. 1843, Joseph Smith, first person, to Israel Daniel Rupp, [July], 1843, letter written by W. W. Phelps for J. Smith; follows *T&S*, "Church History"; published in, Israel Daniel Rupp, *An Original History of the Religious Denominations at Present Existing in the United States*, 1844, CHL (JSP, H1:503–516).[69]

CONTEMPORARY ACCOUNTS

1. 1840, Orson Pratt, apostle, third person, pamphlet entitled, "A[n] Interesting Account of Several Remarkable Visions...," first published in English at Edinburgh, Scotland, CHL, (JSP, H1:517–546).[70]
2. 1842, Orson Hyde, apostle, third person, and pamphlet entitled, Ein Ruf aus der Wüste" (A Cry out of the Wilderness), published in Frankfurt, Germany, MS, CHL; (Dean C. Jessee, ed., PJS, 1:402–426).[71]
3. 1843, Levi Richards, third person, Thomsonian physician and secretary to Joseph Smith. Member of the Council of Fifty; Journal, June 11, 1843, MS, CHL, (published in John W. Welch, ed., *Opening the Heavens, Accounts of Divine Manifestations, 1820-1844*, 2005, pp. 23-24, 49; WJS, p. 215).[72]
4. 1843, David Nye White, first person, interview of Joseph Smith at Nauvoo, Illinois on August 28, 1843, published in the September 15, 1843 issue of the *Pittsburg Weekly Gazette* and later in the *New York Spectator*, September 23, 1843 (Dean C. Jesse, PJS, 1:438-444).[73]
5. 1844, Alexander Neibaur, a member of the Seventy, third person, Journal, May 24, 1844, MS, LDS Church History Library, a German dentist and the first Jewish convert to Mormonism. (John W. Welch, ed., *Opening the Heavens, Accounts of Divine Manifestations, 1820-1844*, 2005, pp. 25–26, 50).[74]

Returning to the first reference to the First Vision of the Prophet Joseph Smith, it has been generally overlooked by Church members, scholars, and critics, perhaps understandably because it only includes one aspect of Joseph's theophany, forgiveness of sins. This 1830 revelation in Section 20 of the Doctrine And Covenants, verses five through eight and specifically verse five is unmistakable as a First Vision account or reference. Section 20 was first published as "Revelations" entitled "The Articles and Covenants of The Church of Christ" in the first issue of the *Evening and Morning Star* in June of 1832, the first newspaper of the Church (E&MS, 1832, pp. 1–2). It was later printed in the *Book of Commandments* of 1833 and in the Doctrine and Covenants of 1835.[75] Joseph's mentioning of having "received a remission of his sins" in this revelation in Doctrine & Covenants Section 20 prior to the visitation of the angel Moroni corresponds to five other accounts of the First Vision, the 1832, 1835, 1842, Orson Pratt's and Orson Hyde's as noted above.

The quotation below retains the original spelling from the 1835 Doctrine and Covenants version:

> *After it was truly manifested unto this first elder [Joseph Smith, Jr.] that he had received a remission of his sins [1820] he was entangled again in the vanities of the world*; but after repenting, and humbling himself, sincerely, through faith God ministered unto him by an holy angel [1823–1827] whose countenance was as lightning, and whose garments were pure and white above all other whiteness, and gave unto him conmandments which inspired him, and gave him power from on high, by the means which were before prepared, to translate the book of Mormon, which contains a record of a fallen people, and the fullness of the gospel of Jesus Christ to the Gentiles, and to the Jews also, which was given by inspiration, and is confirmed to others by the ministering of angels, and is declared unto the world by them, proving to the world that the holy scriptures are true, and that God does inspire men and call them to his holy work in this age and generation, as well as in generations of old, thereby showing that he is the same God yesterday, to-day, and forever.—Amen. (1835 Doctrine And Covenants, Section II:2; compare current D&C 20:5–8, original spelling retained and text in brackets added)[76]

Here in the 1835 scriptural record of Doctrine and Covenants 20:5-8, it is easily seen that Joseph Smith was guardedly and minimally referring to himself at age fourteen and what he was told during his First Vision of the Father and the Son in 1820. Joseph then refers to his later need for repentance at age seventeen, leading to the first visit of the angel Moroni in September of 1823, who would prepare him to eventually obtain and translate the plates of gold of the Book of Mormon.

A dozen years had passed since 1820, before Joseph attempted in the summer of 1832 to record his First Vision in his journal. Constant persecutions, the movement of the Church from New York to Ohio and then to Missouri, and the sacred nature of Joseph's First Vision itself kept him from writing or publishing it earlier.

Joseph would again provide more firsthand details beyond his first 1832 account on November 9, 1835 to "Joshua, the Jewish Minister" also known as Robert Matthias. Again in 1838, Joseph dictated perhaps his most eloquent account of his first vision of Deity in his manuscript "Church History." Joseph's last two firsthand accounts were prepared for the *Chicago Democrat* editor John Wentworth in 1842 and for Israel Daniel Rupp who compiled a book on religious denominations of the United States in 1843.[77]

Of course there are discrepancies in the First Vision accounts as would be expected, as there are in the three New Testament synoptic gospels, Matthew, Mark, and Luke. It is perhaps beneficial to consider the fourteen firsthand and contemporary accounts of the First Vision as a whole and as separate documents.

It should be repeated that because Joseph Smith did not record his First Vision until 1832, and did not publish it in America until 1842, the earlier anti-Mormon works such as Eber D. Howe's *Mormonism Unveiled* (1834) did not include this aspect of Church history because at that time there were no published records yet revealing it. Additionally, persecutions that Joseph experienced in the 1820s were forthcoming from those relatively few locals around Palmyra who knew of Joseph's first vision of Deity, either because he told them or they heard by the grape vine, but they had no basis or official written record put out by Joseph to prove or publish opinions against him regarding his First Vision, such as in local newspapers, until a few years before his martyrdom in 1844 (DofS 3:327–328).

Joseph Smith's 1832 account of his first vision of Deity is the only account known to be partly written and partly dictated by the Prophet. As far as is known, all the other accounts were entirely dictated to clerks, or copied by clerks, or written by associates or a journalist. Joseph's 1832 First Vision account gives us details as to when

Joseph first began attending church meetings and how their teachings compared to the Holy Scriptures he was reading. This was from late 1817 to 1820.

Frederick G. Williams and Joseph Smith alternately wrote of the First Vision in the summer of 1832. Original spelling is retained and Joseph's handwriting is in bold:

> A History of the life of Joseph Smith Jr. an account of his marvelous experience and of all the mighty acts which he doeth in the name of Jesus Ch[r]ist the son of the living God of whom he beareth record and also an account of the rise of the church of Christ in the eve of time according as the Lord brough(t) forth and established by his hand[:] (firstly) he receiving the testimony from on high[;] secondly the ministering of Angels[;] thirdly the reception of the holy Priesthood by the ministering of Aangels to administer the letter of the Gospel–(–the Law and commandments as they were given unto him–) and the ordinencs, fourthly a confirmation and reception of the high Priesthood after the holy order of the son of the living God[;] power and ordinence from on high to preach the Gospel in the administration and demonstration of the spirit[;] **the Kees of the Kingdom of God** conferred upon him and the continuation of the blessings of God to him &c . . . At about the age of twelve years my mind become seriously imprest with regard to the all importent concerns for the wellfare of my immortal Soul which led me to searching the Scriptures believeing as I was taught, that they contained the word of God thus applying myself to them and my intimate acquaintance with those of different denominations led me to marvel excedingly for I discovered that they did not adorn their profession by a holy walk and Godly conversation agreeable to what I found contained in that sacred depository this was a grief to my Soul . . . (JSP, H1:10–11, punctuation added in brackets)[78]

Joseph continued to write saying that his parents "spared no pains in instructing [him] in the Christian religion" and when he was ten years old his father moved the family to Palmyra, New York. As to

Joseph's studying the holy scriptures and pondering them and his dismay with the conflicting teachings of the different churches, who "did not adorn their profession by a holy walk and Godly conversation agreeable to what I found contained in that sacred depository [The Holy Bible] this was grief to my soul." It was then when Joseph was twelve years old that he first became interested in religion, which culminated in his two years of study and investigation leading to his vision at the age of fourteen or during his "fifteenth year" (PofGP, JS-H 1:7). Joseph wrote those feelings in his first 1832 account of his First Vision that continues as follows:

> . . . thus from age twelve years to fifteen I pondered many things in my heart concerning the sittuation of the world of mankind the contentions and divi[si]ons the wicke[d]ness and abominations and the darkness which pervaded the minds of mankind my mind become exceedingly distressed for I become convicted of my sins and by searching the scriptures I found that mankind did not come unto the Lord but that they had apostatized from the true and liveing faith and that there was no society or denomination that built upon the gospel of Jesus Christ as recorded in the new testament and I felt to mourn for my own sins and for the sins of the world for I learned in the scriptures that God was the same yesterday to day and forever that he was no respecter to persons for he was God for I looked upon the sun the glorious luminary of the earth and also the moon rolling in their magesty through the heavens and also the stars shining in their courses and the earth also upon which I stood and the beast of the field and the fowls of heaven and the fish of the waters and also man walking forth upon the face of the earth in magesty and in the strength of beauty whose power and intiligence in governing the things which are so exceding great and marvilous even in the likeness of him who created him <them> and when I considered upon these things my heart exclaimed well hath the wise man said the <it is a> fool <that> saith in his heart there is no God my heart exclaimed all all these bear testimony and bespeak an omnipotant and omnipreasant power a being

> who makith Laws and decreeeth and bindeth all things in their bounds who filleth Eternity who was and is and will be from all Eternity to Eternity and when <I> considered all these things and that<that> being seeketh such to worshep him as worship him in spirit and in truth therefore I cried unto the Lord for mercy for there was none else to whom I could go and to obtain mercy and the Lord heard my cry in the wilderness and while in<the> attitude of calling upon the Lord <in the 16th year of my age>a piller of fire light above the brightness of the sun at noon day come down from above and rested upon me and I was filled with the spirit of god and the <Lord> opened the heavens upon me and I saw the Lord and he spake unto me saying Joseph <my son> thy sins are forgiven thee. go thy <way> walk in my statutes and keep my commandments behold I am the Lord of glory I was crucifyed for the world that all those who believe on my name may have Eternal life <behold> the world lieth in sin and at this time and none doeth good no not one they have turned asside from the gospel and keep not <my> commandments they draw near to me with their lips while their hearts are far from me and mine anger is kindling against the inhabitants of the earth to visit them acording to thir ungodliness and to bring to pass that which <hath> been spoken by the mouth of the prophets and Ap[o]stles behold and lo I come quickly as it [is?] written of me in the cloud <clothed> in the glory of my Father and my soul was filled with love and for many days I could rejoice with great Joy and the Lord was with me but could find none that would believe the hevnly vision nevertheless I pondered these things in my heart (JSP, H1:10–13).[79]

Joseph's first hand account of his 1832 vision did not mention any religious revivals. Nor did Orson Pratt's 1840 contemporary account. In the 1832 account Joseph speaks of being in his "sixteenth year" while in his 1835 and 1838 accounts he speaks of being in his "fifteenth year" or "about fourteen years old." These are common journalist differences. Each account gave important factual and supplementary information. The 1832 account informed us that Joseph became interested in the welfare of his soul and in religious things "from age twelve years to fifteen." Orson Pratt's account told us that Joseph was told by the Lord that he would, at a future time, receive more information about the fullness of the gospel, as did the first hand 1838 and 1842 accounts (PofGP, JS-H 1:5, 7, 26; JD 7:220-21; PWJS, p.242).

It remains that Joseph Smith's combined personal journal and history accounts from 1832, 1835, 1838, and 1842 tell us that he saw God the Father, Jesus Christ the Son of God, and holy angels. Dissecting the differences between the different accounts does not change the composite and final history. The fact that in the 1832 account Joseph said he had his First Vision "in the sixteenth year of my age" and in the 1835, 1838, and 1842 accounts Joseph latter corrected himself and said he was in his "fifteenth year" or was "fourteen years of age," is of little consequence in understanding Joseph's message. Secondly, Joseph's 1832 account only mentions one "personage" while his 1835 and later accounts speak of "two personages." To comparatively discredit one or another or all of the accounts for reason of discrepancies or anachronisms ignores the realities of journal writing and Joseph's human literary progression. Of course, Joseph was human and therefore he included anachronisms in his several accounts. Joseph often corrected himself as most good journalists do. The world would be fortunate to have just one account of such an epochal event. The Prophet Joseph Smith, his clerks and associates left the saints and the world many!

Not including the nearly identical accounts, to have six personally written or dictated firsthand accounts and five contemporary accounts written by reputable associates who heard Joseph's telling of the visitation of God the Father and His Son Jesus Christ as well as angels to the young man Joseph Smith in 1820, is a blessing beyond the expectations of every seeker of truth, historian, and true saint. Adding the Prophet's motivations, questions, and the Lord's responses and rejection of the various religious sects of that day gives the honest investigator a clear understanding of how God feels about everything. To expect perfect synoptic agreement between the different accounts of Joseph's First Vision is to expect what does not exist in either The Holy Bible or The Book of Mormon.

Besides the Doctrine and Covenants Section 20 account, the four 1835 accounts of Joseph's First Vision are shorter and less detailed compared to the other accounts Joseph wrote or dictated himself. The November 9, 1835 telling of his vision to "Joshua the Jewish minister" or Robert Matthias of New York City indicates that Joseph said he saw "a pillar of fire above my head" and that "a personage appeared in the midst of this pillar of flame which was spread all around, and yet nothing was consumed[;] another personage soon appeared like unto the first, he said unto me thy sins are forgiven thee, he testified unto me that Jesus Christ is the Son of God; (and I saw many angels in this vision)[.] I was about 14 years old when I received this first communication" (punctuation added in brackets).[80]

The other very short 1835 account came just five days later when Joseph spoke to a gentlemen named Erastus Holmes on the afternoon of November 14th, saying: ". . . I commenced and gave him a brief relation of my experience while in my juvenile years, say from 6 years old up to the time I received my first visitation of Angels which was when I was about 14 years old and also the visitations I received afterward, concerning the Book of Mormon, and a short account of the rise and progress of the church, up to this, date he listened very attentively and he is a very candid man indeed and I am much pleased with him" (punctuation left).[81]

Above we see that the Prophet Joseph Smith delineated between his First Vision of the Father and the Son as well as "of Angels" which occurred when he was "about 14 years old" *and* his visitation later by the angel Moroni regarding the Book of Mormon when he was seventeen years old.

The most popular and canonized version of Joseph's First Vision accounts is the 1838 version he dictated to his clerk George Robinson. This manuscript account was later copied and edited by clerks James Mulholland and Howard Coray in 1841 as part of Joseph's "Manuscript History" published in early Church newspapers and in The Pearl of Great Price, a latter-day book of scripture canonized by the Church in 1880 giving revelations about the lost books of Enoch, Abraham, Moses, and the history of the Prophet Joseph Smith.[82]

The First Presidency of the Church chose the 1838 account which was dictated by the Prophet Joseph and was the most detailed account initially intended for the Manuscript History of the Church. That account was then also approved by the Council of the Twelve Apostles, the Quorums of the Seventy, and by common consent of the Saints during a General Conference in 1880 and designated as latter-day holy scripture in what is today the Joseph Smith—History portion of The Pearl of Great Price, one of four books of scripture used by the Saints.

As noted earlier, the 1842 account of the First Vision was written by Joseph Smith in the form of a letter to John Wentworth, editor and proprietor of the *Chicago Democrat* newspaper. This account of the vision was published in the Nauvoo newspaper *Times and Seasons* and gives a brief yet very consecutive and doctrinal statement of what Joseph learned from his heavenly interview:

> My father was a farmer and taught me the art of husbandry. When about fourteen years of age I began to reflect upon the importance of being prepared for a future state, and upon enquiring the plan of salvation I found that there was a great clash in religious sentiment; if I went to one society they referred me to one plan, and another to another; each one pointing to his own particular creed as the summum bonum of perfection: considering that all could not be right, and that God could not be the author of so much confusion I determined to investigate the subject more fully, believing that if God had a church it would not be split up into factions, and that if he taught one society to worship one way, and administer in one set of ordinances, he would not teach another principles which were diametrically opposed. Believing the word of God I had confidence in the declaration of James;
>
> "If any man lack wisdom let him ask of God who giveth to all men liberally and upbraideth not and it shall be given him."
>
> I retired to a secret place in a grove and began to call upon the Lord, while fervently engaged in supplication my mind was taken away from the objects with which I was surrounded, and I was enwrapped in a [p. 706] heavenly vision and saw two glorious personages who exactly resembled each other in

> features, and likeness, surrounded with a brilliant light which eclipsed the sun at noon-day.
>
> They told me that all religious denominations were believing in incorrect doctrines, and that none of them was acknowledged of God as his church and kingdom. And I was expressly commanded to "go not after them," at the same time receiving a promise that the fullness of the gospel should at some future time be made known unto me. (T&S, 1842, pp. 705–706; JSP, H1:431–501)[83]

Why did Joseph Smith make so many different accounts and references of his First Vision? It is apparent that Joseph Smith attempted to improve the record of his vision by giving details which were left out of the earlier accounts as well as to correct discrepancies. After the Church was organized in 1830, Joseph more readily responded to those who inquired about his theophany, giving them sometimes abbreviated accounts, such as the two given in 1835 which became four when clerks recopied them in the third person.

Joseph Smith desired to put his First Vision experience into better context with the historical background in which he lived as he got deeper insights and perspectives. Additionally, official requests from newspaper editors and a Christian author including David Nye White, John Wentworth, and Israel Daniel Rupp gave Joseph pause to prepare or dictate lengthy and well-thought-out letters which eventually became major contributions to the history of the Restored Church.

The Articles of Faith were drawn from the 1842 Wentworth Letter, which is a treasure trove of information about many teachings of the Restoration including the First Vision. Between 1820 and 1842, in every case, the Prophet wanted to share divine revelations God had given him, yet regarding his First Vision of the Father and the Son, only when the people were ready and if possible worthy to hear it. Joseph was slow to share his most sacred experiences (D&C 84:57; "Letter IV," M&A 1:5:77-80).

The Church had become international by 1842 and the Prophet was ready to proclaim the First Vision to the world. In March of that year the 1838 and Wentworth Letter accounts were published in the Church's newspaper the *Times and Seasons* over Joseph Smith's name.

It is this writer's opinion that a second reason Joseph Smith published his First Vision in 1842 was Joseph's feeling that his mortal mission was drawing to a close. It was of course this 1838 account published in 1842 which became the standard account and scripture of the Church.

No two accounts or documents of the First Vision are exactly the same. Four accounts or documents are very similar because of the rewriting of the November 9th and 14th, 1835 "Ohio Journal 1835–1836" accounts from first person to third person for the "History 1834–1836" accounts. Two other later accounts are very similar, the 1842 Wentworth Letter and 1843 Rupp Letter. The former apparently being used to produce the latter.[84]

Improving or rewriting the historical record of the First Vision over time would be expected of any journal writer and author, like Joseph Smith. The Prophet was not afraid to be criticized later for variations which might exist in one account compared to another if the succeeding accounts were more complete, accurate, and beneficial. The historical record shows that the several accounts have many corresponding or parallel harmonies and related similarities which confirm their overall meaning. Joseph knew that honest observers would understand the message he was trying to convey and that those willing to call upon God as he did could obtain their own independent and divine witness from the Holy Spirit or confirmation of the veracity of the First Vision and what it means.

Whether personally written or dictated to a clerk, more or fewer words, Joseph Smith's firsthand accounts were written under different circumstances, during different periods in the Prophet's life and for different reasons and audiences.

Regarding four of them, the 1832; Nov. 9, 1835; 1838; and 1842 accounts, Dr. Milton V. Backman, Emeritus Professor of Church History at Brigham Young University, further related in his 1986 book, *Eyewitness Accounts of the Restoration*, "It is not surprising, therefore, that each of them emphasize different aspects of his experience. If one were relating the incident to a group of high priests, for example, he would undoubtedly tell it somewhat differently than he would to individuals who had never heard of Joseph Smith or of the Restoration of the gospel."[85]

Alexander Neibaur left a remarkable account of Joseph's First Vision. He was born in 1808 in Ehrenbreitstein, Germany and attended the University of Berlin where he studied dentistry and later practiced in Preston, England. In 1834, he met and married Ellen Breakel (1811–1870) of the Church of England. When the first Mormon missionaries arrived in England in 1837, the young Neibaur couple were among the first converts. Alexander Neibaur was baptized on April 9, 1838 by Isaac Russell after being taught the restored gospel by Elders Heber C. Kimball, Willard Richards, Orson Hyde and others. The Neibaurs migrated to Nauvoo, Illinois on April 19, 1841, where Alexander further pursued his profession in dentistry and as a matchmaker or manufacturer of matches. He was ordained an elder by Willard Richards in 1841 and a Seventy in 1844. Alexander taught the Prophet Joseph Smith both German and Hebrew while in Nauvoo. Ellen was pregnant when the persecuted Saints evacuated Nauvoo in 1846, so Alexander remained with her as one of the defenders of the besieged city during the Nauvoo War. The Neibaurs later moved to Winter Quarters, now Florence, North Omaha, Nebraska to join the Saints before heading west on the Mormon Trail. Alexander Neibaur was the first Jew to join The Church of Jesus Christ of Latter-day Saints and the first dentist to practice in the Salt Lake Valley after his arrival with his wife on September 24, 1848, about a year after the first pioneer companies arrived with President Brigham Young on July 24, 1847. Alexander and Ellen had fourteen children. Alexander died in Salt Lake City, December 15, 1883. [86]

Alexander Neibaur recorded in his diary for May 24, 1844 that he visited and had dinner at the home of the Prophet Joseph Smith with Edward Bonney. He noted that after dinner he read German with the Prophet. Following this study, the Prophet related his first vision with Deity to these men and Brother Neibaur recorded it. Brother Neibaur's account is recorded below, the original spelling and lack of punctuation are retained:

> May 24 called at J: Smith 10 oc'lk foren[oon] took Dinner (read German) after dinner met the Sax & fox Indians Dance their Waar Danc = 24 called at Br J.S met Mr Bonnie = Br Joseph tolt us the first call he had a Revival Meeting his Mother &

> Br & Sister got Religion, he wanted to get Religion too wanted to feel & shout like the Rest but could feel nothing, opened his Bible the first Passage that struck him was if any man lack Wisdom let him ask of God who giveth to all Men liberallity & upbraidat not went into the Wood to pray kneelt himself down his tongue was closet cleavet to his roof— could utter not a word, felt easier after a while= saw a fire towards heaven came near & nearer saw a personage in the fire light complexion blue eyes a piece of white cloth drawn over his shoulders his right arm bear after a while a other person came to the side of the first Mr Smith then asked must I join the Methodist Church= No= they are not my People, th all have gone astray there is none that doeth good no not one, but this is my Beloved son harken ye him, the fire drew nigher Rested upon the tree enveloped him [illegible, page torn] comforted Indeavoured to arise but felt uncomen feeble= got into the house told the Methodist priest, said this was not a age for God to Reveal himself in Vision Revelation has ceased with the New Testament. (Jessee, PJS, 1:459–461)

Of interest in Brother Neibaur's account is his abbreviated yet thorough coverage of the main points of Joseph's vision. Dr. Neibaur recorded more than twenty separate details from Joseph vision using not very many words. Also unique about Dr. Neibaur's firsthand account is that he records Joseph's description of the first arriving personage, God the Father, who was followed by a second personage, Jesus Christ. Brother Neibaur writes that Joseph, "saw a personage in the fire [of] light complexion [with] blue eyes [and] a piece of white cloth drawn over his shoulders[,] his right arm bear[.] [A]fter a w[h]ile a[n]other person came to the side of the first" (letters, words and punctuation in brackets added).

Above Joseph Smith describes to a contemporary witness that during his First Vision of 1820 he saw that God the Father has a "light complexion" and "blue eyes" and was dressed in "a piece of white cloth drawn over his shoulders his right arm bear." This is perhaps the most singular and detailed account of any prophetic description of God the Father ever given! On April 3, 1836, Joseph Smith and Oliver

Cowdery would witness and Joseph would later dictate to his clerk a remarkable description of Jehovah or Jesus Christ when he appeared in glory at the Kirtland Temple (D&C 110:2–3). We have no equivalent records giving such descriptive human and divine information about the Father and the Son.

Without considering how twenty-first-century sociological and ethnocentric opinions would respond to the Prophet Joseph's description of God the Father having a "light complexion" or being essentially Caucasian with "blue eyes," one is left to consider the sacred words of the Prophet recorded by an honest contemporary witness, Alexander Neibaur.

The prophet Nephi said in the Book of Mormon regarding the love of God and of his mediator Jesus Christ, "he denieth none that come unto him, black and white, bond and free, male and female . . . all are alike unto God" (BofM, 2 Nephi 26:33). And in having their own identity, person, and color, God and Christ do not lose their divine natures and power to redeem.

If one discovers by his or her own faith, belief, prayer, and revelation that Joseph's First Vision is true, then any discussion of the sociological ramifications of Dr. Neibaur's account is rightly tabled until further revelation can answer all the questions. The Prophet Joseph Smith shared what he saw with Dr. Neibaur. It is then incumbent upon the reader or investigator to discover the truth of Dr. Neibaur's account and all of the accounts independently from God. What anyone can know is what all the prophets have told us and what the Lord has confirmed by His Holy Spirit (HBKJV, Amos 3:7; John 14:26).

All known firsthand and contemporary accounts and references of Joseph Smith's first vision of Deity have been identified and each firsthand and several key or noteworthy contemporary accounts have been discussed.

A subject matter harmony chart of the different accounts is presented later in this writing which will further show the integrity of the overall collection of First Vision records when they are compared.

Chapter 10

Believing Joseph's First Vision

Regarding the variations in the Prophet Joseph Smith's First Vision accounts, President Gordon B. Hinckley said:

> I am not worried that the Prophet Joseph Smith gave a number of versions of the first vision any more than I am worried that there are four different writers of the gospels in the New Testament, each with his own perceptions, each telling the events to meet his own purpose for writing at the time. I am more concerned with the fact that God has revealed in this dispensation a great and marvelous and beautiful plan that motivates men and women to love their Creator and their Redeemer, to appreciate and serve one another, to walk in faith on the road that leads to immortality and eternal life.[87]

The late Professor Richard Lloyd Anderson, who taught ancient Greek, the early Christian Church and early Latter-day Saint Church History at Brigham Young University, wrote about Joseph Smith's First Vision accounts as follows:

> What are the main problems of interpreting so many accounts? The first problem is the interpreter. One person perceives harmony and interconnections while another overstates differences. Think of how you retell a vivid event in your life—marriage, first day on the job, or an automobile accident. A record of all your comments would include short and long versions, along with many bits and pieces. Only by blending these glimpses can an outsider reconstruct what originally

> happened. The biggest trap is comparing description in one report with silence in another. By assuming that what is not said is not known, some come up with arbitrary theories of an evolution in the Prophet's story. Yet we often omit parts of an episode because of the chance of the moment, not having time to tell everything, or deliberately stressing only a part of the original event in a particular situation. This means that any First Vision account contains some fraction of the whole experience. Combining all reliable reports will recreate the basics of Joseph Smith's quest and conversation with the Father and Son.[88]

Author and religious studies scholar Stephen Prothero, who is not a member of The Church of Jesus Christ of Latter-day Saints, further stated:

> Critics of Mormonism have delighted in the discrepancies between the canonical [1838 and Pearl of Great Price] account and earlier renditions, especially one written in Smith's own hand in 1832. For example, in the 1832 version, Jesus appears to Smith alone, and does all the talking himself. Such complaints, however, are much ado about relatively nothing. Any good lawyer (or historian) would expect to find contradictions or competing narratives written down years apart and decades after the event. And despite the contradictions, key elements abide. In each case, Jesus appears to Smith in a vision. In each case, Smith is blessed with a revelation. In each case, God tells him to remain aloof from all Christian denominations, as something better is in store.[89]

Latter-day Saint historian Steven C. Harper, writing of the difference between the believer's approach to the First Vision and the skeptic's or unbeliever's said the following:

> One will arrive at the same conclusions as the skeptics if one shares their assumptions about what the facts mean. But if one is open-minded, other meanings for the same facts are possible. The danger of close-mindedness is as real for believers as for skeptics. Many believers seem just as likely to begin

> with preconceived notions rather than a willingness to go where Joseph's accounts lead them. They might assume, for instance, that Joseph told his family of the vision immediately or wrote it immediately, that he always understood all of its implications perfectly or consistently through the years, that he would always remember or tell exactly the same story, or that it would always be recorded and transmitted the same. But none of those assumptions is supported by the evidence. Some believers become skeptics in short order when they learn of the accounts and find that their assumptions of what would happen if Joseph told the truth are not supported by the historical record.
>
> There is an alternative approach to the evidence. It is humble, believing, and thoroughly informed. It does not assume that one already knows how Joseph would respond to and tell a heavenly vision. Instead it allows his accounts to shape that understanding. This is the historical method. It is the method of the believing scholars who study all of the accounts and the context in which Joseph lived and wrote or told them.[90]

There can be no doubt for the need in the world of such a revelation as Joseph's First Vision and for the ensuing plan of happiness that the Lord revealed through the young prophet. Focusing on differences rather than on the combined whole of the various accounts of Joseph's vision will give the reader a warped view of Joseph's vision. To disbelieve the five contemporary accounts witnessed by those who heard Joseph relate his first vision of Deity, is to prejudge without reason. No secular or divine truth was ever discovered by applying a negative attitude or a doubting mind. Proving a negative or that something did not happen for lack of evidence is impossible, and considering Joseph's many First Vision accounts in their historic settings, there is no legitimate lack of evidence to discredit him.

To believe that Joseph was not being honest is to prejudge him unfairly. His integrity was intact before, during and after the experience he eventually shared. Studying the details of Joseph Smith's First Vision and prayerfully considering each of the accounts in their correct historical settings will lead a seeker of truth to the point of a personal connection with our Father in Heaven and His Son Jesus Christ, as never before.

The apostle Peter of the Early Church declared long ago, "that God is no respecter of persons" (HBKJV, Acts 10:34) and his fellow apostle James said, "If any of you lack wisdom, let him ask of God . . . and it shall be given him" (HBKJV, James 1:5). Why did these two apostles of Jesus Christ say that? Because they had applied that same faith as Joseph Smith did and had received a witness from God themselves. They did not see God the Father as Joseph Smith did, it is true. But they did gain a divine witness by the Holy Spirit. When Jesus asked, "Whom say ye that I am?" Peter answered, "Thou art the Christ, the Son of the living God." Jesus perceived that Peter had gained a heavenly knowledge. The Savior then said to Peter, "Blessed art thou Simon Bar-jona: for flesh and blood hath not revealed it unto thee, but my Father which is in heaven" (HBKJV, Matthew 16:15–17). Peter received a witness of Jesus Christ from the Holy Spirit through his prayer to God the Father.

The principle of revelation applies to modern Christian saints and inquirers as much as it applies to ancient saints! Searching the words of the prophets both anciently and in the latter days with a humble determination to understand and draw closer to God and Christ, is not only the historically honest way, but it is the only way one may see their seed of faith grow and blossom into a pure knowledge of truth and its accompanying joy. Joseph Smith was foreordained before he was born like Jeremiah to fulfill a great mission (BofM, 2 Nephi 3:6; HBKJV, Isaiah 11:1–11; Jeremiah 1:5). While most people will not see a pillar of light come down from heaven, or see the face of God the Father, or of the Son, or of angels, as Joseph did, yet all may feel the power of the Holy Spirit in their bosoms burn with the truths of the restored gospel. Each may also have faith to believe on the words of those who have seen, or have received this divine witness of the Spirit, which *belief* in itself is a *gift of the Spirit* and they can be filled with the Spirit of God and with great joy because of that belief! (D&C 46:13–14).

As children of God, we don't know all the answers to every question of life. No two people are born in this mortal life with the same premortal intelligence and the same spiritual gifts from God (PofGP,

Abraham 3:18–19). Yet, anyone can grow and develop extraordinary faith and spiritual gifts during this mortal life. But if one cannot muster the faith to see the face of God, or an angel from heaven, then one should seek to be ministered to by the Holy Spirit through the prayer of faith. There is no greater witness than the Holy Ghost! This gift is available to all who call upon God with all the energy of their hearts with true undying faith and repentance. As recorded by the apostle Luke, the Savior said to the unbelievers who mocked Him, "If ye then, being evil, know how to give good gifts unto your children: how much more shall your heavenly Father give the Holy Spirit to them that ask him?" (HBKJV, Luke 11:13).

Joseph Smith received a revelation in April of 1829 for his friend and clerk Oliver Cowdery, who wanted to have the gift of translation like Joseph Smith had while translating the Book of Mormon, apparently without the Urim and Thummim, but by the Holy Spirit and Joseph's seer stone. By the Spirit of the Lord the revelation reads, "Yea, behold, I will tell you in your mind and in your heart, by the Holy Ghost, which shall come upon you and which shall dwell in your heart. Now, behold, this is the spirit of revelation; behold this is the spirit by which Moses brought the children of Israel through the Red Sea on dry ground" (D&C 8:2–3).

The Holy Ghost is the power of God and the source of true knowledge for those that believe. Those who will call upon the Lord in faith will receive it, by repentance, then by baptism and by the laying on of hands by those in authority, they will receive the *gifts of the spirit* and do great things which are told in the Holy Scriptures (D&C 46).

Chapter 11

Harmony of the First Vision Accounts

A HARMONY OF SUBJECTS FOR ELEVEN OF THE FIRST VISION ACCOUNTS in relation to the historical setting, truths revealed, and the aftermath of Joseph's vision of Deity are presented below, closely following the late Dr. Milton V. Bachman Jr.'s 1986 harmony of subjects related to Joseph's accounts by the year they were written.[91] The 1830 partial account (D&C 20:5) that Bachman omitted and the 1832 first major account are included here. The four November 1835 documents will be considered as one 1835 account. Of course the canonized 1838 account is included. The 1842 Wentworth Letter account is included, while the nearly identical 1843 Rupp Letter account is left out. The contemporary accounts of others by letter are as follows: Orson Pratt (P), Orson Hyde (H), Levi Richards (R), David Nye White for the *New Spectator* (S) and Alexander Neibaur (N). Groupings of accounts by numeric year indicate Joseph Smith's firsthand accounts, while groupings with an alphabetic letter designation indicate contemporary accounts.

Historical Setting	Harmonizing Accounts
Joseph's quest to be forgiven of his sins, his concern for his soul and/or his preparation for his future estate or reward	(1830, 1832, 1835, 1842) (P, H)
Joseph's concern for mankind in general	(1832) (P, H)
Joseph's investigation of various churches	(1832, 1835, 1838, 1842) (P, H, R)
Joseph's concern because the different churches proclaimed conflicting doctrines	(1838, 1842) (P, H)
Joseph's desire to know which church to join or his desire to find Christ's church	(1832, 1835, 1838, 1842) (P, H, S, R)
Joseph's search continued several years	(1832)
Unusual religious excitement in the area, district, region and country where he lived	(1838) (N)
Contention existed among denominations	(1838, 1842, P, H)
Joseph read James 1:5 from the HBJKV	(1835, 1838, 1842) (P, H, S, N)
Joseph sought an answer through prayer	(1832, 1835, 1838, 1842) (P, H, S, N, R)
Vision occurred when Joseph was about fourteen or fifteen years of age	(1832, 1835, 1835-2, 1838, 1842) (P, H, S, N)
Joseph's vision occurred in the spring of 1820	(1838)

Truths Revealed in the Vision	Harmonizing Accounts
God hears and answers prayers and intervenes in the affairs of men	(1832, 1835, 1838, 1842) (P, H, S, N)
The power of evil is real and strong	(1835, 1838) (P, H)
The power of God is stronger than the influence of evil	(1835, 1838) (P, H)
Joseph was engulfed in a pillar of light and filled with unspeakable joy which was the Spirit of God.	(1832, 1835, 1838) (P, H)

Truths Revealed in the Vision	Harmonizing Accounts
Joseph saw two personages	(1835, 1838, 1842) (P, H, S, N)
The two personages resembled each other in features and likeness	(1835, 1838, 1842) (P, H)
The two personage were identified as the Father and the Son and that man was created in the image of God	(1838) (S)
Joseph saw many angels	(1835, 1835-2)
Jesus Christ is the Son of God	(1835, 1838) (S)
The Savior was crucified for the world and all who believe in Him will have eternal life	(1832)
Second Coming of Jesus Christ was imminent in this dispensation of time	(1832)
Joseph was forgiven of his sins	(1830, 1832, 1835) (P, N)
God's true church was not upon the earth in 1820	(1832, 1838, 1842) (P, H, N, R)
Professors of religion taught incorrect doctrine	(1832, 1838, 1842) (P, H, N)
Professors of religion denied the power of God	(1838)
Fullness of the Gospel would be revealed to Joseph Smith the Prophet in due time	(1842) (P, H)
Joseph learned other truths which are not written	(1838)

Aftermath	Harmonizing Accounts
Joseph rejoiced for he was filled with peace and love from his experience	(1832) (P, H)
Joseph was not successful in his attempt to convince ministers and others of his vision	(1838) (N)
Joseph was persecuted after sharing his vision	(1832, 1838) (S)

Dr. Bachman's harmony of Joseph Smith's First Vision gives the reader a good sense and appreciation for the consistency and consolidation over time of Joseph's reflections of his heavenly experience in the grove at Palmyra. As every serious journal writer knows, the story is never completely covered in the first writing. It is clear that major principles and events are mentioned in several accounts.

Six times, reflected in the chart above, the Prophet Joseph Smith mentioned a key principle or event in his vision only once in a single account. Had Joseph not included these singular principles and events, each found only once in the several accounts, the precious knowledge they contain would have been lost. As Joseph Smith added more remembrances and reflections in later accounts over time, the story of his great vision became more complete.

Chapter 12

Contemporary Witnesses Testify

Eleven primary accounts in fourteen documents including a short reference in D&C 20:5 of Joseph Smith's First Vision have been identified, six of which were produced or dictated to clerks by the Prophet himself, and five were contemporary reports by others who heard him relate his experience and made a record of it during the Prophet's lifetime.

Orson Pratt was one of the early converts to the Church and one of the contemporary witnesses to Joseph Smith's telling of his First Vision. Elder Pratt was baptized in September of 1830 after traveling two-hundred miles to meet the young Prophet Joseph Smith in Manchester, New York. In December of 1830 Orson Pratt was ordained an elder. Orson would follow the Prophet to Kirtland, Ohio in 1831 where he lived in Joseph's home for two months. Orson Pratt knew the Prophet Joseph Smith as intimately perhaps as Oliver Cowdery and was ordained one of the original Twelve Apostles of the Church on April 26, 1835.

While serving as an apostle and a missionary for nine months in Edinburg, Scotland in 1840, Elder Pratt raised up a church of 200 converts (*MS* 27:88).[92] While there Elder Pratt published a pamphlet entitled, *Remarkable Visions*. From this source the world received another testimony of the First Vision as follows:

> And he was en[w]rapped in a heavenly vision, and saw two glorious personages who exactly represented each other in their features and likeness. He was informed, that his sins were forgiven him [. . .] that all the religious denominations

> were believing in incorrect doctrines; and, consequently that none of them was acknowledged by God, as his church and kingdom. And he was expressly commanded, to go not after them; and he received a promise that the true doctrine, the fullness of the gospel, should at some future time, be made known to him; after which the vision withdrew, leaving his mind in a state of calmness and peace, indescribable.[93]

In a later message to the Saints in Great Britain entitled, "Are the Father and the Son Two Distinct Persons?" published in the *Millennial Star* for September and October of 1849, Elder Orson Pratt declared that Joseph had seen both the "Father and the Son" as two distinct persons (MS 11:281–284, 309–302).[94]

President Brigham Young (1801–1877) knew Joseph Smith beginning in 1832, was one of the first apostles of the new Church ordained in 1835 and after Joseph Smith's death would become the Second President of the Church. On June 23, 1867, President Young stated:

> Joseph was naturally inclined to be religious, and being young, and surrounded with this excitement, no wonder that he became seriously impressed with the necessity of serving the Lord. But as the cry on every hand was, "Lo, here is Christ," and "Lo, there!" Said he, "Lord, teach me, that I may know for myself, who among these are right." And what was the answer? "They are all out of the way; they have gone astray, and there is none that doeth good, no not one." When he found out that none were right, he began to inquire of the Lord what was right, and he learned for himself. Was he aware of what was going to be done? By no means. He did not know what the Lord was going to do with him. (JD 12:67)

Another witness of the First Vision not yet mentioned was an early British convert from Canada who heard the restored gospel from Elder Parley P. Pratt. President John Taylor (1808–1887) was baptized a member of the Church on May 9, 1836, was ordained an apostle December 19, 1838, and became the Third President of the Church, serving from 1877 to 1887. John Taylor was a contemporary intimately acquainted with Joseph Smith from 1836 to 1844 and described the

First Vision as it was related to him by the Prophet Joseph Smith. After the Prophet's death in 1844 President Taylor testified of the First Vision and of Joseph's character:

> . . . A message was announced to us by Joseph Smith the Prophet, as a revelation from God wherein he stated that holy angels had appeared to him and revealed the everlasting Gospel as it existed in former ages; and that God the Father and God the Son had also appeared to him: the Father pointing to the Son said, "This is my beloved Son, hear ye him." (John Taylor, "Three Nights' Public Discussion," Liverpool, 1850, 23–24; PofGP, JS-H 1:17)

> I was acquainted with Joseph Smith for years. I have traveled with him; I have been with him in private and in public; I have associated with him in councils of all kinds; I have listened hundreds of times to his public teachings, and his advice to his friends and associates of a more private nature. I have been at his house and seen his deportment in his family. I have seen him arraigned before the tribunals of his country, and have seen him honorably acquitted, and delivered from the pernicious breath of slander, and the machinations and falsehoods of wicked and corrupt men. I was with him living, and with him when he died, when he was murdered in Carthage jail by a ruthless mob . . . I have seen him, then, under these various circumstances, and I testify before God, angels, and men, that he was a good, honorable, virtuous man—that his doctrines were good, scriptural, and wholesome—that his precepts were such as became a man of God—that his private and public character was unimpeachable—and that he lived and died as a man of God and a gentleman. (John Taylor, Deseret News: Semi-Weekly, SLC, Utah, 18 April 1882; The Gospel Kingdom, p. 355)[95]

Recalling what Joseph told him prior to 1844, President Taylor said in 1879:

> I can tell you what he told me about it. He said that he was very ignorant of the ways, designs and purposes of God, and knew nothing about them; he was a youth unacquainted with religious matters or the systems and theories of the day. He went to the Lord, having read James' statement . . . He believed that statement and went to the Lord and asked him, and the Lord revealed himself to him together with his Son Jesus, and, pointing to the latter, said: "This is my beloved Son, hear him." He then asked in regard to the various religions with which he was surrounded. He enquired which of them was right, for he wanted to know the right way and to walk in it. He was told that none of them was right, that they had all departed from the right way. (JD 21:161)[96]

John Taylor later continued his testimony regarding Joseph Smith in a sermon in October of 1881 to the Saints:

> We all look upon Joseph Smith as being a Prophet of God. God called him to occupy the position that he did. How long ago? Thousands of years ago before this world was formed. The Prophets prophesied about his coming, that a man should arise whose name should be Joseph, and that his father's name should be Joseph, and also that he should be a descendant of that Joseph who was sold into Egypt. This prophecy you will find recorded in the Book of Mormon. He had very great and precious promises made to him by the Lord. I have heard him say on certain occasions, "You do not know who I am." The world did not like him. The world did not like either the Savior, or the Prophets; they have never liked revealed truth; and it is as much as a bargain for the Saints even to bear the truth.
>
> In the commencement of the work, the Father and the Son appeared to Joseph Smith. And when they appeared to him, the Father, pointing to the Son, said, "This is my beloved Son, hear him." As much as to say, "I have not come to teach and instruct you; but I refer you to my Only Begotten, who is the Mediator of the New Covenant, the Lamb slain from before the foundation of the world; I refer you to Him as your

> Redeemer, your High Priest and Teacher. Hear Him." (JD 26:106)

Professor Milton V. Backman in 1986 observed , "Elder Taylor not only declared that he personally learned from Joseph Smith the basic truths unfolded during the First Vision, but proclaimed that Joseph Smith's 1838 history discussing events preceding the organization of the Church was accurate" (PofGP, JS-H 1:1–75).[97]

President Wilford Woodruff (1807–1898), an early apostle and a President of the Church, was also a contemporary associate and friend of the Prophet Joseph Smith. Many years after his association with the Prophet Joseph Smith, President Woodruff declared:

> I have never read anywhere, that I know of, of the same power manifested in any dispensation to the children of men, which was manifested to the Prophet of God in the organization of this Church, when the Father and the Son both appeared to the Prophet Joseph in answer to his prayer. . . .This was an important revelation, which has never been manifested in the same manner in any dispensation of the world, that God has given concerning His work. So in its organization, the Prophet of God was administered to by the angels of heaven. They were his teachers, they were his instructors, and all that he did, and all that he performed from the commencement, from that day to the day of his martyrdom, was by the revelation of Jesus Christ. (MS 52:258)[98]

Joseph Smith was alone in the sacred grove when the Father and the Son, after descending in a pillar of light, visited him, and conversed with him. Contemporary witnesses mentioned above have told us and recorded for all time and eternity what Joseph told them about his marvelous vision.

There is no evidence of their colluding in order to promote a fraud, rather they freely recorded their personal interviews, or corresponded by letters with the Prophet Joseph during the last years of his mortal life. Their most powerful testimonies, in the case of those who became Saints or members, came from the lips of the Prophet himself and from the confirmation of the Holy Spirit.

These contemporary witnesses of Joseph Smith's First Vision were not all his associates in faith. John Wentworth, Daniel Rupp, and David Nye White were an unaffiliated newspaper editor, a religious historian, and a magazine editor, respectively. Another contemporary who heard Joseph's telling of his vision was a traveling Jewish stranger. And as reviewed above, the Prophet's sacred first vision of Deity accounts were recorded, spoken of, and published by faithful leaders and apostles of the Church as well.

To each of these witnesses, the modern Saints are sincerely grateful and indebted for their thoughtful and detailed contemporary records of the Prophet Joseph Smith's First Vision, one of the most important religious events since the creation of the heavens and earth.

Chapter 13

The First Vision and the Angel Moroni's Visits

Some who have denied the reality of the First Vision of the Prophet Joseph Smith have enlisted statements of Joseph's wayward brother and former church leader William Smith (1811–1893) given in his autobiography late in life (1883). They claim that William said there was no religious excitement in Palmyra in 1820 and that Joseph's only visions took place beginning in 1823 when the angel Moroni visited him the first time. Yet, William Smith admits, "A more elaborate and accurate description of [Joseph Smith's] vision, however, will be found in his own history."[99]

Richard Lloyd Anderson noted, "The Prophet does not suggest that he confided his FIRST VISION to his family" (EofM 3:357). Orson Pratt first published the vision in 1840. William Smith was born March 13, 1811 at Royalton, Windsor County, Vermont. He was nine years old in 1820 and became one of the original apostles of the Restored Church in 1835. William asked to be ordained Church Patriarch when Joseph Smith Sr. died and Hyrum and Joseph Smith had both been martyred in 1844. Brigham Young, then President of the Twelve Apostles, agreed and William was ordained May 24, 1845 as requested. Within days William began to usurp authority over the Twelve and claim he was the head of the whole church. William was excommunicated from the Church a year later on October 12, 1846.

William Smith's history should be of interest to investigators of Joseph's First Vision, however, those referring to it should realize that

William's testimony is less consistent than his contemporaries Orson Pratt, Brigham Young, and John Taylor and others. He died in 1893 an apostate who separated himself from the Restored Church and the fullness of the gospel that the Prophet Joseph Smith had revealed and taught to the Saints. While he bore testimony of the First Vision, William Smith is not the most reliable witness for the revelations of the Prophet Joseph Smith.[100]

Three and one-half years after his First Vision, in fulfillment of the Lord's earlier promise to Joseph that he would be "further directed" (JS-H 1:26), the angel Moroni first visited Joseph Smith on September 21, 1823 in Joseph's room in Palmyra, New York. Moroni was a former prophet who lived in ancient America and was now a resurrected being in the service of God. Moroni would visit Joseph at the Hill Cumorah each consecutive year in September over four years, or five visits in all, from 1823–1827. At Moroni's last visit on September 22, 1827, the angel delivered up the gold plates on which the ancient Nephite record of the Book of Mormon was written that Joseph would translate by late June 1829 and publish in March of 1830.

Opponents of Joseph Smith have intentionally confused the First Vision of 1820 and the visits of the angel Moroni between 1823 and 1827. One misunderstood source, used by some who have denied the First Vision of Joseph Smith, comes from Oliver Cowdery's letter to W. W. Phelps giving the early history of the Prophet recorded in the *Messenger and Advocate* newspaper in 1834.[101] Oliver began to write the background details of religious excitement prior to Joseph's First Vision of the Father and the Son in the first installment of his history intending to describe the actual vision in the second or next installment of the church's newspaper. When Joseph Smith read the first article and realized what Oliver was about to do, he stopped Oliver from finishing the story and directed him to instead record the visit of the angel Moroni relative to the already published Book of Mormon.[102] Evidently, in late 1834 and early 1835, Joseph felt that he was not ready to divulge in print his most sacred of all revelations, the vision of the Father and the Son.

Below is the abstract of an essay written by researcher Roger Nicholson which explains in greater detail why some are being confused:

> In 1834, Oliver Cowdery began publishing a history of the Church in installments in the pages of the Latter-day Saints' Messenger and Advocate. The first installment talks of the religious excitement and events that ultimately led to Joseph Smith's First Vision at age 14. However, in the subsequent installment published two months later, Oliver claims that he made a mistake, correcting Joseph's age from 14 to 17 and failing to make any direct mention of the First Vision. Oliver instead tells the story of Moroni's visit, thus making it appear that the religious excitement led to Moroni's visit. This curious account has been misunderstood by some to be evidence that the "first" vision that Joseph claimed was actually that of the angel Moroni and that Joseph invented the story of the First Vision of the Father and Son at a later time. However, Joseph wrote the account of his First Vision in 1832 in which he stated that he saw the Lord, and there is substantial evidence that Oliver had this document in his possession at the time that he wrote his history of the Church. This essay demonstrates the correlations between Joseph Smith's 1832 First Vision account, Oliver's 1834/1835 account, and Joseph's 1835 journal entry on the same subject. It is clear that not only did Oliver have Joseph's history in his possession but that he used Joseph's 1832 account as a basis for his own account. This essay also shows that Oliver knew of the First Vision and attempted to obliquely refer to the event several times in his second installment before continuing with his narrative of Moroni's visit.[103]

In a different vein, critics have claimed that Joseph Smith joined the Presbyterian, Baptist, or Methodist churches prior to 1823 and after he had been told to join none of the churches by the Lord in his 1820 First Vision (PofGP. JS-H 1:19, 20, 26). The three reminiscent statements making such claims came five to seven decades after 1820. One of these critics, Pomeroy Tucker, wrote decades later in his 1867 book, *Origin, Rise, and Progress of Mormonism*, "that Joseph joined the Methodist probationary class in Palmyra but soon 'withdrew from the class' without being converted; announcing that 'all the churches [were] on a false foundation.'" Orson Pratt, who met Joseph Smith in

1830 in Palmyra, also confirms that Joseph did not join any of the churches in Palmyra prior to that year.[104]

Joseph's mother Lucy and siblings, Hyrum, Sophronia, and Samuel joined the Presbyterian Church, the only church which had a meetinghouse in Palmyra, and Joseph may have attended with them a few times. About three and a half years after his remarkable vision of Deity in 1820, and after the death of Joseph's eldest brother Alvin, who died November 19, 1823, Joseph Smith's mother Lucy Mack Smith recalled in her autobiography several related facts about Joseph.

First, that Joseph "utterly refused" to attend church services with the intent to convert, and he made the specific request: "do not ask me to join them." Secondly, Joseph remarked at this time that he could "go into the woods" and learn more in a couple hours than his family could obtain from attending church for two years anywhere else. These statements in themselves are proofs that Joseph was referring to his 1820 First Vision in the *grove of woods* and not the first visitation of the angel Moroni, who appeared *in Joseph's room* and not "in the woods" on September 21, 1823. Lucy Mack Smith's comments are very telling as to Joseph's confidence in his religious convictions and his direction for the future:

> Shortly after the death of Alvin, a man commenced laboring in the neighborhood, to effect a union of the different churches, in order that all might be agreed, and thus worship God with one heart and with one mind. This seemed about right to me, and I felt much inclined to join in with them; in fact, the most of the family appeared quite disposed to unite with their numbers; but Joseph, from the first, utterly refused even to attend their meetings, saying, "Mother, I do not wish to prevent your going to meeting, or any of the rest of the family's; or your joining any church you please; but, do not ask me to join them. I can take my Bible, and go into the woods, and learn more in two hours, than you can learn at meeting in two years, if you should go all the time." To gratify me, my husband attended some two or three meetings, but peremptorily refused going any more, either for my gratification, or any other person's. During this excitement,

> Joseph would say, it would do us no injury to join them, that if we did, we should not continue with them long, for we were mistaken in them, and did not know the wickedness of their hearts. One day he said, that he would give us an example, and that we might set it down as a prophecy; viz: "You look at Deacon Jessup," said he, "and you hear him talk very piously. Well, you think he is a very good man. Now suppose that one of his poor neighbors should owe him the value of a cow, and that this poor man had eight little children; moreover, that he should be taken sick and die, leaving his wife with one cow, but destitute of every other means of supporting herself and family—now I tell you, that Deacon Jessup, religious as he is, would not scruple to take the last cow from the poor widow and orphans, in order to secure the debt, notwithstanding he himself has an abundance of everything." At that time, this seemed impossible to us, yet one year had scarcely expired when we saw Joseph's prophecy literally fulfilled.[105]

It seems clear that no contemporary record exists to support the claims that Joseph Smith joined the Presbyterian, Baptist, or Methodist churches prior to 1823 or before the organization of the Restored Church in 1830, after he had been told to join none of the churches by the Lord in 1820. Joseph was true to the Lord.[106]

Joseph's mother Lucy was baptized as an independent in 1802 at Randolph, Vermont. Lucy said, "I concluded that my mind would be easier if I were baptized and I found a minister who was willing to baptize me and leave me free from membership in any church after which I pursued the same course until my oldest son [Alvin] attained his 22nd year." Lucy's history implies that she did not join any church until the year before Alvin's 22nd birthday in 1820, "I stepped forward and yielded obedience to this ordinance; after which I continued to read the Bible as formerly until my eldest son had attained his twenty-second year."[107]

Alvin Smith "attained his twenty-second year" on 11 February 1820, placing Lucy Mack Smith's joining the Presbyterian Church early that year, before Joseph's First Vision. Joseph's 1838 First Vision account indicates the same (PofGP, JS-H 1:7). Critics following the late Reverend Wesley P. Walters (1926–1990) will have a hard time proving that Lucy and three of her children joined the Presbyterians several years after in 1824 during a revival in Palmyra. Joseph Smith was not influenced greatly by the 1820 Presbyterian membership of his mother, nor by the revival of 1824 in Palmyra. While Joseph was influenced by religious excitement between 1816–1820, he was first influenced according to his 1832 First Vision account by the revivals of 1816 and 1817 beginning at age "twelve" (JSP, H1:10–13).[108]

In her autobiography Lucy Mack Smith wrote regarding that first interview of Joseph and the angel Moroni and the family's reaction to this wonderful news:

> Furthermore, the angel told him, at the interview mentioned last, that the time had not yet come for the plates to be brought forth to the world; that he could not take them from the place wherein they were deposited until he had learned to keep the commandments of God—not only till he was willing, but able, to do it. The angel bade Joseph come to this place every year, at the same time of the year, and he would meet him there and give him further instructions. The ensuing evening, when the family were all together, Joseph made known to them all that he had communicated to his father in the field, and also of his finding the Record, as well as what passed between him and the angel while he was at the place where the plates were deposited.
>
> We were now confirmed in the opinion that God was about to bring to light something upon which we could stay our minds, or that he would give us a more perfect knowledge of the plan of salvation and the redemption of the human family. This caused us greatly to rejoice, the sweetest union and happiness pervaded our house, and tranquility reigned in our midst.[109]

Mother Lucy Smith and the Smith family were content in the Lord's direction for their family. Lucy and her three children, Hyrum, Sophronia, and Samuel, quit attending the Western Presbyterian Church during the year after Joseph's last visit from the angel Moroni when he received the gold plates, breastplate, and Urim and Thummim at the Hill Cumorah on September 22, 1827. This fact is known because Presbyterian Church records date the suspension of Lucy and her three children.

In January of 1830, while Joseph Smith held the copyright, portions of the Book of Mormon text were illegally obtained from the printer, modified, and published in advance by Abner Cole under his pseudonym "Obadiah Dogberry" in the short-lived *Palmyra Reflector*. Soon after, Lucy and Hyrum were visited by Deacon George Beckwith of the Presbyterian Church who pressured them to renounce the Book of Mormon and Joseph's story of his visitation by the angel Moroni, however, to no avail. Deacon Beckwith said, "I wish—that if you do believe those things, you never would proclaim anything about them, I do wish you would not." Lucy replied, "Deacon Beckwith . . . even if you should stick my body full of faggots and burn me at the stake, I would declare, as long as God should give me breath, that Joseph has that record, and that I know it to be true." Lucy and her three children would be "censured" and "suspended" from the Presbyterian Church "for eighteen month's neglect of worship" on March 29, 1830, the month before Joseph organized the Restored Church of Jesus Christ on April 6, 1830 (EofM 3:1357).[110]

The key to understanding Joseph's relationship to the churches of his youth in Palmyra, is in realizing the fact that he occasionally attended the Methodist and perhaps other churches but was not converted to their doctrine, nor was he baptized as a member of those churches. Joseph knew he was told by the Lord to join none of the churches and that the Lord had something in mind for him to do.[111]

Joseph's brother, William Smith, in his 1883 autobiography, said that Joseph Smith's vision came in 1822–1823 when he saw an angel, conflating the First Vision of 1820 and the visit of the angel Moroni in 1823. However, during a speech William gave published June 9, 1883 in *The Saints Herald* newspaper, the same year of his autobiography, he partially clarified his story of Joseph's First Vision, though he was still confusing the two events and Joseph's age. William Smith said:

> About four years after my father removed with his family from Vermont to New York [1820], my brother Joseph became concerned on the subject of religion. My mother and brother Hyrum and a sister were members of the Presbyterian

Church. We knew that Joseph's mind was engrossed on religious subjects for some time . . . "Was there a revealed plan by which man could find out that way?" My brother told me there was a lack of wisdom; he did not know which way to go. He retired to the woods to ask the Lord for guidance. While praying he saw a bright light, like the brightness of the sun. In that light he saw a personage; and that being pointed him [Joseph] out as the messenger to go forth and declare his truth to the world; for "They had all gone astray;" "Every man was going his way". . .[112]

Chapter 14

The Prophet Joseph Becomes a Seer

JOSEPH'S MISSION REQUIRED REVELATION BEYOND THAT RECEIVED IN his First Vision. A seer is an inspired prophet who can receive divine revelations directly from God and can also translate sacred records written in ancient and lost languages into the current language of the people. It is done not by scholastic ability, rather by "the gift and power of God." Joseph revealed this in his "Preface" to the Book of Mormon, 1830 edition, and Wilford Woodruff noted this concept in his journal (November 28, 1841, CHL). This power of God to translate ancient scripture was the definition of a seer given by Ammon to King Limhi in the Book of Mormon (Mosiah 8:13). A Urim and Thummim was the instrument the Prophet Joseph Smith used to receive directions from the Lord and to translate part of the ancient Nephite record, the Book of Mormon and several early revelations found in The Doctrine and Covenants, sections 3, 6, 7, 11, 14, and 17, which appeared first in the Book of Commandments in 1833.[113]

Joseph would act as a "seer" on many occasions during the remaining fourteen years of his life. Whether translating the Book of Mormon in 1829 or receiving revelations later published in the Book of Commandments in 1833, renamed two years later as The Doctrine and Covenants, he used his spiritual gifts from heaven. The four types of revelation that the Prophet Joseph Smith received can be described as: (1) divine visitations of God the Father, the Savior Jesus Christ, and of resurrected angels; (2) the instrument identified as the Urim and

Thummim; (3) a seer stone separate from the Urim and Thummim; and (4) the gifts, voice and burning power of the Holy Ghost or Holy Spirit, the third member of the Godhead.

The earliest known prophet mentioned in the Holy Scriptures who possessed a Urim and Thummim was the brother of Jared or Mahonri Moriancumer in 2200 BC, who received it upon the mount. This same Urim and Thummim was used by Joseph Smith and seen also by the Three Witnesses of the Book of Mormon (BofM, Ether 5:2; D&C 17:1; DofS 3:223–225). There are seven references in the Bible to the "Urim and Thummim," sometimes referenced only as "Urim": Exodus 28:29–30; Leviticus 8:8; Numbers 27:21; Deuteronomy 33:8; 1 Samuel 28:6; Ezra 2:63; Nehemiah 7:65. There are four references in the Book of Mormon to a similar device called the "interpreters" used by ancient American prophets and seers: Mosiah 8:13; Mosiah 8:19; Mosiah 28:20; and Ether 4:5. The Urim and Thummim, consisting of a breastplate and spectacles with two crystal-like seer stones held in two metal bows or rims of the spectacles, was used to receive divine revelations by Abraham, Moses, and perhaps other Biblical prophets. The two prophets Ezra and Nehemiah seem to indicate that there was no "priest with Urim and Thummim" when the Jews returned from their Babylonian Captivity in 539 BC (PofGP, Abraham 3:1; HBKJV, Exodus 28:29–30; Ezra 2:63; Nehemiah 7:65).

A different Urim and Thummim than Abraham's was possessed by Moriancumer in ancient America and was later used by King Mosiah II, Nephi IV (assumed), and by Moroni in the ancient American branch of the Church of Christ. Later, the angel Moroni, as a resurrected being, loaned this Urim and Thummim to the Prophet Joseph Smith in 1827. Two years later the angel Moroni took it back after the Book of Mormon was translated in the fall of 1829 (BofM, Ether 4:5; D&C 3; DHC 1:21–22).

A second physical tool of revelation mentioned in the scriptures is the individual seer stone without the spectacles and breastplate. We read in the Book of Mormon how Alma recorded an ancient prophecy, prior to his time, that referred to a single stone, "And the Lord said: I will prepare unto my servant Gazelem, a stone which shall shine forth in darkness into light" (BofM, Alma 37:21, 23). Here in the Book of Mormon, as in the Old Testament of the Bible, are accounts of ancient prophets using a single stone or "Urim" as tools of divine communication (HBKJV, 1 Samuel 28:6). It is possible that references to "Urim" in the Bible can also mean either a single stone, or the Urim and Thummim with two stones and a breastplate.

The New Testament refers to a single "white stone" given to those who will receive eternal life (HBKJV, Revelation 2:17). This theme was continued in a revelation given to Joseph Smith on April 2, 1843 which referenced Revelation 2:17 and the white stone "that will become a Urim and Thummim to each individual who receives one, whereby things pertaining to a higher order of kingdoms will be made known: And a white stone is given to each of those who come into the celestial kingdom, whereon is a new name written, that no man knoweth save he that receiveth it. The new name is the key word" (D&C 130:10–11).

The First Vision and the other revelations which came soon after set the stage for an explosion of revolutionary doctrine. A marvelous revelation called "The Vision" was given to Joseph Smith and Sidney Rigdon from Jesus Christ at Hiram, Ohio, February 16, 1832. Sidney Rigdon was Joseph's future Counselor in the Presidency of the Church. Not since his First Vision in 1820 had Joseph seen such marvelous things, and this time the vision was seen and the voice of Jehovah was heard with a fellow member of the Church. In this personal vision of Jesus Christ, the Lord said:

> For thus saith the Lord—I, the Lord, am merciful and gracious unto those who fear me, and delight to honor those who serve me in righteousness and in truth unto the end.
>
> Great shall be their reward and eternal shall be their glory.
>
> And to them will I reveal all mysteries, yea, all the hidden mysteries of my kingdom from days of old, and for ages to come, will I make known unto them the good pleasure of my will concerning all things pertaining to my kingdom.
>
> Yea, even the wonders of eternity shall they know, and things to come will I show them, even the things of many generations.
>
> And their wisdom shall be great, and their understanding reach to heaven; and before them the wisdom of the wise

> shall perish, and the understanding of the prudent shall come to naught.
>
> For by my Spirit will I enlighten them, and by my power will I make known unto them the secrets of my will—yea, even those things which eye has not seen, nor ear heard, nor yet entered into the heart of man (D&C 76:5–10).

By these first words of the Savior, Joseph Smith and Sidney Rigdon learned that the Lord intended to reward their faithfulness with great understanding of many secrets and things no other men on earth knew or understood. This revelation lasted several hours, and later required the efforts of six scribes to record that portion of the vision which was allowed to be written, as seen and heard by these two men. These two seers were wrought upon by the Holy Ghost in such a way that they could see the Lord Jesus Christ and other worlds and kingdoms in relation to the final destiny of all humanity.

The revelation revealed the ancient doctrine taught by the Apostle Paul of three degrees of glory, or that every person would be rewarded differently in the resurrection based on what they did with what was given to them in mortality. After reading *John* 5:29, the two prophets determined, "that if God rewarded every one according to the deeds done in the body, the term 'Heaven,' as intended for the Saint's eternal home, must include more kingdoms than one" (D&C 76 Synopsis).

The Lord continued the revelation saying:

> We, Joseph Smith, Jun., and Sidney Rigdon, being in the Spirit on the sixteenth day of February, in the year of our Lord one thousand eight hundred and thirty-two—
>
> By the power of the Spirit our eyes were opened and our understandings were enlightened, so as to see and understand the things of God—
>
> Even those things which were from the beginning before the world was, which were ordained of the Father, through his Only Begotten Son, who was in the bosom of the Father, even from the beginning;
>
> Of whom we bear record; and the record which we bear is the fullness of the gospel of Jesus Christ, who is the Son, whom we saw and with whom we conversed in the heavenly

vision. (D&C 76:11–14; JSP, R2:413 419; E&MS, pp. 1–2; JSP, R2:225–233)

The remainder of the vision revealed the nature of the three degrees of glory, which included the celestial, the terrestrial, and the telestial worlds and the qualifying requirements and limitations of each world. These three kingdoms and worlds differed in glory as the sun, moon, and stars differ in brightness as Paul noted in 1 Corinthians 15:40–42. The revelation included a description of Perdition.

Regarding the revelation known as the "new and everlasting covenant" found in D&C 132, which was received on July 12, 1843 at Nauvoo, Illinois, an interesting aspect of the prophetic abilities of Joseph Smith was displayed. Though Joseph had already received it once, Hyrum Smith and William Clayton encouraged Joseph Smith to "write the revelation by means of the Urim and Thummim" which was probably referring to Joseph's white seer stone, since Joseph had returned the Urim and Thummim and breastplate to Moroni not too long after the translation of the Book of Mormon was finished. To this suggestion Joseph replied, that "he did not need to [use urims or a seer stone], for he knew the revelation perfectly from beginning to end" (DHC 5:501–507; D&C 132:4).[114]

The subject of this revelation, D&C 132, the new and everlasting covenant, was of great importance to the saints both anciently and in the latter days as it defined how husbands and wives could be sealed together for both mortality and eternity in a celestial marriage. When authorized by the Lord, this covenant and blessing included the plurality of wives, a doctrine not currently practiced in the Church. The Lord revealed to Joseph Smith that he had justified Abraham, Isaac, and Jacob, and other servants of the Lord, including Moses, David, and Solomon, in their having more than one wife. By the power of the Holy Ghost, Joseph Smith received this revelation, and it was recorded by his clerk at that time, William Clayton.

The new and everlasting covenant includes the baptismal and marriage covenants as well as covenants made at other times, such as the oath and covenant of the priesthood and temple covenants. These are eternal principles and covenants, having existed in past dispensations or periods of time when the kingdom of God was operating on the earth with God's authorized prophets or servants, from the days of Adam to the present time (JST, Genesis 13:13; PSDP, Testament of Adam, 3:2–3; Testament of Abraham 3:2–3; D&C 84:33–38; TPJS, 237).

The first seven verses of the much longer revelation is related below:

> Verily, thus saith the Lord unto you my servant Joseph, that inasmuch as you have inquired of my hand to know and understand wherein I, the Lord, justified my servants Abraham, Isaac, and Jacob, as also Moses, David and Solomon, my servants, as touching the principle and doctrine of their having many wives and concubines—
>
> Behold, and lo, I am the Lord thy God, and will answer thee as touching this matter.
>
> Therefore, prepare thy heart to receive and obey the instructions which I am about to give unto you; for all those who have this law revealed unto them must obey the same.
>
> For behold, I reveal unto you a new and an everlasting covenant; and if ye abide not that covenant, then are ye damned; for no one can reject this covenant and be permitted to enter into my glory.
>
> For all who will have a blessing at my hands shall abide the law which was appointed for that blessing, and the conditions thereof, as were instituted from before the foundation of the world.
>
> And as pertaining to the new and everlasting covenant, it was instituted for the fullness of my glory; and he that receiveth a fullness thereof must and shall abide the law, or he shall be damned, saith the Lord God.
>
> And verily I say unto you, that the conditions of this law are these: All covenants, contracts, bonds, obligations, oaths, vows, performances, connections, associations, or expectations, that are not made and entered into and sealed by the Holy Spirit of promise, of him who is anointed, both as well for time and for all eternity, and that too most holy, by revelation and commandment through the medium of mine anointed, whom I have appointed on the earth to hold this power (and I have appointed unto my servant Joseph to

> hold this power in the last days, and there is never but one on the earth at a time on whom this power and the keys of this priesthood are conferred), are of no efficacy, virtue, or force in and after the resurrection from the dead; for all contracts that are not made unto this end have an end when men are dead. (D&C 132:1–7)

Being a national public figure or a famous preacher of scriptural themes alone is not necessarily what constitutes a holy prophet and a seer. A prophet and seer is not solely defined as a founder of a great religious movement or a worldwide church. However, a servant of God and a holy prophet, seer, and revelator could be all those things and at times more. A prophet may prophecy of things to come. He may have revelations or be a revelator wherein God directly speaks to him or reveals his truths and his will by the power of the Holy Ghost. These revelations will often contain information not known to anyone else, perhaps never known before, and sometimes they are teachings which were lost for centuries during periods of past spiritual darkness and apostasy.

A prophet, seer, and revelator is one who is made holy before God and must be clean from the blood and sins of his generation. A prophet must walk in all the commandments of God and especially those currently given to him. A true prophet must be filled with the Holy Spirit and be able to speak and teach by pure inspiration. At times, a prophet may speak in the name of the Lord of those things which must surely come to pass, or of things which the Lord wishes the Saints to understand, or of revelations which are to become new scripture (DHC 5:27, 181).

Similar is the nature of a prophetess, who is the wife of a prophet or of a righteous man, and is herself a righteous woman called by the Lord and filled with the Spirit of the Holy Ghost, as were Miriam and Deborah, Elizabeth and Mary, to perform great works: to prophesy or to be a judge in Israel; or to give birth to a prophet or to the Son of God (HBKJV, Exodus 15:20; Judges 4:4–5; Luke 1:26–38).

The Prophet Joseph Smith became such a prophet, seer, and revelator as Enoch, Abraham, Moses, Samuel, Nephi, King Mosiah, Alma, and others. Joseph spoke with the Lord "face to face" as Moses did (HBKJV, Exodus 24:9–11; 33:11). Like the ancient prophets before him Joseph received visions from God and visitations of angels (PofGP, JS-H 1:18–20, 29–43; D&C 76:5–14; D&C 110). The Lord told Moses, "Hear my words: If there is a prophet among you, I the Lord make myself known to him in a vision; I speak with him in a dream" (HBKJV, Numbers 12:6).

According to what is revealed in both the ancient and modern scriptural records, since the time of Adam to the present day, prophets had seen the Lord, the Son of God (Jehovah), and entertained and wrestled with angels or translated beings (HBKJV, Genesis 32:24, 30). But since the time of the Garden of Eden, no prophet had been physically visited in person by both God the Father and His Son Jesus Christ like the young Seer and Prophet Joseph Smith Jr. was in 1820 (DofS 1:27). This gives us an idea of the great importance, within the Father and Son's eternal plan, of Joseph Smith's First Vision, regarding his mission to restore the fullness of the gospel to the earth with all of its principles and doctrines, ordinances and blessings.

The Deacon and later Seventy of the Early Church, Stephen, who, "full of faith and power, did great wonders and miracles among the people." Stephen saw a vision of God and the Son of Man in heaven just prior to his death by stoning, ordered by the Jewish high priests in Roman controlled Jerusalem. We noted earlier that there is no record of Stephen having a conversation with God or the Savior in that vision (HBKJV, Acts 6:8; 7:56; ANF 5:254–256). While Joseph did not converse with God the Father, he was personally introduced by the Father to the Savior who gave Joseph instructions and answered the fourteen-year-old boy's question as to which church he should join. The answer was that he should join none of them, "to continue as [he] was until further directed" as the Lord had special mission for this young prophet to fulfill in the latter days (PofGP, JS-H 1:18–20, 26; MS 52:258).

To review, "a seer is revelator and a prophet also." This definition is in accordance with the Book of Mormon. A seer also has a special ability when called upon to translate ancient records written in lost languages using a special and often heavenly controlled instrument containing two stones called the Urim and Thummim (BofM, Mosiah 8:13–18). This instrument or these stones were called the Nephite "interpreters" in the Book of Mormon (Mosiah 8:13). Separately these stones are called *seer stones* (HBKJV, Revelation 2:17; D&C 130:6–11).

As a latter-day seer, the Prophet Joseph Smith learned that the Lord had a work for him to do, line upon line, revelation upon revelation, using all the gifts which God and angels would give to him. These spiritual gifts included the Urim and Thummim, individual seer stones, holy angels, the Holy Ghost, and the words of Jesus Christ Himself over a course of twenty-four years. No other prophet of God achieved so much in such little time as the young Seer and Prophet Joseph Smith.

Chapter 15

The Magical and the Miraculous

When considered in the light of the Second Great Awakening of nineteenth-century New England, the world where Joseph Smith grew up, the magical and miraculous rods and seer stones used by Moses and Aaron anciently would seem odd to most church-goers, yet very interesting to some Christians of Joseph's day. After being used by ancient prophets, designated objects became part of the latter-day Seer's standard prophetic tools. In other words, because they did not let the advances of the preceding Age of Reason or of science block their faith in Biblical miracles, and the use of sacred instruments by ancient prophets and seers, Christians of the early and mid-nineteenth century could consider the authenticity of such sacred things.

Those who did consider the idea of new revelation, currently living prophets and translation of ancient records with miraculous instruments of righteous divination, would become the early converts of the Church which Joseph later established. This becomes even more true as Joseph Smith questioned the religious doctrines of his day, prepared to ask the Lord which church he should join and became the recipient of the greatest and most important heavenly vision from God in nearly two thousand years (HBKJV, Leviticus 8:8; Numbers 27:21; Deuteronomy 33:8; 1 Samuel 28:6; PofGP, JS-H 1:1–19).

Eric A. Eliason, a Professor of English at Brigham Young University, recently wrote of how the ancient Biblical Hebrews considered magic and how Latter-day Saints and other Christians today should likewise look at Joseph Smith's use of miraculous instruments to assist in his prophetic work as a modern-day seer:

> While some contemporary Evangelicals may be myopic in their criticisms of Joseph Smith, they are correct to see the Bible as a key to understanding Joseph Smith's "magical" practices. According to Bible scholar Shawna Dolansky, a magic-versus-religion distinction "is not represented in . . . ancient Near Eastern literatures," and ancient Hebrews did not make a distinction between licit and illicit magico-religious practices based on form or content. In the cultural context of ancient Israel, the prohibitions found in Deuteronomy 18 and Leviticus 19–20 do not categorically condemn magic. "Magic as a category . . . was not illegal," says Dolansky. "The mediation of divine power . . . in the hands of priests and prophets [was] perfectly legal." According to Bible scholars, Moses turning his staff into a snake was not the same as Pharaoh's magicians doing so, since Moses was a prophet of God and Jannes and Jambres were not. From a biblical perspective, determining whether Joseph Smith's treasure seeking, seer-stone gazing, blessing of "magic" handkerchiefs, alleged Kabbalistic dabbling, and so forth were proper should not be based on whether moderns see them as weird or formally similar to pagan practices, but on whether or not Joseph Smith was an authorized prophet of God. Presumably, since Joseph Smith claimed to be God's instrument for restoring biblical priesthood authority, he would have welcomed this basis for determination.[115]

Those unfamiliar with religious life and seer stones in nineteenth-century New England may struggle with this part of the Prophet Joseph Smith's history. Scholars have long debated this issue without consensus. The obvious presence of these principles in the Bible and in the Book of Mormon contrast with the Age of Reason and reliance on science over religion. Such is a dilemma that is older than the period here being discussed. The Apostle Paul warned his associate Timothy nearly two thousand years ago not to be overcome by the tenets of "false science." Students of the Bible must remember that Paul lived in his own Age of Reason, or the Hellenist world of Greek

Philosophers and read and preached from a Greek Old Testament called the *Septuagint* (HBKJV, 1 Timothy 6:19–21).

By the late twentieth century, Professor Eliason informs us, most sincere non-Latter-day Saint historians deemed Joseph Smith's use of seer stones as inexplicable, yet identified them as one of the following three things—real magic and divination, cultural folklore, or unnecessary tools for salvation in terms of modern Christian doctrine. By "unnecessary tools for salvation" it should be pointed out that this opinion is based on twentieth-century rather than nineteenth-century Christian doctrine and belief regarding the use of objects as tools in receiving divine guidance.[116]

At least one twentieth-century, modern anti-Mormon historian, Reverend Wesley P. Walters, went so far as to claim that Joseph Smith's use of seer stones was akin to practicing "the occult" and led to the "creation of a cult." Revisionist Latter-day Saint historian Dr. D. Michael Quinn was the first Mormon scholar in the twentieth century to venture into the magical world of prophets and seers as related to Joseph Smith. Unlike Reverend Walters, Dr. Quinn ultimately pointed out that such things as seer stones and rods should be expected in the world and works of a real prophet.[117]

Chapter 16

Joseph Smith and His Seer Stones

It is recorded in the Bible that Moses turned his rod or staff into a serpent and that Aaron's rod blossomed in the spring like a tree and produced almonds. Aaron's ephod and breastplate contained twelve stones for the Twelve Tribes of the House of Israel and two additional "memorial" stones which rested upon the shoulders of Aaron's priestly ephod or robe. Upon the breastplate over his heart were connected the two seer stones called the Urim and Thummim. Were these the same stones called the Urim and Thummim elsewhere in the text? It would seem so. If the illuminated left stone was a "no" answer from God and if the illuminated right stone was a "yes" answer, then could a textual or other vision be seen within the stones, such as in the "spectacles" which Joseph Smith had used? If we could only have been there (HBKJV, Exodus 4:1–4; Exodus 28:12; Numbers 17:8).

Realizing that the Prophet Joseph Smith was entrusted with a Urim and Thummim connected to a breastplate, which were functionally similar yet configured perhaps differently than what Moses gave Aaron, is to understand in part what it means for a man to be called of God as a prophet and a seer (HBKJV, Hebrews 5:4). To have in one's possession the Urim and Thummim is a rare occurrence and one of the signs that God is with that man and that he is a true prophet, seer, and revelator. However, it is not required for a prophet of God to always have the Urim and Thummim. Many prophets whose lives are described in the Holy Scriptures did not have it, yet by the power of the Holy Ghost were able to do great and marvelous works and were a conduit for many miracles in the name of the Lord.

From the *Encyclopedia of Mormonism,* we read the following about the ancient seer stones called the Urim and Thummim:

> In Antiquity at least two different Urim and Thummim existed, and possibly three. Chronologically, the brother of Jared received the first known one (Doctrine and Covenants 17:1). This same set came into the hands of Mosiah 2 and other Book of Mormon prophets, subsequently being deposited with the gold plates [that Joseph Smith received] (JS-H 1:35). The fate of the second set, given to Abraham (Abraham 3:1), remains unknown. Unless Abraham's Urim and Thummim had been passed down, Moses received a third set mentioned first in Exodus 28:30. The Urim noted in 1 Samuel 28:6, probably an abbreviated form of Urim and Thummim, was most likely the one possessed by Moses (cf. Num. 27:18–21). What happened to this one is also unknown, though certainly by postexilic times the Urim and Thummim were no longer extant. (Ezra 2:63; Nehemiah 7:65; EofM 4:1499–1500)[118]

At first, while translating the gold plates of the Book of Mormon, which were inscribed with a language the book itself calls "Reformed Egyptian" (BofM, Mormon 9:32), Joseph Smith used the Urim and Thummim which was deposited with the plates, which the angel Moroni loaned to him for that purpose. As Joseph progressed, his wife Emma, who was his first scribe, tells us he no longer needed to use the more cumbersome Urim and Thummim and instead used his personal seer stone, which history records he possessed as early as 1822.[119]

Following his translation of the Book of Mormon in March of 1830, Joseph said, "by the wisdom of God, [the plates and the Urim and Thummim] remained safe in my hands, until I had accomplished by them what was required at my hand. When, according to arrangements, the messenger called for them, I delivered them up to him; and he has them in his charge until this day" (PofGP, JS-H 1:60).

The Prophet Smith Joseph possessed two separate seer stones by 1826, in addition to his later temporary possession of the Urim and Thummim that Moroni took back after the Book of Mormon translation was finished. One of these stones was whitish in color, oval in shape, and crystalline yet opaque in appearance, while the other stone was "dark" or "chocolate colored" with swirls of light and dark brown and also oval in shape, about the size of an egg. Joseph found a seer stone while digging "a well" for treasure in the garden of Willard Chase in 1822 who lived about a half mile from Joseph's home in Palmyra. Emma Smith, David Whitmer, and Martin Harris said Joseph used this stone to translate part of the Book of Mormon when the Urim and Thummim became too cumbersome. Emma wrote in a letter that this was the "dark" or "chocolate" stone. After the translation of the Book of Mormon was completed in late June of 1829, Joseph Smith gave his brown seer stone to Oliver Cowdery, the soon to be Second Elder of the Church. President Wilford Woodruff said the Prophet Joseph was "shown of the Lord" the location of "the [white] seer stone known as Gazelem . . . to be some thirty feet under ground, which he obtained by digging under the pretense of digging a well." Mackay and Frederick suggest that "Gazelem" here refers to the white seer stone that Joseph "carried with him through life."[120]

Joseph's friend Martin Harris, a farmer in Palmyra, who would become one of the three Book of Mormon witnesses, reported an account from the early 1820s of Joseph's abilities in using a seer stone. Martin said that he hid a pin in a haystack and that Joseph found it immediately without even looking in the hay by gazing at his seer stone in his hat while reaching into the haystack with his hand to extract the pin. This account shows that Martin Harris had faith in Joseph Smith's spiritual abilities and that the seer stones Joseph possessed really could be used to see and find things that nobody else could.[121]

Some Latter-day Saints are not aware that Joseph Smith retained a seer stone for his entire adult life, even after 1829 when he finished translating the Book of Mormon. While in Nauvoo, Illinois, Joseph retained his white seer stone and used it for the translation of ancient scripture. According to both Wilford Woodruff and Parley P. Pratt, two of the latter-day apostles in 1842, Joseph used his "Urim and Thummim," which then commonly referred to Joseph's white seer stone, to translate the Book of Abraham and the Book of Joseph, the latter of which was never recorded or published, while the former became part of the latter-day scripture known as The Pearl of Great Price first published in England in 1851.[122]

David Whitmer was one of the original Three Witnesses to the Book of Mormon, as was Martin Harris and Oliver Cowdery, who each saw the angel Moroni, the Urim and Thummim and breastplate, and the gold plates from which the book was translated. These three witnesses also saw the sword of Laban taken by Nephi from Jerusalem and the miraculous "ball" or "director" called the Liahona, which means "compass," given to Lehi to lead him and his family from Israel to the New World (BofM, Alma 37:38; D&C 17:1). David Whitmer, an early associate of the Prophet Joseph and a "president" of the Church in Missouri, left the church in 1838 and accused Joseph Smith of being a fallen prophet. David felt that none of the revelations Joseph Smith had received by the seer stone should be printed or made public. David Whitmer also felt that only revelations received by Joseph from the "stone" could be called scripture, not the revelations

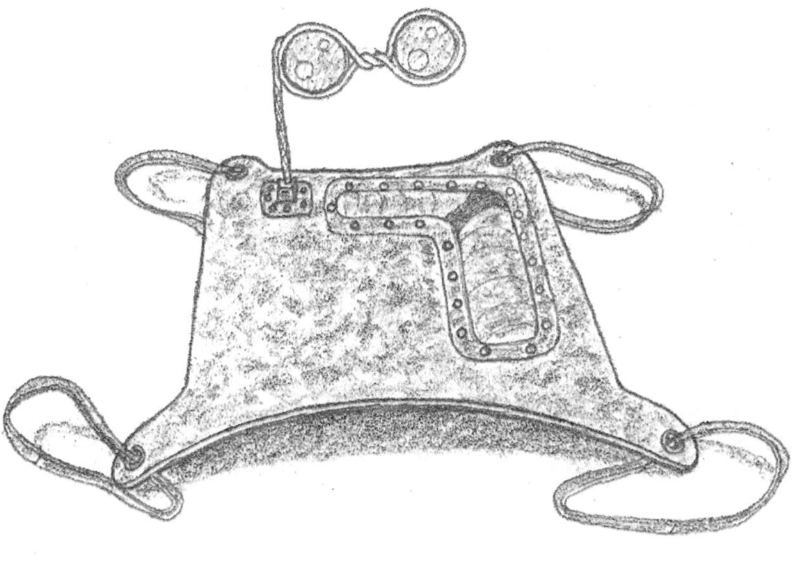

3. The Urim and Thummim or Jaredite and Nephite "interpreters" and breastplate loaned to the Prophet Joseph Smith in September 1827 to facilitate the translation of the *Book of Mormon*. Sketch by the author. Reference: Replica made by David Baird and photographs by Daniel Smith.

4. Joseph Smith's layered brown seer stone or "dark-colored chocolate stone" (MacKay p. 69), approx. 6 centimeters or 2-3/8 inches long. This seer stone appears to be made of chatoyant or "tiger-eye." Sketch by the author. Reference: photographs of the stone by Weldon C. Andersen and Richard E. Turley, Original stone is kept in the Church Historical Museum, Salt Lake City, Utah.

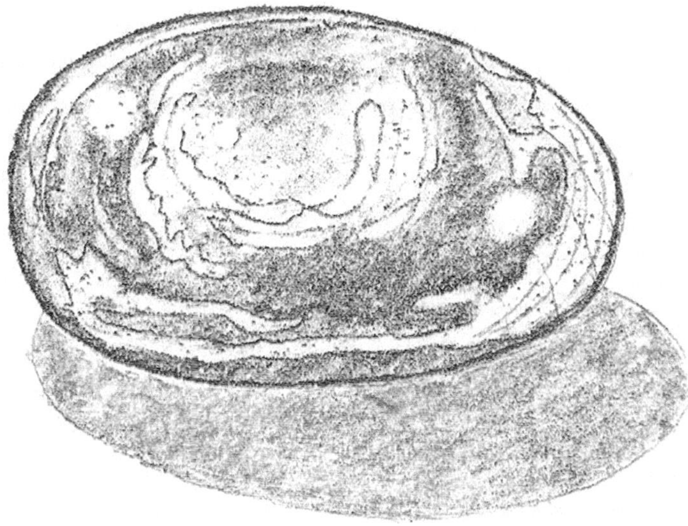

5. Joseph Smith's white crystalline seer stone that he carried with him throughout his adult life. Sketch by the author. Reference: painting of the white seer stone by Anthony R. Sweat, 2016. Original stone is kept in the First Presidency's Vault, Church Administration Building, Salt Lake City, Utah.

Joseph received from Jesus Christ through prayer and by the power of the Holy Ghost, a contradiction.[123]

Joseph possessed and used other single seer stones as well. In 1855 President Brigham Young told the Apostles that the Prophet Joseph Smith had as many as five seer stones and stated that Joseph "did not regard his seer stones simply as relics of his youth" and obtained some of them after 1830 while President of the Church. Importantly, in less than a year from his translation of the Book of Mormon, Joseph learned to receive direct revelation from the Holy Ghost regarding new scripture without having to use any of his seer stones, if he desired (JS-H 1:60).

We can name the five seer stones Joseph Smith is said to have possessed during his life: (1) the Urim and Thummim, loaned to the Prophet by the angel Moroni which Joseph used to translate part of the Book of Mormon and receive some of the early revelations in the Doctrine and Covenants up to June 1829 (D&C 18); (2) the brown egg-shaped stone traditionally used for the translation of the remainder of the Book of Mormon; (3) the whitish crystalline, opaque, and egg-shaped seer stone retained by the Prophet Joseph until his death which he used to translate the Book of Abraham and Book of Joseph from Egyptian papyri; (4) a green crystalline hollow cylindrical-shaped seer stone; and (5) a sandy colored disk-shaped "Nauvoo" seer stone near the size of a US quarter coin. While relatively little is known about these five stones, it appears that Joseph Smith valued and used both the brown and whitish or crystalline seer stones more than the others.[124]

Almost immediately after the publication of the Book of Mormon and organization of the Church in the spring of 1830, Joseph began his translation of the Holy Bible now known as the Inspired Version or Joseph Smith Translation of the Bible. Joseph's vision of the Book of Moses was given to him in June 1830 and his work in translating Genesis continued until March of 1831. One of the original apostles of the Restoration, Orson Pratt, was watching as Joseph and Sidney Rigdon worked together on this new version of the Bible. Elder Pratt remembered, "Joseph, as if he read his thoughts, looked up and explained that the Lord gave him the Urim and Thummim when he was inexperienced in the Spirit of inspiration. But now he had advanced so far that he understood the operations of that Spirit, and did not need the assistance of that instrument" (MS 36:488–499).[125]

Latter-day Saint Historians Michael Hubbard MacKay and Nicholas J. Frederick, in their landmark book *Joseph Smith's Seer Stones* relate the following:

> In addition to translating at least a portion of every scriptural text of the Restoration with a seer stone, it is significant that at least some of Joseph's contemporaries believed that revelation through a seer stone was the surest way of receiving revelation from God. As early as 1830 and 1831, members of the Church tried to separate Joseph Smith's prophetic voice from his own personal voice, especially when challenging new revelations or commandments.
>
> Joseph Smith embraced the idea of seer stones within his prophetic calling, eventually infusing them with deeper religious meaning that affected Mormon theology more broadly. Even if not every prophet or member would use a seer stone on earth, everyone in the celestial kingdom would. Joseph Smith's seer stone theology implicitly rejects any scenario that makes Joseph Smith's seer stones mundane objects, especially considering the prophetic provenance and prophecies of his seer stones. Though some historians point toward folk religion and magic cultures to understand them and others see the seer stones as cultural artifacts that God used to His advantage, Joseph Smith and his Restoration scripture provided an ancient provenance to the seer stones with major theological implications about how we understand the nature of God and how sacred scripture is delivered to prophets.[126]

Joseph Smith and Brigham Young confirmed that a seer stone is not always required for a prophet to be a seer and a revelator or to translate. As noted above, in 1831 while in Kirtland, Ohio, Joseph was translating the Bible, he did not feel the need to use his white seer stone, even though he had used it and saw a vision of the creation while studying the first chapters of Genesis. About ten years later, while translating the Book of Abraham from Egyptian papyri in Nauvoo, Illinois, the Prophet would again use his white seer stone. Certainly having or possessing a seer stone would give Joseph Smith or any prophet additional faith and confidence in translating ancient records, both when he used it and when he did not.[127]

Joseph taught that every faithful Saint would eventually have a seer stone. With this stone one can continue to progress in the celestial kingdom and learn all those "things pertaining to a higher order of kingdoms" (HBKJV, Revelation 2:17; D&C 130:10).

Joseph showed his white seer stone to the Twelve Apostles in a council meeting on December 27, 1841, in Nauvoo, Illinois. In 1855, President Brigham Young reminisced about that meeting and the *Millennial Star* later published as part of the "History of Brigham Young" what the Prophet Joseph Smith had told the Twelve Apostles that day, as follows:

> He said that every man that lived on the earth was entitled to a seer stone, and should have one, but they are kept from them in consequence of their wickedness, and most of those who do find one make an evil use of it; he showed us his seerstone. (MS 26:119).[128]

One would think that President Young assumed that those who will receive a seer stone in this life will also receive the fullness of the gospel of Jesus Christ and become a member of The Church of Jesus Christ of Latter-day Saints.

Michael Hubbard MacKay and Nicholas J. Fredericks reported in their important book *Joseph Smith's Seer Stones* that, "While speaking at Joseph Smith's funeral, William W. Phelps stated that *Gazelem* was Joseph Smith's name in the pre-earth life: 'Joseph Smith, who was Gazelem in the spirit world, was, and is, and will be in the progress of Eternity: —The Prince of Light'" (MacKay and Fredericks, p. 104; emphasis added; Wilford Woodruff's Journal, Dec. 27, 1841, 2:144; 8:500, CHL; D&C 78:9, 1835 edition).

Joseph Smith as a prophet and seer, is a mortal forerunner for all the Latter-day Saints and for all the children of Adam and Eve who now live or will live on this earth in the coming years. Joseph Smith is an example of truth and righteousness like the prophets before him and also the forerunner for the Second Coming of Jesus Christ. Through the revelations of Jesus Christ to Joseph Smith, he points the way for every modern person toward their baptism and living a life of covenants, where eventually the faithful will arrive in the celestial kingdom of heaven spoken of by the ancient Apostles Paul and John (HBKJV, 2 Corinthians 12:2; Revelations 2:17).

According to later revelations given to the Prophet Joseph Smith, this earth will be transformed and become a celestial kingdom, "a sea of glass" or a great seer stone itself. The glory of the earth will be like that of the sun. Joseph said, "The place where God resides is a great Urim and Thummim. This earth, in its sanctified and immortal state, will be made like unto crystal and will be a Urim and Thummim to the inhabitants who dwell thereon . . . and this earth will be Christ's" (D&C 130:7–9; See also HBKJV, Revelation, chapters 21 and 22).

Chapter 17

Sacred Truths of the First Vision

JOSEPH SMITH'S GREATEST REVELATION, HIS FIRST VISION OF 1820, should be considered as the most transformational event since the death and resurrection of Jesus Christ; and never before has a prophet of God recorded such a vision since Moses wrote that God spoke to Adam and Eve in the Garden of Eden (DofS 1:27). In this rare dispensational event, the Prophet Joseph recorded the words that the Father spoke to him in 1820, "This is My Beloved Son, Hear Him!" (PofGP, JS-H 1:17).

The Book of Mormon prophet Nephi heard "the voice of the Son" speaking to him about baptism and the gift of the Holy Ghost, and in the next verse, "the voice from the Father" declaring to Nephi that the testimony of His Son is true (BofM, 2 Nephi 31:14–15). But there was no vision. John the Baptist heard the voice of the Father while baptizing Jesus in the Jordan River. Matthew wrote, "the Spirit of God descended like a dove and lighting upon him [Jesus]: And lo a voice from heaven, saying, 'This is my beloved Son, in whom I am well pleased.'" And there was no vision. A similar declaration by the Father is given on the Mount of Transfiguration, "This is my beloved Son, in whom I am well pleased; hear ye him" (HBKJV, Matthew 3:16–17; Matthew 17:5). The Father did not appear. And when the resurrected Savior visits the Nephites of the New World in AD 34, the Father says, "Behold, my Beloved Son, in whom I am well pleased, in whom I have glorified my name—hear ye him," but the Father does not appear (BofM, 3 Nephi 11:7). Last, we read Luke's account of Saint Stephen seeing the heavens opened and the "Son of man standing on the right hand of God," as two separate beings, during the early days of Saul or Paul. In this revelation there is no descent of deity to earth or dialogue between the Father, the Son, and Stephen (HBKJV, Acts 7:56).

The early Christians of Palestine and the Nephite Christians of the New World worshipped the "One God." They considered both the Father and the Son "as one God, yea, the very Eternal Father of heaven and earth" and the God of Abraham, Isaac, and Jacob, who said, "I and my Father are one" (BofM, Mosiah 15:4; Mormon 9:11–12; HBKJV, John 10:30). This at first seems like the Trinity doctrine of two or three Gods in one person. How do Christians and Latter-day Saints harmonize the separateness of the Deities revealed to Saint Stephen anciently and to Joseph Smith in 1820, with these scriptural statements indicating their divine *oneness*?

A very long-standing dear friend, a fellow high priest and a physician, Dr. Mark E. Mitchell, recently shared with me his understanding of the "One God" or the Oneness of the Godhead as spoken of in the Bible and in the Book of Mormon. After our earlier electronic mail discussion and his own personal, earnest, and sincere prayer about this doctrine, it was given to him by the Spirit to understand that the "One God" or Oneness doctrine is much more than we think, yet not necessarily what the world of modern Christianity currently thinks. Below is a significant part of what Dr. Mitchell related on this subject:

> We are one with others when we have set aside our own egos, and been willing to make the things of theirs ours, and the things of ours theirs. It requires a sacrifice on our part, but thus it requires a sacrifice on the parts of those with whom we become one. We all must give in order to accept more. Thus in the eternities, we subject ourselves eternally to the wills of others, even as they subject themselves to our will. Thus the humility that is required of us is required of God and gods as we wend our eternal way. Thus in our eternal pathway, we have not just One, but an infinite One with us as we suffer, as we struggle, as we strive. . . .
>
> God the Father is a single Entity, yet He is all who seek to become like Him, beginning with Jesus Christ. As we can see, Jesus Christ had a great and mighty mission to perform, one

that made Him infinitely necessary to the Father. [Jesus said, "I and my father are one" (John 10:30).] Now let us expand our minds and our imaginations here. Even as Jesus Christ had a great and mighty mission, so do we all have a great and mighty mission, one that makes us infinitely necessary to God the Heavenly Host. As our numbers grow, the number of great and mighty missions grow, and each is crucial to God. As the song, the "Spirit of God" says, "The knowledge and power of God are expanding," and it is because we are the knowledge and power of God. This means that Godhood and Godhead continue to redefine themselves as they move forward, for though God is an unchanging God, He is mostly unchanging in His eternal changing. God is not God the Father without God the Mother. He is not God the Father and Mother without God the Son. They are not God the Father, Mother, and Son without the Holy Ghost. The Holy Ghost and the Heavenly Host are synonymous [in truth and purpose], and as Jesus says, denying the Holy Ghost is the unpardonable sin. Why? Because by denying the Holy Ghost, we are rejecting our own identity. We are cutting ourselves, who will ascend to that position, off from our destiny. Thus we must languish in a place of eternal sameness forever if we are not willing to join with the Heavenly Host, to join with the mind of God. . . .

Therefore in all this the name God becomes the name of an eternal corporation [or an eternal family], where any member of the corporation [by keeping eternal covenants] can [eventually] say he or she is God. This does not take away from the specific mission or the identity of God the Father or Mother or Son. And since the inheritance is without end, when we reach the place where we have individually grown to the place where He was when He became the Father [or He became like his Father], the corporation will divide, and give us our inheritance where we will begin what He began in His beginning, and we will be [still speaking of separate beings] our own God the Father, God the Mother, and God the Son, and we will make our own God the Holy Ghost. We

> are still, and always will be, part of the original corporation [or original family] of God.[129]

It would be twenty-three years after the First Vision, or 1843, before Joseph Smith would fully define the separate natures of the Godhead and the ability of every child of God to become what Paul calls "joint-heirs with Christ," which is that "Oneness" with the "One God" that Jesus Christ and the ancient prophets were speaking of, which Dr. Mitchell has elaborated on (HBKJV, Romans 8:16–17; D&C 130:22). Four years previous to this revelation in D&C 130:22, and without a formal revelation, Joseph Smith indicated that there was a Mother in heaven associated with God the Father. While not much is known about our eternal Mother in Heaven, Sister Elaine Anderson Cannon wrote in the *Encyclopedia of Mormonism*:

> As early as 1839 the Prophet Joseph Smith taught the concept of an eternal mother, as reported in several accounts from that period. Out of his teaching came a hymn that Latter-day Saints learn, sing, quote, and cherish, "O My Father," by Eliza R. Snow. President Wilford Woodruff called it a revelation. 'In the heav'ns are parents single? No, the thought makes reason stare! Truth is reason; truth eternal Tells me I've a mother there.' When I leave this frail existence, When I lay this mortal by, Father, Mother, may I meet you In your royal courts on high? [Hymn no. 292]. (EofM 2:961)[130]

Returning to our narrative, from the death of the first apostles of the Early Church until the Prophet Joseph Smith's era, no clear and specific doctrinal statement of the true anthropomorphic and separate nature of the Father and the Son had been provided to the ancient Church in the extant Biblical record. The Eastern and Western churches of the Middle Ages were only given the *Apostle's Creed* and the *Nicene Creed* which declared the Trinitarian view of the Godhead, that they were all three—Father, Son, and Holy Ghost—a single spiritual entity, without a physical body, who mainly through the bodily Jesus Christ during his earthly ministry or by the Holy Ghost manifested themselves as needed to men on earth.

When quoting the Savior's words, it becomes more clear that this knowledge of the Godhead was one of the most sacred of all God's mysteries and teachings, "All things are delivered unto me of my Father: and no man knoweth the Son, but the Father; neither knoweth any man the Father, save the Son, and he to whomsoever the Son will reveal him" (HBKJV, Matthew 11:27).

It is apparent that these "great and marvelous things" and "the greater things" as Moroni called them in the Book of Mormon concerning the Godhead had been reserved by divine decree for the most holy of the saints anciently (BofM, Ether 4:2), and for the Dispensation of the Fullness of Times, to be revealed in the latter days by the Prophet Joseph Smith to those saints and open-minded among the Gentiles who would believe the Savior's words as found first in the Holy Bible and then in the Book of Mormon (BofM, Mormon 8:34; Ether 4:13; HBKJV, John 17:3).

The three separate bodily Deities doctrine of the Godhead recorded in D&C 130:22 states that the Father and the Son each have a glorified body of flesh and bones, except the Holy Ghost which is a glorified spirit or the Holy Spirit. These three Deities are unified in a divine purpose as "One God" (BofM, 2 Nephi 31:21).

This doctrine was revealed to the Prophet Joseph Smith in his First Vision of 1820 and four more times during heavenly visions to him and other witnesses between 1831 and 1836, wherein the separate natures of the Godhead were manifested.

The first of these post-1820 manifestations was at Kirtland, Ohio on June 4, 1831 at the schoolhouse on a hill near Isaac Morley's farmhouse when both the Father and the Son appeared (Levi Hancock's Journal). The second post-1820 Father and Son vision to Joseph Smith was with Sidney Rigdon on February 16, 1832 at Hiram, Ohio when the "Vision of the Degrees of Glory" was received (D&C 76:19–23). The third was March 18, 1833 in Kirtland, Ohio when God the Father and the Son made a brief personal appearance to the members of the School of the Prophets including Joseph Smith and Zebedee Coltrin (SLSP, Oct. 3, 1883). A fourth appearance occurred on January 21, 1836 as Joseph Smith saw in heavenly vision "the blazing throne of God, whereon was seated the Father and the Son," and also those who became heirs of the celestial kingdom of God (D&C 137).[131]

As nearly all Christians from the fourth century forward and like nearly all American Christians of nineteenth-century New England, Joseph Smith would have been taught to believe the "Trinity" doctrine of the Godhead. Having seen the Father and the Son as two distinct beings in his First Vision of 1820, as described in his 1835 account, he very likely at the age of fourteen would have at least been surprised to learn that God the Father and Jesus Christ were anthropomorphic and had separate bodies. Joseph saw what the ancient Saint Stephen, the first deacon and first martyr, saw when he was stoned by the Jews in Jerusalem centuries before (Acts 7:56). During the years since his First Vision, Joseph must have pondered this scriptural yet untaught doctrine of the Godhead having separate bodies before recording it in his second 1835 account of his first vision of Deity.[132]

From his limited understanding of the prevailing doctrine of Deity prior to his vision, the young Joseph would have naturally struggled and was unable to record for many years what he saw in his vision of 1820. From the multiple accounts of his earliest vision and his doctrinal teachings along the way, it is clear that over time Joseph began to comprehend the nature of the Godhead enough to write it. These accounts were written twelve, fifteen, and eighteen years after the First Vision. The timing of the accounts would be expected of one as young as Joseph was during his First Vision. Joseph having seen the Father and the Son four additional times between 1831 and 1836, would have gotten used to the idea that the Father and the Son were separate and distinct beings. Yet, they were unified in purpose as One God as he read in the scriptures of the Holy Bible and the Book of Mormon.

In the *Lectures on Faith* first published with the Doctrine and Covenants in 1835, the early Church brethren wrote that God the father and the Son Jesus Christ were two separate beings or personages of spirit. They had not yet received revelation telling them that both the Father and the Son had bodies of glorified flesh and bone:

> There are two personages who constitute the great, matchless, governing, and supreme power over all things . . . They are the Father and the Son—the Father being a personage of spirit, glory, and power, possessing all perfection and fullness; the Son, who was in the bosom of the Father, a personage

> of tabernacle, made or fashioned like unto man, or being in the form and likeness of man, or rather man was formed after his likeness and in His image; he is also the express image and likeness of the personage of the Father, possessing all the fullness of the Father, or the same fullness with the Father; being begotten of him, and ordained from before the foundation of the world to be a propitiation for the sins of all those who should believe on his name, . . . (Lectures on Faith 5:2, 1835, p. 52)

By the end of 1835, Joseph had recorded three major accounts of his 1820 vision of Deity, the 1832 account and two accounts in 1835. Additionally, he and Sidney Rigdon had published the "Lectures on Faith" in the first edition of the Doctrine and Covenants in 1835. But Joseph would not share a definitive revelation on the glorified yet corporeal bodies of the Father and the Son until April 2, 1843, "The Father has a body of flesh and bones as tangible as man's; the Son also; but the Holy Ghost has not a body of flesh and bones, but is a personage of Spirit. Were it not so, the Holy Ghost could not dwell in us" (D&C 130:22).

The Savior Jesus Christ Himself, when He appeared to His apostles in Galilee, had declared that His own resurrected body is composed of "flesh and bones" (HBKJV, Luke 24:39). Joseph was given more confirming witnesses of the separateness of the Father and the Son between 1835 and 1842 as he translated the Book of Abraham which tells of a conversation between God the Father or the "Lord" and the "Son of Man" who is Jesus Christ, during the grand council in the premortal heaven where it was decided that Jesus Christ would be the Savior of this world (PofGP, Abraham 3:27). Joseph Smith gradually learned the nature of the Godhead.

These scriptures and events show the developmental nature of revelation. Joseph had no four volume *Encyclopedia of Mormonism* in 1820 to refer to following his First Vision experience. "For precept must be upon precept, precept upon precept; line upon line, line upon line; here a little, and there a little: For with stammering lips and another tongue will he speak to this people" (HBKJV, Isaiah 28:10–11; Acts 2:1–18). The Lord gradually reveals doctrine by revelation. The gift of tongues is to teach foreigners the gospel and if given otherwise require an interpreter and are not considered doctrine (Article of Faith no. 9; TPJS, pp. 162, 212, 229, 247–248).

It is a natural conclusion that several of the key revelations of the Restored Gospel, including the First Vision (PofGP, JS-H 1:1–26) and the nature of the Godhead (D&C 130:22), were not immediately published or spelled out at first. This is further substantiated by the fact that the Prophet Joseph made four significant attempts to record his first vision of 1820 in the years 1832, 1835, 1838, and 1842.[133]

As mentioned earlier, Joseph did not first record his First Vision until 1832, twelve years after the event. One should remember that Joseph was only fourteen years old when he had this experience, and did not begin to value the importance of keeping a journal until he was fully of age and had begun translating the Book of Mormon. He had received several informative visitations from the angel Moroni from 1823 to 1827, and six revelations in sections in the Doctrine and Covenants via the Urim and Thummim in 1829, all important to the work to which he was called, or the Restoration of God's earthly kingdom.[134]

On April 6, 1830, the day the Restored Church of Jesus Christ was organized, the Lord commanded the Prophet Joseph Smith, "Behold, there shall be a record kept among you" (D&C 21:1). From that day forward and considering the revelations he already had received from the angel Moroni, Joseph fully recognized how important it was to make a record of his revelations from angels, the Savior Jesus Christ, and the historic workings of the newly organized Church of Christ.

Once Joseph, his scribes, and church historians began to record and eventually publish the marvelous events of the Restoration, the critics and antagonists would use those records against the Prophet and the Church. The shear scope and epic nature of Joseph's experiences or revelations were too large and grand for the scholastic doctors of academia. Those steeped in the tenets of modern reason and science, which had long ago removed both an active Deity and all miraculous events from their minds, libraries, and laboratories, could find little room for a repeat of the divine and revelatory experiences of Abraham or Moses or Daniel or Stephen or Paul. Perhaps one of the most popular and also equally unfair of Joseph's historian-critics, Fawn M. Brodie, unreasonably claimed that because Joseph didn't write his most sacred experience, the First Vision of 1820, until 1832 it must be condemned as "sheer invention."[135]

Such was the approach of many of Joseph's critics, both in academia and in the professional ranks of the clergy. If Joseph didn't play by their prior or latest rules, or if his revelation was not in line with their creeds, then any chance of acceptance was removed. Judgment was rendered against the young prophet regardless of the natural progression of Joseph's religious tutoring by an angel and his required daily manual labor in order to help his father's family meet their temporal needs.

Such poor historical appraisals from dissenting and anti-Mormon scholars cannot be proof by any reasonable standard of whether Joseph Smith had a vision or not. The overall harmony of the accounts of the First Vision alone, given by Joseph and other associates and apostles of the Restored Church, make it clear that Joseph's testimony of God the Father and of the Son Jesus Christ was undeniable to the young prophet and consistent with his mission throughout his life.

Some scholars have wondered why Joseph did not include his First Vision in the Book of Commandments first published in 1833, nor in the later Doctrine and Covenants of 1835. Some critics have claimed that this is evidence that the First Vision of 1820 did not really happen. However, it is very evident that the Prophet was very hesitant to share his most sacred personal experience at this time with the entire world or with all the Saints.

This explanation is made clear by the early Saints' struggle to accept what they had already received, namely the Book of Mormon. Thus, it rightly appears that the Prophet Joseph left out the First Vision from the early publications of the young latter-day Church of Jesus Christ intentionally.

In a revelation of September 22, 23, 1832 in Doctrine and Covenants, the Lord said to the Prophet Joseph Smith:

> And your minds in times past have been darkened because of unbelief, and because you have treated lightly the things you have received—Which vanity and unbelief have brought the whole church under condemnation. And this condemnation resteth upon the children of Zion, even all. And they shall

> remain under this condemnation until they repent and remember the new covenant, even the Book of Mormon and the former commandments which I have given them, not only to say, but to do according to that which I have written—(D&C 84:54–57).

It is interesting that the ancient prophets of the Bible and the Book of Mormon followed a similar course of withholding the "great and marvelous things" or most sacred of the scriptures for the prophets and the most worthy saints and in some cases withheld them or "sealed" them entirely (BofM, Mormon 8:34; Ether 4:1–15).

The Apocrypha is a collection of fifteen books of ancient Hebrew scripture. Some of the books were probably assembled as they now exist later than their authors lived or in New Testament and medieval times between 200 BC and AD 400. The Apocryphal books were originally considered of hidden origin or intended for the initiated or the prophets. Regarding the Apocrypha, the Lord told the Prophet Joseph Smith by a revelation on March 9, 1833, "There are many things contained therein, that are true, and it is mostly translated correctly; There are many things contained therein that are not true, which are interpolations by the hands of men . . . Therefore, whoso readeth it, let him understand, for the Spirit manifesteth truth" (D&C 91:1–2, 4).

With this information in mind, an interesting passage from the Apocrypha repeats an important concept of how the Lord reveals Holy Scripture and allows certain portions of revelation or scripture to be given to the people while other portions are withheld for a time or indefinitely. The Lord told the prophet Ezra, or Esdras as he was known in the Latin world, regarding the restricted revelations given to Moses and to himself, in the following verses:

> I told him [Moses] many wonderful things, showed him the secrets of the times, and disclosed to him the end of times. I instructed him as follows: These things you are to make known, but those [you must] keep secret. I command you now: The signs I showed you, the dreams you saw, The interpretations you heard—keep them in your mind! (APCR, 2 Esdras 14:5–8).

The revelations given to Moses which he shared were his five books, Genesis thru Deuteronomy, or what the Jews called the Torah. While the apocalypses or heavenly visions given to Moses of the creation, history, and end of this earth were kept sacred and not to be given to the House of Israel until the last days (PofGP, Moses 1; APCR, The Apocalypse of Moses; ANF 8:565–570, Revelation of Moses).

Unbelieving historians have also criticized the reliability of Joseph Smith's most comprehensive account of the First Vision, or his 1838 account published in his history and in The Pearl of Great Price as scripture, when it differs from Joseph's 1832 and 1835 journal accounts in details (JSH 1:1–26).

The first or 1832 account spoke of repentance and forgiveness, the Spirit of God and Joseph beginning his quest for religious knowledge at age twelve; while the second account of 1835 spoke of two divine beings descending in turn in a shaft of light followed by angels; and the third account of 1838 spoke of the Father and the Son descending in a pillar of light and Joseph's dialogue with them at age fourteen without the mention of angels and his culminating desire to follow the Biblical charge to ask God what he should do in relation to the many different sects, or what church he should join. In the second or 1835 account Joseph added as an afterthought, noting, "I was about 14 years old when I received this first communication." All combined, the reader gets a broad and more complete idea of what Joseph Smith experienced and how he ultimately at age fourteen had his most glorious First Vision (PofGP, JS-H 1:1–19).[136]

Any writer or journalist knows that the more times you write the same story with time in between to reflect and understand, the more accurate and complete the final product becomes. Sometimes, later accounts leave out parts earlier versions included and vice versa. Such is the nature of journal and history writing. Yet, overall, in the case of Joseph's First Vision and with his later revelations to the Church directly, Joseph managed to deliver by his own hand or by the hand of scribes, a consistent message that all can understand with reasonable and dedicated effort. Dean C. Jessee, the premier modern organizer of *The Joseph Smith Papers*, tells us that "Joseph struggled to record the events of his life." Dean Jessee writes further, "The conditions in which he was raised did not facilitate a literary course—indigent circumstances, which required the labor of the entire Smith family to meet their daily needs, limited Joseph's schooling. He later wrote that he had been 'deprived of the benefit of an education suffice it to say I was mearly instructed in reading writing and the ground rules of Arithmatic which const[it]uted my whole literary acquirements'" (original spelling retained).[137]

It should also be noted that there was no systematic method for recording any of the revelations Joseph Smith received between 1820 and April 6, 1830 when the Church was organized. This sheds light on why there were no written records of Joseph's First Vision prepared prior to 1830 and actually until 1832 (D&C 21:1).[138]

The problem of record keeping persisted throughout the Prophet's leadership in the Church. Joseph had appointed clerks to keep records for him, but most of them either apostatized or died between 1836 and 1841. Clerks came and went, James Mulholland and Robert Thompson died within two years between 1839–1841 and Joseph lamented not having all the words of inspiration and revelation which had been given to him and the other presidents and apostles who led the church with him.

Speaking to the recently appointed Quorum of Twelve Apostles in Kirtland in 1835, Joseph said:

> If I now had in my possession every decision which has been had upon important items of doctrine and duties, since the commencement of this work, I would not part with them for any sum of money; but we have neglected to take minutes of such things, thinking perhaps that they would never benefit us afterwards . . . [A]nd now we cannot bear record to the church and to the world of the great and glorious manifestations which have been made to us, with that degree of power and authority we otherwise could, if we now had these things to publish abroad. ("A Record of the Transactions of the Twelve Apostles")[139]

A very deep reading of the Prophet Joseph Smith's transformational teachings is possible for all with the records now available, which have already been published. According to Dean C. Jessee, the "father of the Joseph Smith Papers Project," Joseph Smith delivered about 250 sermons from 1830 through 1844 of which only about 50 were recorded. That means that 80 percent of all Joseph Smith's sermons were not recorded and of the 20 percent or 50 sermons that were, only a handful are complete. Those periods when Joseph did not have a scribe in 1831 and 1832 in Kirtland attributed much to what is missing from his record. On the other hand, "There is no [religious] group that has the [foundational] historical record of the depth and quality that the Latter-day Saints have," said Church Historian Dr. Ronald K. Esplin in 2009, managing editor of *The Joseph Smith Papers*, noting that the early Saints were commanded to keep records. "The people tried and worked at it." Dr. Esplin continued, "At the beginning [church members] expected him to deliver the word of God [in Kirtland and Missouri], but they didn't expect him to be teaching beyond the revelations," Esplin said. According to Dr. Esplin, "Once this revelatory foundation was laid, especially in Nauvoo [1839–1844], they realized that they wanted to treasure everything that he said."[140]

Shorthand skills were not perfected in the mid-nineteenth century among the Saints and considering all, it is a great blessing to have those sermons of the Prophet which were recorded. Were it not for the dedicated work of Elders Willard Richards, who used a rudimentary shorthand, Wilford Woodruff, and a few others, who kept detailed records of many of Joseph sermons and conversations, the Latter-day Saints would have far less than has been preserved in the Church Archives.

Church Historian Dean C. Jessee, interviewed by the *Deseret News* in 2009, said, "Willard Richards did more to record what (Joseph Smith) did and said than any other person . . . He kept his journal day-by-day for the last two-and-a-half years of his life . . . The church has 1,500 pages from Joseph Smith's journals, but only 36 pages were written in his own hand . . . Three-fourths of the pages were written by Richards." One third of the Prophet's letters of correspondence have not survived. Dean Jessee estimates that "around 250 pages were dictated by the Prophet."[141]

The *Deseret News* reported, "The first volume of the Joseph Smith Papers Project was published in November of 2008. In addition to journal pages, the church maintains correspondence [or letters], meeting minutes, sermon recordings and other documents from the life of the Prophet. The first volume of *The Joseph Smith Papers*, a collection of the Prophet's journals from 1832–39, was published last November [2008]."[142]

The Church Historian's Press has indicated that the Joseph Smith Papers Project will eventually include twenty-seven volumes. These are sacred records of the life and revelations of the great Seer of Palmyra and the latter-day forerunner of Christ.

Elder Richard J. Maynes, of the Presidency of the Seventy of The Church of Jesus Christ of Latter-day Saints, after serious study of Joseph Smith's First Vision accounts has recently identified twenty eternal truths as follows:

1. We learn that the scriptures are true and can be taken literally and applied in our lives.
2. We learn that pondering the scriptures brings power and insight.
3. We learn that knowledge alone isn't enough; acting on what we know results in God's blessings.
4. We learn to put our trust in God and look to Him for answers to life's most important questions and not to put our trust in man.
5. We learn that prayers are answered according to our unwavering faith and according to Heavenly Father's will.
6. We learn the reality of Satan's existence and that he has actual power to influence the physical world, including us.
7. We learn that Satan's power is limited and superseded by God's power.
8. We learn that Satan will stop at nothing to destroy the work of God and that Satan must have known the importance of Joseph Smith in his role as the Prophet of the Restoration.
9. We learn that we can overcome Satan by calling upon God and putting our complete faith and trust in Him.
10. We learn that where there is light, darkness must depart.

11. We learn that God the Father and His Son, Jesus Christ, are two separate and distinct beings, resembling each other in features and likeness.
12. We learn that we are created in God's image.
13. We learn that Christ is risen.
14. We learn that God knows us personally and is aware of our needs and concerns. He called Joseph by name.
15. We learn of the relationship between the Father and the Son. Jesus defers to His Father, and the Father communicates with mortals here upon the earth through His Son.
16. We learn that Jesus Christ is beloved of His Father by the Father's designating Jesus as His Beloved Son.
17. We learn that the true Church of Jesus Christ as He originally organized it was not found upon the earth at the time of Joseph Smith, confirming the reality of the Great Apostasy foretold by Paul the Apostle.
18. We learn that when we care enough to desire God's input in our life, He will reveal a refining course for us. At Joseph's time all the denominations and sects were wrong.
19. We learn that every dispensation of time receives the visions, blessings, and glories of God. We learn insight into how God chooses His prophets.
20. We learn that God chooses the pure in heart who are righteous and have righteous desires to do His work, confirming the teaching from the Bible that God looks upon the heart and does not choose based on outward appearance or social status or standing (see HBKJV, 1 Samuel 16:7).

> Joseph Smith's First Vision is the key to unlocking many truths that had been hidden for centuries. Let us not forget or take for granted the many precious truths we have learned from the First Vision.[143]

These twenty sacred and eternal principles reflected from the First Vision of Joseph Smith given above by Elder Richard J. Maynes of the

Seventy are truly "precious truths" which are spiritually comprehensive and should be considered by anyone seeking as the young Joseph did for eternal truths that only God knows.

Whether one is young or old, a believer in God or an agnostic or atheist, a new convert or a mature saint, an intrepid searcher for truth or an academic scholar, the First Vision of Joseph Smith has a message for everyone. The late emeritus Professor of Church History, Milton V. Backman Jr., said that the First Vision of Joseph Smith "undergirds the doctrine of an anthropomorphic God and theomorphic man [a man formed or born of God], of the relationships of the persons of the Godhead, and of continual revelation" (EofM 2:515–516).

Thus, the whole world can learn, regardless of cultural background—whether Jew, Gentile, Christian, Muslim, or Eastern Philosopher, or Practitioner of New Age religions—from Joseph Smith's First Vision and the associated revelations that followed.

Among the many important principles revealed to the Prophet Joseph Smith during his short life, we can learn that God the Father and His Son Jesus Christ each have a glorified and eternal body of flesh and bone like man's in form and appearance, and that we are truly created "in the image of God . . . male and female" (HBKJV, Genesis 1:27). We can be assured of our eternal connection to Deity and understand further what Paul meant when he wrote, "we are the children of God" (HBKJV, Romans 8:16), not just by our faith and belief, but by our actual being and origin.

Chapter 18

The First Vision and the Major Critics

From the days of the young Prophet Joseph Smith Jr. to the present there have been many literary attempts to cast doubt on or destroy the latter-day prophet's testimony of the First Vision. Crediting Mormon historical documents compiler and historian Dan Vogel, the Church Historical Department's Professor Steven C. Harper, now editor-in-Chief of BYU *Studies Quarterly*, identified three major critics and solidified the three main criticisms used by those skeptical of Joseph Smith's First Vision:

The first critic was the Methodist minister to whom Joseph shared his experience in the grove at Palmyra. According to Joseph's 1838 account, "he treated my communication not only lightly, but with great contempt, saying it was all of the devil, that there were no such things as visions or revelations in these days; that all such things had ceased with the apostles, and there never would be any more of them" (PofGP, JS-H 1:21).

More than a century later, the second major critic of the First Vision was Dr. Fawn Brodie, eventually a tenured history professor at UCLA, who wrote very eloquently, as Dr. Steven C. Harper tells us, to "mask her historical deficiencies" and convince readers that Joseph had contrived the vision many years after he said it happened.

Less than thirty years later, Rev. Wesley Walters, a Presbyterian minister, began to write in 1967 against Joseph Smith and The Church of Jesus Christ of Latter-day Saints. Reverend Walters accused Joseph

Smith of creating a spirit of revivalism in Palmyra, where Walters said that a lack of historical records indicated there was none. Without debating whether the "absence of evidence is not evidence of absence," Wesley Walters claimed that because there was an historical records gap, which has been addressed in an earlier chapter, in the revivals at Palmyra between 1819–1823, therefore Joseph could not have had any vision during that time.[144]

These three critics and their criticisms combined provide the three legs of doubt used most often by skeptics to promote the idea that no such thing as visions of God happen anymore, that Joseph Smith invented his First Vision, and that he also invented the revivalist environment of 1820 in Palmyra in order to substantiate it.[145]

It is not sure who the "Methodist preacher" was that condemned Joseph's sharing of his vision. It was likely not the Presbyterian Reverend George Lane of Pennsylvania who came to upstate New York to preach regularly and was accredited by Joseph's brother William Smith and Oliver Cowdery of "awakening Joseph spiritually." Perhaps it was a local traveling Methodist minister from nearby Phelps just thirteen miles southeast of Palmyra. Both of these ministers would be aware of the trend toward treating secular reason above spiritual experiences such as what Joseph had described in his vision (PofGP, JS-H 1:19–20). The Smith family then lived in what Dickens called, the "age of railways" where everything in past ages could be challenged.[146] It is interesting if not ironic, as Dr. Steven C. Harper has pointed out, that John Wesley, the founder of Methodism, was very concerned about a future lack of spirituality in his flock as they grew in numbers, that they might become "a dead sect, having the form of religion without the power."[147]

During the early nineteenth century, men like Eber D. Howe published criticisms of Joseph Smith and his prophetic gifts which were limited mainly to personal, psychological, and libelous attacks condemning Joseph Smith as "lazy, indolent, ignorant and superstitious" and guilty of "fraud and deception" in his claims of revelations, translating the Book of Mormon and establishing the latter-day kingdom of God.[148] All this in spite of the fact that a local physician, Dr. Gain Robinson, gathered sixty signatures in one hour from responsible neighbors who attested to the reliability and uprightness of the

Smith Family in 1825 in order to help them save their farm from dishonest men who had purchased their loan.[149] It appears that these early antagonist writers were in no position scholastically to attempt any other critique of the Prophet, a position each successive generation of antagonists seems to lose themselves at, in spite of the presence of contemporary historical information which supports Joseph Smith's own testimony of the First Vision and his later revelations.

By the mid-twentieth century this approach with a PhD and more footnotes added was still being employed, anti-Mormon historians often quoting the same one-sided or false claims of the nineteenth-century antagonists. The bestselling biographer of Joseph Smith writing in 1945, Fawn M. Brodie, used a similar veiled psychological attack to explain how Joseph Smith, in her view, pretended his revelations and was able to so successfully turn himself into a prophet and create a latter-day kingdom of God which became a Mormon Empire. Not all reviewers of Dr. Brodie's book, *No Man Knows My History: The Life of Joseph Smith,* gave favorable reviews. A *New York Times* book reviewer in 1945 said Fawn Brodie's work often presented "conjecture as fact." Writing about Fawn M. Brodie's book in 1960, apologist and renowned scholar of the classics and ancient scripture at Brigham Young University, Dr. Hugh W. Nibley was struck "by the brazen inconsistencies that swarm in its pages."[150] A non-Mormon scholar, Dr. Jan Shipps, in her book, *Sojourner in the Promised Land: Forty Years Among the Mormons*, acknowledges Fawn Brodie's book in more glowing terms as "beautifully written biography . . . the work of a mature scholar [that] represented the first genuine effort to come to grips with the contradictory evidence about Smith's early life."[151] The one concern with Dr. Shipps's assessment is that while Dr. Brodie confronted much of the available evidence in well-written English, Brodie never honestly came to grips with the plain evidence that supported the conclusion that Joseph Smith truly was a prophet.

Fawn Brodie responded to the First Vision by saying Joseph was influenced by his religious environment to eventually imagine he was a seer or a prophet. She concluded the young Prophet was an imposter who copied his religious ideas from others or invented them. As a former Mormon and UCLA History Professor, Fawn McKay Brodie (1915–1981) acknowledged that Joseph Smith lived in a time where the Bible was used to interpret both world, regional, and local history. Rather than acknowledge how Joseph's environment enhanced his great faith in Biblical prophets and scripture, Brodie proposed that Joseph Smith invented his First Vision experience in the grove at Palmyra due to his environment and imagination. Dr. Brodie wrote, "It should not be forgotten, however, that for Joseph's vigorous and completely undisciplined imagination[,] the line between truth and fiction was always blurred." Fawn Brodie used her scholastic position to claim Joseph Smith was a fraudulent "genius of improvisation," yet made no effort to investigate the Prophet on his own terms, or from a position of historical faith.[152]

After this head-on personal attack, Dr. Brodie's dubious and so-called empirical evidence for denying the authenticity of the First Vision was, the fact that Joseph's mother Lucy and siblings Hyrum, Samuel, and Sophronia continued to attend the Presbyterian Church until 1828, eight years after Joseph's vision in 1820, in which he was told to join none of the Churches. The historical records do not reveal from spring 1820 to September 22, 1827 when the angel Moroni gave Joseph the gold plates and further instructions, that Joseph's father, mother, and siblings knew that Joseph was going to be commanded by God to organize a new church at some later date, which up until April 1830 he had not yet been commanded to do.[153]

Joseph did know this much, as Orson Pratt related in his 1840 account of Joseph's 1820 First Vision, which coincides well with Joseph's 1842 Wentworth letter account, "he received a promise that the true doctrine, the fullness of the gospel, should *at some future time*, be made known to him (italics added)."[154] This of course does not tell us that as of 1820 Joseph knew he would organize a new church, neither that Joseph's parents nor his siblings new of this detail at the time immediately after the First Vision, nor for nearly eight years after it. Joseph's mother and siblings did cease attending the Presbyterian Church in 1828 within a year from the angel Moroni's fifth visit on September 22, 1827 and about eighteen months before the Lord commanded Joseph Smith to organize the Church of Jesus Christ in April 1830 (D&C 20:1–2).

When fact or fiction didn't matter, Fawn Brodie repeated tales of fake miracles, such as the "apocryphal story about Joseph Smith, which holds that he too boasted he would walk upon the water, but that he secretly built a plank bridge underneath the surface of the pond."[155] After reading this kind of approach to "biography" one must ask what kind of scholarship and literary judgment is that?

Joseph respected his family's religious preferences and did not confide everything he had learned in his vision of 1820 until years later. By the time Joseph began translating the gold plates in April 1828, his family was in support of his divine calling, to translate and publish the Book of Mormon, and to do whatever the Lord might ask. Joseph received a revelation in February 1829 that "a marvelous work was about to come forth" (D&C 4:1). Nearly all the immediate Smith family joined the new church by 1831. We each should ask, would Joseph's family members have joined the new church had he been an imposter as Fawn Brodie assumed?[156]

As unfortunate for her readers as it was for herself, Dr. Brodie had little patience for the divine or the miraculous, and called Joseph Smith's works thoroughly "cabalistic wizardry" and "hocus pocus," the latter she applied to the translation of the Book of Mormon, which Brodie considered "frontier fiction."[157]

No Man Knows My History, full of footnotes, wit, and fanciful prose, sells a thousand copies each year, and has a very big axe to grind. According to her biographer, Newell G. Bringhurst, Fawn M. Brodie disliked Mormonism and more directly her "parochial life" under it and grew to disdain about everything related to The Church of Jesus Christ of Latter-day Saints into which she was born in Huntsville, Utah in 1915.

Six months after *No Man Knows My History* was published in 1945, as she expected and wanted, Fawn M. Brodie was excommunicated from the Church. It has been revealed that Fawn Brodie did not take criticism well against any of her writings and typically reacted in three repetitive ways: first, to be annoyed at all criticisms and especially her Latter-day Saint critics; second, to assign an emotional or psychological attachment to the Church to those Mormon scholars that criticized her work; and third, she generally refused to respond to scholarly challenges to the "soundness" of her biographies. Following *No Man Knows My History*, Fawn Brodie had written controversial biographies about Thomas Jefferson and Richard Nixon which received some strong criticisms from her colleagues at UCLA as well as by other related American history specialists.[158]

On June 19, 1946, President William H. Reeder of the New England Mission issued the excommunication letter. The charges against her were given in President Reeder's May 23, 1946 letter requesting her to appear before the Mission Court "for investigation of alleged wrong-doing and to show cause, if any you have, why you should not be excommunicated from The Church of Jesus Christ of Latter-day Saints for apostasy, in this among other matters: That in a book recently published by you, you assert matters as truths which deny the divine origin of the Book of Mormon, the restoration of the Priesthood, and of Christ's Church through the instrumentality of the Prophet Joseph Smith, contrary to the beliefs, doctrines, and teachings of the Church."[159]

A later interview in 1975 would reveal the inner preconceived opinions of Fawn Brodie before she had done significant research on the life of Joseph Smith. This oral history project from California State University quotes Dr. Brodie saying, "I was convinced before I ever began writing the book [*No Man Knows My History: The Life of Joseph Smith*] that Joseph Smith was not a true prophet . . ."[160]

Dr. Brodie acknowledges in the same interview that she did not review any of the autobiographic journals and writings of the Prophet himself, which at that time were not publicly available, even though David O. McKay, President of the Quorum of the Twelve Apostles, had agreed to let her have access to them.[161]

Joseph Smith's 1832 and 1835 journals were not available to all scholars so Dr. Brodie used Joseph's 1838 account of his First Vision, giving her the false impression that Joseph had not written of his most glorious revelation until twenty years after it happened when Orson Pratt published his 1840 pamphlet version of the 1838 Joseph Smith History. In the second edition of 1971, Brodie corrected that misunderstanding and used the earlier 1832 and 1835 accounts of the First Vision to support her "evolutionary" theory of Joseph Smith's history.[162]

Fawn Brodie admitted her own need at an early age for a psychological understanding of herself and a separation, or "liberation," as Steven C. Harper put it, from the Latter-day Saint Church, and acknowledged finally going to a psychologist during the 1950s and '60s. This expressed psychological need to separate herself from the restored Church of Jesus Christ from early adulthood had the effect of her applying similar psychological analysis to the life of the Prophet Joseph Smith in her biography. Dr. Brodie's conclusion about Joseph Smith was not that of paranoia because she acknowledged Joseph's persecution was real, rather as Brodie would explain it years later, she compared Joseph to the psychological model of the "imposter," which she states both in her 1971 "Supplement" in later editions of *No Man Knows My History* and in her 1975 oral history interview.[163]

Fawn Brodie's biographer, Newel Bringhurst, who also left the Church as a young adult, admired Professor Brodie as an early feminist historian writing about Mormonism. Dr. Brinkhurst, a professor of politics and history at the College of the Sequoias in California, researched and read Fawn Brodie's correspondence thoroughly. Brigham Young University Professor Louis Midgley, after reviewing Brinkhurst's biography made this observation, Professor Brinkhurst "does not maintain that Fawn Brodie's disbelief was caused by 'research' on the Mormon past, merely that it was thereby 'reinforced.'"[164]

Fawn Brodie had left the Church and her childhood faith long before she wrote, *No Man Knows My History*, first published in 1945. She framed the arguments for decades ahead that would be used against Joseph Smith's testimony of his most important experiences and works, beginning with the First Vision. Fawn Brodie did not change her opinion of Joseph Smith twenty-five years later with the second edition of her biography when the earlier accounts of 1832 and 1835 were made available to her. She simply incorporated them into her evolutionary and psycho- environmental theories of Joseph's life.[165]

Professor Brodie's 1971 second edition of *No Man Knows My History* confirms the author's final position, "The awesome vision he described in later years was probably the elaboration of some half-remembered dream stimulated by the early revival excitement and reinforced by the rich folklore of visions circulating in his neighborhood. Or it may have been sheer invention, created some time after 1830 when the need arose for a magnificent tradition."[166] While it is not hard to pity Fawn Brodie, she being raised a member of the Church and no longer being a Latter-day Saint, yet one must identify the historiographical pitfall which her biography entails. Fawn Brodie had psychological and pre-determined reasons to oppose what Joseph Smith experienced in his First Vision and drew her conclusions about the available evidence by applying superimposed reactions to that evidence.

Dr. Steven Harper concluded his evaluation of *No Man Knows My History* with this statement, "Critical interpretations of Joseph's vision like hers share a common hermeneutic or explanatory method. They assume how a person in Joseph's position, or persons in his neighborhood, must have acted if his story was true and then show that his accounts vary from the assumed scenarios. They usually postulate a hypothetical alternative to Joseph's own explanation."[167]

Reverend Wesley P. Walters claimed there was no evidence of revivalism in 1820 Palmyra when Joseph said he experienced his First Vision. With the help of several historians we have shown that this is not the case and that there were several major revivals in Palmyra during the period of Joseph's youth from 1818 to 1822, except none in the year 1819. To that we can add other major revivals in Palmyra during 1816–1817 which likely also influenced Joseph when his family first arrived there.

According to Richard L. Bushman, Reverend Walters, who first wrote against the historicity of Joseph's First Vision in 1967, "performed a positive service to the cause of Mormon History" by delving deep into the archives and showing us that Latter-day Saint Historians can't assume as Walters noted, "that Joseph Smith's account [or accounts] must be correct," as many had done prior to the mid-twentieth century. Walters is accredited with "awakening [Latter-day Saint historians] to investigate the context of Joseph's account's, but faulted for forcing his thesis."[168]

Professors Richard L. Bushman and Marvin S. Hill did not overemphasize in their research the very late June 25, 1820 revival in Palmyra. However, they did recognize the 1818 revival, as this writer does, as one of the key events that first inspired the young Joseph Smith to seek the truth. They also noted historically that there was also "unusual excitement" over religion in the area around Palmyra, New York in 1820 as Joseph Smith recorded in 1838 (JS-H 1:5).[169]

Whether Professor Bushman thinks Reverend Walters was correct about there being no revival in 1820 is not clear.

Dr. Backman and Dr. Quinn, as expressed in an earlier chapter, have shown historically that there was a revival in late spring 1820 on June 25th. It has been reported that it snowed on May 28, 1820 in Palmyra and it is easy to see that Joseph could have considered June 25th still part of spring while technically summer began on June 21st or solstice four days earlier.[170]

According to the contemporary Benaijah Williams diaries, Reverend George Lane was in that district or region of country in both 1819 and 1820 and in July 1820 "spoke on Gods method in bringing about Reffermations [sic]."[171] The Williams diaries confirm the religious excitement of 1820, yet historians unaware of these records continue to repeat Reverend Walters claim "that there was no significant revival in or around Palmyra in 1820" contrary to the evidence that supports what Joseph Smith wrote in his journals and history.

It is clear to believing Latter-day Saints and to competent and faithful historians that what Joseph Smith wrote in his several accounts of his First Vision about the excitement over religion or revivalism, his own desire to know which church was correct and his acceptance of the challenge of the Apostle James (HBKJV, James 1:5) to inquire of the Lord for wisdom, are all verifiable in historical context.

While we cannot here address them all, Marvin S. Hill, Professor of American History at BYU, further summarizes the obvious historical biases of several major critics of Joseph Smith:

> To some extent Reverend Walters, and to a considerable extent, the Tanners, suffer from what Sidney E. Mead called an anti-historical bias. They allow for no development in Joseph Smith's thought, holding up a very absolutistic model to which he is supposed to conform. They always assume that the worst motives influenced the Mormon prophet. They begin with Brodie's absurd notion that unless Joseph Smith told about his vision sufficiently that the newspapers picked it up and unless all the details are exactly alike, Joseph made the story up. It makes no difference to them that the story does appear in the first history which Joseph wrote in 1832 and

> that it appears in some form in all the accounts with which he had anything to do.[172]

> Professor Hill continues:

> A tolerant viewpoint is required in handling any religious sources. Sectarians like Walters and the Tanners will allow for it in their own religious preference but will not extend the same courtesy to the Mormons. Walters accepts the gold digging stories told by Obadiah Dogberry in the Palmyra Reflector quite uncritically, as he does the testimonies of E. D. Howe. These stories have been examined with care by Hugh Nibley and Richard Anderson, and they have demonstrated that there are major inconsistencies and an extreme one-sidedness. Why should one give unqualified credence to Dogberry, who so often resorts to hyperbole and who had a run-in with Joseph Smith regarding his publishing part of the Book of Mormon without permission? Dogberry was obviously contemptuous and this biased what he wrote. Why accept E. D. Howe when Hurlbut [Howe's source] went to Palmyra deliberately to get something on the Mormons? Walters' scholarship is one of sectarian advantage, not objectivity.[173]

The honest observer will find that while Joseph Smith lived in a favorable time to believe in prophets and seers, as compared to today, his own experiences in revealing hidden divine mysteries of God, seeing and speaking with God the Father and Jesus Christ face to face and later with holy angels and translating and publishing new scripture from ancient records, as real seers did and should do, all proved he was more than a product of his New England environment or his own imagination. Joseph Smith truly was, as evidenced by the works which he produced during his life, a prophet and a seer!

Professor Richard L. Bushman makes this clear in his first book about the latter-day prophet, *Joseph Smith And The Beginnings Of Mormonism*, published in 1984. Dr. Bushman is convinced after investigation of the historical record that Joseph Smith was no pretender and not just an important religious figure among many. Professor Bushman confirms that the life of Joseph Smith follows a scripturally predicted and historically verified path consisting of at least *four great achievements*: the First Vision; the Translation of the Book of Mormon; the establishment of the Church of Christ which included receiving the priesthood authority by divine visitations from angels; and the Restoration of all things including temple rites. All four are major preparations for the Second Coming of the Savior.

Dr. Bushman shows that unlike Alexander Campbell, who was a child of the Enlightenment, shown by his Christian theological writings, Joseph Smith on the other hand, was far more like a prophet and seer, bringing forth new revelations, doctrines and ordinances whose writings both in the Book of Mormon and in the Doctrine and Covenants were more like those found in the Bible.[174]

It occurred to this writer several years ago while studying the accounts of Joseph Smith's First Vision which Joseph personally wrote or dictated in 1832, 1835, 1838, and 1842, that these several accounts were complementary, supplementary, and naturally what would be expected from a young man that was progressing in his knowledge of Deity and divine doctrine, as a young prophet who was eventually given the task to re-establish the kingdom of God on the earth.

It became even more clear to this writer after thus far producing thirty-three volumes of handwritten personal journals, four handwritten volumes of ward clerk and high council journals, and numerous volumes of work-related daily planners, that the understanding of life's events when recorded over time will expand and become more accurate or complete. As one's personal record is reviewed, clarity and inspiration may be obtained, memory is renewed, and details can be defined and further recorded. It is noticed that Joseph's 1838 and 1842 accounts of his First Vision were longer and more detailed than his 1832 and 1835 accounts for similar reasons. Some precious elements may be missing from the earlier accounts, but the later accounts benefit from this process. Certainly, this has been my experience, and this was the Prophet Joseph Smith's experience as he tried to make a record, and as all should acknowledge, quite eloquently so, of the marvelous things that he experienced during his short life (1805–1844), all initiated by his First Vision in the spring of 1820.

Unfortunately, nonbelievers and critics of the Prophet will not give Joseph Smith the same developmental tolerance in his history writing as they would give themselves or others they would esteem as worthy of human development. This predetermined unfairness has shown itself in the writings of such enemies or critics of Joseph Smith and Mormonism as Obadiah Dogberry, Eber D. Howe, Philastus Hurlbut, Alexander Campbell, David Whitmer, John C. Bennett, and others in the nineteenth century. Fawn M. Brodie, Jerald and Sandra Tanner, Rev. Wesley P. Walters, Lavina Fielding Anderson, H. Michael Marquardt, Grant H. Palmer, and Dan Vogel and others make up a significant part of the antagonists of the twentieth century.

While several of the critics of Joseph's testimony from Fawn Brodie (1945) forward did considerable research in major libraries and archives of America and made contributions to Mormon literature, each of them made critical mistakes in their individual source preferences, emphasis, and methods of evaluation, leaning to anti- Mormon and non-Mormon historians as much as to the faithful histories of Joseph Smith and The Church of Jesus Christ of Latter-day Saints. As Fawn Brodie stated, "I was just putting all the versions together and then, as I say, it was a little like building a mosaic."[175]

The main problem with this "mosaic" approach to historical biography is that all three contradicting sources, Mormon, non-Mormon, and anti-Mormon, cannot all be right at the same time and give an accurate portrayal of the big picture. Using all three to construct a true history is impossible. To solve this, on matters of the character of Joseph Smith and the divine manifestations he and others testified of, Professor Brodie and the other critics, when there were contradictions, deferred to the anti-Mormon and non-Mormon opinions, that of fraud and unbelief.

By doing so they refused to look at Joseph Smith and his experiences on his own terms, that of an honest person, learning and growing in knowledge as he went, "from grace to grace," seeking in faith and receiving actual personal revelation. Joseph's detractors more often than not made negative preconceived assumptions related to their own religious needs and conditions, followed by disparaging conclusions mingled with numerous footnotes. Such a formula can never be expected to produce reliable history or accurately represent in biography a great religious leader and the restored Church of Jesus Christ he founded.

Investigators of the Prophet Joseph Smith and his First Vision today and in the future would do far better to seek historical literature from Joseph's own hand and from his many clerks. Since the nearly completed twenty-seven volume Joseph Smith Papers Project has become available from the Church Historian's Press in Salt Lake City, investigators of the Prophet Joseph Smith should seek out those original documents. Then they should seek out scholars who have studied Joseph Smith's life deeply in an unbiased and balanced historical light for many decades, rather than from the estranged and often unbelieving critics with an axe to grind.

New detractors of Joseph Smith's First Vision and The Church of Jesus Christ of Latter-day Saints in general are now developing in the twenty-first century, largely repeating what these earlier antagonists or critics have already promoted.

At the same time a new generation of faithful and believing prophets, apostles, and saints, and among them gospel scholars and church historians, are each moving forward and rising upward to fill the ranks of the Restored Church and its growing academic community of scholars.

Chapter 19

A Great Seer and a Restoration Foretold

The coming of Jesus Christ prior to His Second Coming to restore the truth to the earth in a distant latter day had been prophesied by the Apostle Peter in his sermon at Jerusalem during Pentecost, which was the beginning of the Early Church of Christ in AD 34. Peter preached to a large audience at Jerusalem, to "Jews, devout men, out of every nation under heaven" (Acts 2:5), and reminded them of the prophecies of Christ's first coming in the flesh as the promised Messiah. He reminded them that in that day, Peter's day, and again in the latter day, this day, as the prophet Joel had predicted, "your young men shall see visions, and your old men shall dream dreams: and on my servants and on my handmaidens I will pour out in those days of my Spirit; and they shall prophesy . . ." (HBKJV, Joel 2:28–29; Acts 2:17–18; D&C 95:4).

Then later in the week, after visiting the temple with John, Peter again spoke to a large crowd and prophesied himself by saying:

> Repent ye therefore, and be converted, that your sins may be blotted out, when *the times of refreshing shall come* from the presence of the Lord; And he [God] shall send Jesus Christ, which before was preached unto you: *Whom the heaven must receive until the times of restitution of all things,* which God hath spoken by the mouth of all his holy prophets since the world began (HBKJV, Acts 3:19–20, emphasis added).

These oft quoted passages in the Book of Acts look forward to the world in a time beyond Peter's day when the Lord Jesus Christ would come again and restore all things in preparation for His glorious Second Coming.

Elder Bruce R. McConkie explained the "times of refreshing" scripture as follows:

> This designated period, this times of refreshing, is to take place at the second coming of the Son of Man, in the day when the Lord sends Christ again to earth.[176]

The Apostle Paul wrote to the Ephesians, "That in the dispensation of the fullness of times he might gather together in one all things in Christ, both which are in heaven, and which are on earth; even in him" (HBKJV, Ephesians 1:10).

Jewish Tradition records *two separate messiahs* who would be born in the latter days, as Matthew B. Brown explained, "one from the tribe of Judah, *the Messiah ben David,* or "son of" David, and one from the tribe of Joseph, the *Messiah ben Joseph-Ephraim* or "son of" Joseph. The *Messiah ben Joseph* concept first arose when Rachel, the mother of Joseph of Egypt prophesied that Joseph would be the ancestor of a messiah who would "arise at the end of days." Scholars who have studied this remarkable legend have determined that it was "a standard article of faith, early and firmly established and universally accepted" (emphasis added).[177]

The Apostle Peter was not the first to prophesy of the Restoration of the fullness of the gospel in the latter days, nor of the coming of that seer who would deliver it. Joseph, son of Jacob, Vizier of ancient Egypt, prophesied of this seer in the Book of Genesis before editors removed it. A thousand years after Joseph, in 600 BC, Lehi, a prophet in ancient America, took a pristine Biblical record out of Jerusalem called the brass plates from which he recorded this prophecy about the latter-day seer from the seed of ancient Joseph. This seer would restore the knowledge of the Lord's covenants and his name would be "Joseph" after his father. Isaiah and Ezekiel both quoted part of this prophecy (BofM, 2 Nephi 3:11–14; HBKJV, Isaiah 29:10-14; Ezekiel 37:15–17).

This prophecy by ancient Joseph of Egypt that refers to the Prophet Joseph Smith Jr. is found in the Joseph Smith Translation of the Bible (translated 1831–1833):

> And again, *a seer will I raise up out of the fruit of thy loins*, and unto him will I give power to bring forth my word unto the seed of thy loins; and not to the bringing forth of my word only, saith the Lord, but to the convincing them of my word, which shall have already gone forth among them in the last days;
>
> Wherefore *the fruit of thy loins shall write [the Book of Mormon]*, and *the fruit of the loins of Judah shall write [The Holy Bible]*; and that which shall be written by the fruit of thy loins, and also that which shall be written by the fruit of the loins of Judah, shall grow together *unto the confounding of false doctrines, and laying down of contentions, and establishing peace among the fruit of thy loins, and bringing them to a knowledge of their fathers in the latter days; and also to the knowledge of my covenants*, saith the Lord.
>
> And out of weakness shall he be made strong, in that day when my work shall go forth among all my people, which shall restore them, who are of the house of Israel, in the last days.
>
> And that seer will I bless, and they that seek to destroy him shall be confounded; for this promise I give unto you; for I will remember you from generation to generation; and his name shall be called Joseph, and it shall be after the name of his father; and he shall be like unto you; for the thing which the Lord shall bring forth by his hand shall bring my people unto salvation. (JST, Genesis 50:30–33, emphasis added; HBKJV, Ezekiel 37:15–17)

Isaiah prophesied of the future heresies or "deep sleep" that would follow the Early Church that Jesus Christ and His Apostles established, and of an unlearned prophet in the latter days who would translate an ancient record of the Jews:

> For the Lord hath poured out upon you the spirit of deep sleep, and hath closed your eyes: the prophets and your rulers, the seers hath he covered.

> *And the vision of all is become unto you as the words of a book [the Book of Mormon] that is sealed,* which men deliver to one that is learned, saying, Read this, I pray thee: and he saith, I cannot; for it is sealed:
>
> And the book is delivered to him [Joseph Smith Jr.] that is not learned, saying, Read this, I pray thee: and he saith, I am not learned.
>
> Wherefore the Lord said, Forasmuch as this people draw near me with their mouth, and with their lips do honour me, but have removed their heart far from me, and their fear toward me is taught by the precept of men:
>
> Therefore, behold, I will proceed to do a marvellous work among this people, even a marvellous work and a wonder: *for the wisdom of their wise men shall perish, and the understanding of their prudent men shall be hid.* (HBKJV, Isaiah 29:10–14, emphasis added)

In the latter days, modern prophets have confirmed the role of Joseph Smith as the Lord's designated prophet of this last dispensation. On October 9, 1859 in Salt Lake City, Joseph Smith's successor President Brigham Young declared:

> It was decreed in the counsels of eternity, long before the foundations of the earth were laid, that he should be the man, in the last dispensation of this world, to bring forth the word of God to the people, and receive the fullness of the keys and power of the Priesthood of the Son of God. The Lord had his eye upon him, and upon his father, and upon his father's father, and upon their progenitors clear back to Abraham, and from Abraham to the flood, from the flood to Enoch, and, from Enoch to Adam. He has watched that family and that blood as it has circulated from its fountain to the birth of that man. *He was foreordained in eternity to preside over this last dispensation.* (JD 7:289-290, emphasis added; DBY, 108)

Like Abraham before him, who was included among the valiant spirits in the grand council in heaven before this earth was made, so also the Prophet Joseph Smith was among them, and called to stand at the head of this last dispensation (PofGP, Abraham 3:22–23).

Regarding this foreordination the Prophet Joseph Smith said:

> Every man who has a calling to minister to the inhabitants of the world, was ordained to that very purpose in the Grand Council of heaven before this world was. I suppose that I was ordained to this very office in that Grand Council. (TPJS, 365)

Had Joseph Smith not been prepared from before the foundations of the earth, by this literal and prophetic foreordination, he certainly could not have received his First Vision and the many other divine manifestations throughout his shortened life.

This is not a "predestination" following Augustine and Calvin, where some interpret Romans 8:29–30 and Ephesians 1:4–5 to mean that God causes everything and man is only an effect. *Foreordination* requires each person to voluntarily choose to accept divine callings or not, and to fulfill God's purposes by their own agency with the aid of heaven. "All things are present" to Him (D&C 38:2). "he [God] anticipates our choices. However he does not make the choices for us" (EofM 2:522–523).

Historians have told us that such revelations and manifestations as Joseph's First Vision were condemned by the churches and their leaders in Palmyra in the 1820s and 30s. This attitude was typical of the Age of Enlightenment. Thus, without a divine manifestation from God, Joseph might have been inclined to accept the doctrines of one of the prevailing churches of his day as his mother and siblings did at first, and if that had happened, Joseph would have been generally led astray.

Fortunately, for Joseph, his family and for all who would listen to Joseph's testimony, none need be led astray. The Great Seer Joseph Smith Jr. received many divine revelations from the Lord that brought forth the fullness of the gospel and the restored Church of Jesus Christ which are now among us (D&C 1:17–24).

Chapter 20

Aftermath of the First Vision

THE YOUNG SEER OF PALMYRA EXPERIENCED MARVELOUS THINGS, and the Lord through him restored heavenly knowledge unknown to the world for at least sixteen hundred years. No greater prophet since the Apostles of Christ was appointed, and no other prophet was authorized by God and holy angels to restore the fullness of the gospel and establish the Church of Jesus Christ on earth.

The record of Joseph Smith's First Vision has been considered doctrinal by the Latter-day Saints from its first recording and telling to the world by the Prophet and the latter-day apostles during the 1830s and 40s. The First Vision was given wide distribution among the Saints in March of 1842 when Joseph's 1838 account and the 1842 Wentworth letter account were both first published in the *Times and Seasons* newspaper. The 1838 account was published again in 1851 in *the Pearl of Great Price* in Liverpool, England by Apostle Franklin D. Richards, then also President of the British Mission. Among non-Mormon readers, the First Vision was published also in 1844 by Israel Daniel Rupp in Philadelphia, Pennsylvania in his book, *An Original History of the Religious Denominations at Present Existing in the United States*. This book's source was the 1843 letter of Joseph Smith to Israel Daniel Rupp and its almost identical account taken from the Wentworth letter.[178]

The First Vision record would become part of the standard works of the Church or scripture during General Conference on October 10, 1880 under the direction of President John Taylor, third president of the Church and one of its early witnesses.

With only a few details, the fourteen-year-old Joseph had been instructed by the Savior that "all religious denominations were believing in incorrect doctrines and that none of them was acknowledged of God as his church and kingdom" and to "go not after them." At the same time, Joseph said he was given "a promise that the fullness of the gospel should at some future time be made known unto me."[179]

Three years and six months passed in Joseph's life from the spring of 1820 when he had his First Vision until September 21, 1823. Humbled by his own imperfections and lessor sins, Joseph again sought the Lord in humble prayer in his bedroom, seeking "forgiveness" of his "sins and follies" and "a manifestation" of his standing before the Lord. In the evening of that date, and for the next four years annually, Joseph Smith was visited by the angel Moroni who began to prepare Joseph to translate the plates of the Book of Mormon by the gift and power of God (PofGP, JS-H 1:29, 54). Moroni had deposited the plates anciently in the Hill Cumorah near Joseph's home after the destruction of his people the Nephites.

Joseph Smith learned by faith how to use a seer stone, which he discovered by revelation and had uncovered under the earth reportedly as early as 1822. A second separate seer stone Joseph obtained before 1831. These seer stones were separate from those seer stones associated with the Urim and Thummim which the angel Moroni loaned to him on September 22, 1827. And like the young Joseph who was sold into Egypt, Joseph Smith Jr. was becoming a prophet and a seer himself. Considering his foreordination before his birth, he already was.

About July 15, 1828, the first 116 pages of the Book of Mormon were translated and then lost by Martin Harris, who was one of three men called to be witnesses of the sacred book (BofM, 2 Nephi 27:12–13). Joseph was distraught after Moroni came and took away the plates and Urim and Thummim for a while (D&C 3:14–16). On September 22, 1828, Moroni returned the plates and Urim and Thummim to Joseph (DHC 1:23; EofM 1:210).

After that humbling experience and losing their first child at birth, Emma Smith acted as scribe for several months as Joseph continued the translation. Oliver Cowdery arrived in Harmony, Pennsylvania on April 5, 1829 to relieve Emma as scribe. Joseph eventually began using a seer stone instead of the cumbersome breastplate of the Urim and Thummim as before (CHC 1:119).

This alternate method of translation, reported by one of the three witness, David Whitmer, was similar except that Joseph would place his single seer stone in a hat, put his face over the opening and create a dark space for the stone to illuminate with a "spiritual light." A piece of material like "parchment" would appear and produce to Joseph's view the translated part or segment of the plates in the English language, about ten or twelve words at a time that Joseph would then read to his scribe who would record it and read it back to Joseph before starting the next set of verses, a miraculous occurrence to say the least. Joseph said the translation was by the "gift and power of God" and the Three Witnesses, Martin Harris, Oliver Cowdery, and David Whitmer testified of it, which allowed the Prophet Joseph to produce the English version of the Book of Mormon (EofM 1:210).[180]

Eventually Joseph needed neither Urim and Thummim nor his own seer stones to receive revelation from God. Joseph the Seer would become like a urim or seer stone himself, the Spirit of God would shine through him and speak (EofM 3:1293).

As early as 1823, Joseph Smith was given more information about his prophetic mission that he and Oliver Cowdery would be receiving the keys of the holy priesthood and the office of the apostleship from holy angels who were former prophets on earth. When directed, they would establish the true Church of Christ once again after its absence for sixteen hundred years. The lesser Aaronic Priesthood and its keys were restored to Joseph and Oliver on May 15, 1829 by John the Baptist, and the greater Melchizedek Priesthood and its keys in June of 1829 by Peter, James, and John (D&C 13; DHC 1:39–42; D&C 27:12; DHC 1:106–108).

Latter-day Saint Church Researcher Scott H. Faulring wrote:

> Oliver Cowdery, in the final installment of his history of the "rise of the church," stated that Moroni told Joseph Smith in 1823 that "when they [the Book of Mormon plates] are interpreted the Lord will give the holy priesthood to some, and they shall begin to proclaim this gospel and baptize by

> water, and after that they shall have power to give the Holy Ghost by the laying on of their hands.[181]

A surprisingly large number of documents identify the Restoration of the Aaronic and Melchizedek Priesthoods including the apostleship. Latter-day Saint Historian Brian Q. Cannon and the BYU Studies staff identified *seventy* documents which bear witness of the Restoration of the priesthood authority to Joseph Smith and Oliver Cowdery as "elders" and "apostles" in 1829. The first of these documents is the "Articles of the Church of Christ" (1829) in Oliver Cowdery's handwriting which speaks of the apostleship of Paul, and that "ye [Joseph and Oliver] are called even with that same calling." The document concludes with Oliver Cowdery's statement, "Behold I am Oliver. I am an Apostle of Jesus Christ by the will of God the Father & the Lord Jesus Christ." The article documents scores of similar witnesses and ends with the seventieth document which is Hiram Page's witness in a March 4, 1848 letter confirming the ordination of Joseph Smith and Oliver Cowdery to the offices of an "elder" and an "apostle" before April 6, 1830.[182]

On April 6, 1830, Joseph Smith and five associates obeying a revelation to establish the kingdom of God on the earth, met in Peter Whitmer's log cabin in Manchester, New York. They, along with about sixty others were in attendance as the Church of Christ, later renamed by the Lord, "The Church of Jesus Christ of Latter-day Saints" was organized. In that meeting Joseph Smith was accepted as "First Elder" and Oliver Cowdery as "Second Elder" of the church. By a revelation given on that day, Joseph was named by the Lord, a "seer, a translator, a prophet, an apostle of Jesus Christ, an elder of the church through the will of God the Father, and the grace of your Lord Jesus Christ, Being inspired of the Holy Ghost to lay the foundation thereof, and to build it up unto the most holy faith" (D&C 20:1–4; 21:1–3).

Receiving a divine revelation on "Church Organization and Government" from Jesus Christ through the Holy Spirit, the Prophet Joseph Smith was directed to organize and restore the Church as it had existed anciently upon the earth with apostolic authority. The following is part of that revelation given on April 6, 1830:

The rise of the Church of Christ in these last days, being one thousand eight hundred and thirty years since the coming of our Lord and Savior Jesus Christ in the flesh, it being regularly organized and established agreeable to the laws of our country, by the will and commandments of God, in the fourth month, and on the sixth day of the month which is called April—

Which commandments were given to Joseph Smith, Jun., who was called of God, and ordained an apostle of Jesus Christ, to be the first elder of this church;

And to Oliver Cowdery, who was also called of God, an apostle of Jesus Christ, to be the second elder of this church, and ordained under his hand;

And this according to the grace of our Lord and Savior Jesus Christ, to whom be all glory, both now and forever. Amen.

After it was truly manifested unto this first elder that he had received a remission of his sins, he was entangled again in the vanities of the world;

But after repenting, and humbling himself sincerely, through faith, God ministered unto him by an holy angel, whose countenance was as lightning, and whose garments were pure and white above all other whiteness;

And gave unto him commandments which inspired him;

And gave him power from on high, by the means which were before prepared, to translate the Book of Mormon;

Which contains a record of a fallen people, and the fullness of the gospel of Jesus Christ to the Gentiles and to the Jews also;

Which was given by inspiration, and is confirmed to others by the ministering of angels, and is declared unto the world by them—

Proving to the world that the holy scriptures are true, and that God does inspire men and call them to his holy work in this age and generation, as well as in generations of old;

Thereby showing that he is the same God yesterday, today, and forever. Amen.

> Therefore, having so great witnesses, by them shall the world be judged, even as many as shall hereafter come to a knowledge of this work.
>
> And those who receive it in faith, and work righteousness, shall receive a crown of eternal life;
>
> But those who harden their hearts in unbelief, and reject it, it shall turn to their own condemnation—
>
> For the Lord God has spoken it; and we, the elders of the church, have heard and bear witness to the words of the glorious Majesty on high, to whom be glory forever and ever. Amen. (D&C 20:1–16; DHC 1:64–70).

Once given this priesthood authority and apostleship, Joseph and Oliver as the first and second elders of the Church, being inspired by the power of the Holy Ghost were able to baptize each other and new believers into the Church of Christ which was organized on April 6, 1830. They then laid their hands upon the heads of these converts and gave them the gift of the Holy Ghost as done in the Early Church by the ancient apostles. The Lord Jesus Christ Himself would later reveal to Joseph Smith the Prophet in 1838 the official name of His church, "For thus shall my church be called in the last days, The Church of Jesus Christ of Latter-day Saints" (D&C 20:2; 21:2, 3; 33:5; 115:4; HBKJV, Acts 9:17–18; 18:17; 19:6).

Six years later, as persecutions increased, additional priesthood keys were given to Joseph and Oliver to gather the House of Israel from the four corners of the earth, to teach the fullness of the gospel to the Saints, to minister to the Saints as they make and keep sacred covenants in the Holy Temple, to perform baptisms for the dead, and to seal worthy couples, men and women as husbands and wives with their children as families for both time in mortality and for all eternity. These eternal blessings were confirmed upon them in 1836 in the Kirtland Temple in Ohio from Moses, Elias, and Elijah who are now angels, resurrected prophets from earlier gospel dispensations (D&C 110; 128; 132).

Missouri governor Lilburn W. Boggs issued his Mormon Extermination Order of October 27, 1838 declaring that "the Mormons must be treated as enemies and must be exterminated or driven from the state" (DHC 3:175). On November 12, 1838 the Prophet Joseph Smith, his brother Hyrum, Sidney Rigdon, Lyman Wight, Caleb Baldwin, and Alexander McRae were unjustly charged of "treason" and sentenced to die by firing squad at Far West Missouri. One honest leader of that state's militia, General Alexander W Doniphan, refused to carry out the unlawful order of Major General Samuel D. Lucas. Instead, Joseph, and the five brethren named, spent four winter months in the cold and inaptly named Liberty Jail, while the saints were driven by mobs from their homes in Missouri to Illinois in the winter of 1838-1839. While imprisoned the prophet had several important revelations in March of 1839 that are of great worth to the Latter-day Saints (DHC 3:289-305,374,414; JSP D6: 265-429; D&C121; D&C 122; D&C 123; D&C 127:2).

Like the ancient saints of the Early Church, the Latter-day Saints of the nineteenth century were persecuted and driven from state to state until they fled into the western wilderness of America. Between 1830 and 1847, these pioneer Saints were driven from New York to Ohio to Missouri to Illinois and finally to the Great Salt Lake Valley. What at first was a much larger US Territory, in 1896 became the current State of Utah, joining the United States. The Prophet Joseph Smith was martyred by a mob with painted faces in 1844 at Carthage, Illinois. No other religious leader in America has suffered more for his faith in God and his religion than did the Prophet Joseph Smith. No other American religion has suffered more officially sponsored persecution than the members of The Church of Jesus Christ of Latter-day Saints.

As attorney, judge, and apostle, Elder Dallin H. Oaks, now First Counselor in the First Presidency of the Church, testified before Congress on May 13, 1992:

> I know of no other major religious group in America that has endured anything comparable to the officially sanctioned persecution that was imposed upon members of my church by federal, state, and local government officials.[183]

Joseph's glorious First Vision, which inspired the great work of restoration of truth and divine authority to the earth, was carried out by the Prophet and Seer Joseph Smith and assisted by Elder Oliver

Cowdery, both who were instructed and ordained by angels, in order to establish the kingdom of God throughout the world.

Their missions fulfilled, qualifies these two Prophets and the Church—Joseph Smith, Oliver Cowdery, and The Church of Jesus Christ of Latter-day Saints—and their successors—the First Presidency and the Quorum of the Twelve Apostles—to be the heavenly and earthly legal priesthood heirs to Peter, James, and John and the ancient Early Church of Jesus Christ which was established by those original Apostles (HBKJV, John 15:16; DofS 1:213–214).

Without the principle of personal revelation from heaven, Joseph never would have received the gold plates of the Book of Mormon. He and Oliver Cowdery, his scribe and counselor, would never have received the priesthoods of Aaron, Melchizedek, and the apostleship. The keys of the priesthood for the work of the Lord would have never come. Joseph would not have been able or inclined by an unmatched faith to restore the kingdom of God on earth, or the Church of Christ later known as The Church of Jesus Christ of Latter-day Saints. From such reflections, the importance of the First Vision to Joseph Smith is understood.

One may ask, why is there only *one true church* on the earth at a time? Because God is a not the author of the confusion and strife that Joseph saw in the religious world around him, which we can also see today. The Savior told Joseph in 1820 during his First Vision that the other sects had "a form of godliness, but they deny the power thereof." The denial of Joseph Smith's First Vision by the various sects in Joseph's and in our day is another witness of this principle of God's one true Church. Joseph truly experienced "the power of godliness" and he "could not deny it." The sects denied this power and each contradicted the other claiming to be right. Yet all cannot be right at the same time (PofGP, JS-H 1:19, 25).

The importance and purpose of Joseph Smith's First Vision in 1820 cannot be overstated. No other place in America, other than the "burned over district" of upstate New York, could have better inspired and challenged Joseph to seek answers in the Bible, and then by his own faith, directly from God through prayer. It took two years of preparation and study beginning in 1818 for Joseph to develop his faith strong enough to pray for a revelation from God. Reading and pondering the Holy Scriptures gave him the strength and wisdom he needed to achieve that.

"For if any of you lack wisdom, let him ask of God . . ." (James 1:5), are words of the ancient apostle which will be remembered for eternities to come as the wellspring of true faith that set Joseph Smith on the path to call upon and see God face to face, as Moses had anciently (HBKJV, Exodus 33:11). Once his course was set, the young prophet did not look back, rather he pressed forward in his desire to commune with Deity and entered the grove in Palmyra expecting an answer to his prayer.

This epochal and divine event happened in an enlightened age that denied its possibility. Once Joseph received the personal visitation and introduction from God the Father to His Son Jesus Christ accompanied by holy angels, both Joseph and the world were changed forever. Yet, like the Early Church, only a small part of the people of the world would show enough faith to believe or know of its truth.

With this heavenly manifestation, Joseph was introduced to the Godhead and the true natures of God, Jesus Christ, and the Holy Ghost who accompanies them. Joseph was able to reconcile himself with God spiritually and to help himself avoid the religions of his day divinely labeled as unacceptable (PofGP, JS-H 1:19). As previously noted, the records of the Church document four more times, between 1831 and 1836, both the Father and the Son would appear to Joseph Smith. Three of those divine manifestations were witnessed by others.

The young prophet faced persecutions when he told others of his first vision of Deity, yet he eventually shared it with many people including family members and made four personal accounts or records of his vision during his shortened life prior to his martyrdom with his brother Hyrum.

The magnitude of the First Vision is further explained by President Spencer W. Kimball, the Twelfth President of the Church, as follows:

> Nothing short of this total vision to Joseph could have served the purpose to clear away the mists of the centuries. Merely an impression, a hidden voice, a dream could not have dispelled the old vagaries and misconceptions. The God of all the worlds and the Son of God, the Redeemer, our Savior, in person

> attended this boy. He saw the living God. He saw the living Christ. Of all the great events of the century, none compared with the first vision of Joseph Smith.[184]

The current prophet and seventeenth President of The Church of Jesus Christ of Latter-day Saints, Russell M. Nelson, in April of 2019 made the following declaration during General Conference:

> As President of His Church, I plead with you who have distanced yourselves from the Church and with you who have not yet really sought to know that the Savior's Church has been restored. Do the spiritual work to find out for yourselves, and please do it now. Time is running out.[185]

How does one do this "spiritual work" successfully? There is no better way than to follow the *advice* of the Apostle James, "If any of you lack wisdom, let him [or her] ask of God," and the *example* of the young boy Joseph Smith as he took his question to the Lord in humble prayer in a grove of trees in Palmyra, New York on a beautiful spring day in 1820 (HBKJV, James 1:5; PofGP, JS-H 1:1–26).

Those who will humbly ask of the Lord will be answered and filled with love and joy, just as the young prophet described in his 1832 account when he wrote, ". . . my soul was filled with love, and for many days I could rejoice with great Joy" (JSP, H1:13).

Joseph Seer of Latter Day (Cont.)

. . . Hark, the vision of Isaiah,
Sees young Joseph's sealed book.
None can read the ancient scripture,
Learned scoff and will not look.

Yet the lad who was not learned,
Reads it with the urim took.
Message of the ancient gospel,
In this promised land forsook.

Other prophets long departed,
Now in glory they appeared.
Bringing with them keys of heaven,
Priesthood power to the Seer.

See the stone has left the mountain,
Rolling, crushing, fills the earth.
The Church of Jesus Christ, established,
Ancient truths have found rebirth.

No rest given to the Prophet,
Painted mobs with hatred rage.
He and Hyrum died at Carthage,
Martyrs sealed beyond the grave.

Now we sing and praise the hero,
Death no longer bids him pay.
He may now from heaven bless us,
Joseph Seer of Latter Day.

—Steven Anthony Wilden

Appendix 1

The Nicene Godhead

The knowledge given to Joseph Smith during his first vision of Deity in 1820 aligns doctrinally with what Enoch, Noah, Abraham, Moses, Ezra, and other prophets and apostles had taught concerning the Godhead. Like the ancient prophets before him, Joseph Smith's First Vision confirms that God the Father, Jesus Christ, and the Holy Ghost were three separate and distinct beings. The defined separate nature of the Godhead that had existed from before the creation of the earth, the sun, moon, and stars was changed by the Council of Nicaea early in the fourth century AD. (PSDP, 1 Enoch 39:2, 7; 40:1–7; 46:1–5; 48:2–4, 11; pp. 27–28, 31, 32–33; PofGP, Moses 8:23–24; Abraham 3:27; Moses 1:31–33; HBKJV-APCR, 2 Esdras 13:26; HBKJV, Daniel 7:13–14; Matthew 1:17; Acts 7:55–56).

The doctrine of the "Trinity," or the adopted idea of three gods in one being, or in one immaterial substance, was borrowed from Greek Philosophers who influenced the Romanized or Medieval Church. It is interesting to note that the word "Trinity" is not mentioned in the Bible, neither in the Book of Mormon, nor in any other ancient scriptures such as the Apocrypha and Pseudepigrapha.[186]

The apocalyptic writer in the Book of Enoch recorded the ancient or original doctrine that the "Son of Man" or Messiah (Jesus Christ) existed in heaven with the "Lord of spirits" (God the Father) before he was born in the flesh on earth. From the Book of Enoch we read:

> In that hour was the Son of man invoked before the Lord of spirits, and his name in the presence of the Ancient of days. Before the sun and the signs were created, before the stars of

> heaven were formed, his name was invoked in the presence of the Lord of spirits. A support shall He be for the righteous and the holy to lean upon, without falling; and he shall be the light of nations . . . In his presence he visited, and has revealed to the saints and to the righteous the wisdom of the Lord of spirits; because they have hated and rejected this world of iniquity, and have detested all its works and ways, in the name of the Lord of spirits. (PSDP, 1 Enoch 48:2–6; compare HBKJV, Hebrews 1:2; John 1:1–19)

The prophet Ezra, who was called Esdras during the Middle Ages, revealed this same doctrine of the Son of Man who would be our Savior who is a separate being whom God the Father held in reserve for the benefit of the spirits or God's children.

From the Book of Esdras we read:

> The same is he [the Son of Man] whom God the Highest hath kept a great season, which by his own self shall deliver his creature [the saints who are his children]: and he shall order them that are left behind [all the remaining spirits of men and women yet unborn] (HBKJV-APCR, 2 Esdras 13:26).

The three members of the Godhead have always been united in doctrine, purpose and power in order to save as many of Father's children who would choose to follow their plan. This unity of purpose would later be confused by the pre-medieval church with the separate natures and bodily form of the Godhead and the ancient practice of worshipping "one God" who was Yahweh or Jehovah or Jesus Christ. The Old Testament as it has come down to the present does not mention the name of "Jesus Christ" while the Book of Mormon does in its accounts of the Jaredites and the Nephites (HBKJV, John 1:14; 17:3, 21; 1 Corinthians 8:6; Galatians 3:20; D&C 93:3–4; 130:22; BofM, 2 Nephi 26:12; 31:21; Ether 2:12).

The Medieval Church embraced the Greek or Hellenist learning of its day. The leading teachers, deacons, priests, and bishops of the clergy were often taught the Greek language in the schools of the philosophers, who then went to work on creating the orthodoxy of the fourth-century medieval church. Most notable of these recensions was the redefinition of Deity. Ante-Nicene fathers Origen and Tertullian rejected the Gnostic heresy and believed in a bodily resurrection, yet adopted the Trinitarian Godhead view as did the many bishops who led the changing Church.[187]

The linguist, educator, and historian James L. Barker (1880–1958) reminds us in his book, *Apostasy From the Divine Church*, of that principle the Prophet Joseph Smith taught to the Restored Church, "Jesus was resurrected with a perfect material body [Luke 24:39]. The Son is like the Father. The Son is in possession of a material body. God organized the world with pre-existing element. The Father is God, Jesus is God, the Holy Ghost is God. They are numerically distinct."

Professor Barker quotes Professor Alfred Weber (1835–1914) of the University of Strasbourg who wrote about Greek *immaterialism* in his *History of Philosophy*. For Plato, "intelligence must consider matter as its natural enemy . . . as the seat and principle of evil." Prof. Barker further noted that to the Greeks, "God is not in the form of a man. God is immaterial. God is the absolute Idea, is the first and the final cause of all being. There is of (logical) necessity only one God. Matter is evil."[188]

The Godhead, from the earliest Biblical and non-canonical records, including The Book of Enoch, The Book of Abraham, and the Old and New Testaments, functioned as three individuals, the Father, the Son, and the Holy Ghost, not as one being, but as three distinct beings. The Prophet Joseph Smith said that the Father and the Son each have glorified bodies of flesh and bones and the Holy Ghost is a personage of Spirit. Both ancient and modern scripture teach the same (HBKJV, Psalms 110:1; Matthew 22:40; PSDP, Enoch 46:1–3; PofGP, Abraham 3:27; D&C 130:22).

The cause for and most dominating issue at both the Council of Nicaea in AD 325 and the Council of Constantinople in AD 381 was the doctrine of the Godhead and the relationship between the Father and the Son. Two theologians of Alexandria, Egypt—one Arius, a priest, and the other Athanasius, an arch-deacon—led a dispute from opposite sides that engulfed the entire church for more than fifty years. However, the dispute began earlier and lasted far longer than these two councils due to the Sabellian teachings of the third century including those of Noetus of Smyrna dating to AD 230. Both

Sabellius and Noetus taught that God is indivisible, and the Father, Son, and Holy Ghost were three manifestations of one divine being, a concept called Modalism. The second, or Arian controversy of the Godhead, extended the dispute for nearly two centuries.[189]

A small percentage of the bishops of the new state sanctioned Roman Church met at the Council of Nicaea in AD 325. A non-majority of 250 to 300 bishops attended or about 15 percent of the 1,800 bishops in Constantine's empire, according to the fourth-century church historian Eusebius. Of this, a "majority" was desired in order to get a doctrinal "consensus" for the divided church. That questionable "majority" of approving bishops would not come for another half-century at the Council of Constantinople in AD 381 when the Nicene Creed was adopted. Had not Constantine's desire to unite the various bishops of the east and west into one state-run church been so strong, perhaps the Arian controversy would never have come to such a head. The Arian controversy persisted even after the Council of Constantinople, but was eventually silenced. The modern Roman Catholic Church, Eastern Orthodox Church and the Protestant Churches have institutionalized the Trinitarian view identified in the Nicene Creed from that time.[190]

Arius held the original position similar to the ancient Adamic and Semitic prophets, that God the Father was superior to the Son, and that they were two different beings and of different substance. The Son was begotten by the Father, with no mystical oneness of being, while obviously having a oneness of purpose and in that latter sense were "One God." This would fall into alignment with the revelations given to Joseph Smith on the Godhead beginning with his First Vision in 1820.

Athanasius held the now current position of the Catholic, Orthodox, and Protestant churches that God the Father and the Son Jesus Christ are one being and of one substance, yet are also three persons in accordance with the Nicene Creed.[191]

In May of AD 325, "The council condemned Arius and, with reluctance on the part of some, incorporated the non-scriptural [Greek] word *homoousios* [or ὁμός, *homós*] ("of one substance") into a creed to signify the absolute equality [of the nature and identity] of the Son with the Father. The emperor then exiled Arius, an act which, while manifesting a solidarity of church and state, underscored the importance of secular patronage in ecclesiastical affairs."[192]

The Book of Mormon, as well as secular history, reveals that medieval churches and the associated nation-states of the Gentiles have practiced the "secret works of darkness," "murders," and "abominations" that Nephi warned us about (BofM, 2 Nephi 10:15). This includes much "wickedness" that is prophesied by the angel Moroni to still exist in the nineteenth century when Joseph Smith was alive and preparing to bring forth the Book of Mormon and to eventually restore the original Church of Jesus Christ on earth (BofM, Mormon 8:26–36; PofGP, JS-H 1:36–41).

In the first few centuries following the death and resurrection of Jesus Christ the doctrines of the Early Church were gradually changed or corrupted, including the doctrine of Deity. The doctrine of Deity was officially changed in the early or pre-Medieval Church by the Councils of Nicaea in 325 and Constantinople in 381. The intellectual philosophy of the elite and educated class soon influenced the Church's clergy and doctrine. The adoption of Greek Philosophy, or human knowledge, by the early Christians often superseded divine revelation from God to prophets and apostles. For example, Platonism's doctrine of *Logos*, applied to Christ being the *Word of God*, confused the Godhead of three persons who, during centuries of debate, became the basis for a three-in-one deity called the "Trinity" (MDoc, 449).

The Nicene Creed was first drafted in AD 325 and later modified and finally approved in the Council of Constantinople in AD 381. As presently used in the Roman Catholic Church it reads as follows:

> I believe in one God,
> the Father almighty,
> maker of heaven and earth, of all things visible and invisible.
>
> I believe in one Lord Jesus Christ, the Only Begotten Son of God, born of the Father before all ages. God from God, Light from Light, true God from true God, begotten, not made, consubstantial* with the Father; through him all things were made. For us men and for our salvation he came down from heaven, and by the Holy Spirit was incarnate of the Virgin Mary, and became man. For our sake he was crucified under

Pontius Pilate, he suffered death and was buried, and rose again on the third day in accordance with the Scriptures. He ascended into heaven and is seated at the right hand of the Father. He will come again in glory to judge the living and the dead and his kingdom will have no end.

I believe in the Holy Spirit, the Lord, the giver of life, who proceeds from the Father and the Son, who with the Father and the Son is adored and glorified, who has spoken through the prophets.

I believe in one, holy, catholic and apostolic Church. I confess one Baptism for the forgiveness of sins and I look forward to the resurrection of the dead and the life of the world to come. Amen.[193]

*"*Consubstantial*" is often translated as "one in being" or "of one substance"

Much of the Nicene Creed is true, including the belief in God the Father, the Son, and the Holy Spirit, that Jesus Christ is the "Only Begotten Son of God, born of the Father before all ages [Christ's pre-mortal life]," and of course the resurrection of Christ. However, there are a few problems in this creed which should be reviewed:

1. Christian theologians and historians have established that the Nicaean Council of AD 325 "incorporated the non-scriptural [Greek] word homoousios ('of one substance') into a creed." Professor John Burnaby of Trinity College, Cambridge admits, "the Nicene Creed inserts seven phrases, which set forth not what the Primitive Church believed about the 'Jesus of History,' the man who lived and died and rose again, but what was later declared to be implied, by beliefs about Jesus, in regard to the eternal being of God. Only the last of these phrases, 'through whom all things were made' has clear authority in the New Testament" (Burnaby, 70).

   "Consubstantial with the Father" is the critical phrase in the Nicene Creed that changes the Biblical concept of the Godhead and removes their individual persons and characters, their separate beings, and the separate bodily existence of the three members of the Godhead, the Father, the Son, and the Holy Spirit. This created an impossible being which is neither human nor a glorified man as Christ defined Himself after His resurrection (HBKJV, Luke 24:39; D&C 130:22–23; EofM 2:552–553).

When the Nicene Creed, joined the Father and Son as one being, and later, theologians included the Holy Spirit with the Father and Son as "consubstantial" or "of one substance" or one-in-three and three-in-one, this clouded the world's and the Church's understanding of the true nature of God the Father and the Son of God. A God, with a body of flesh and bones as the resurrected Christ has, could not be "immaterial" or "of one-substance" with the Father (HBKJV, Luke 24:39). Absent are the attributes of God the Father in the canonized Bibles as the "Man of Holiness" given in modern scripture, while Jesus Christ is referred to as the "Son of Man" (PofGP, Moses 6:57; 7:35; HBKJV, Daniel 7:13; Matthew 24:30; Mark 8:31; 9:31; 10:33; Revelations 1:13; D&C 130:22; EofM 2:546–553).[194]

2. In the long second paragraph of the creed the phrase "*by the Holy Spirit was incarnate* of the Virgin Mary" expresses a fundamental misunderstanding about the Godhead when we consider that Jesus Christ was the Only Begotten Son of our Heavenly Father. Jesus was not incarnated or sired by the Holy Spirit, and that Mary was actually the mother of Jesus in a natural and biological way, discretely described in the apostle Luke's gospel. It appears that the authors of the Nicene Creed were trying to follow Matthew 1:18 but did not understand that verse. It is much clearer from Luke's gospel, "The Holy Ghost shall come upon thee [the Virgin Mary] and the power of the Highest [the Father] shall overshadowed thee" (HBJKV, John 10:17–18; Luke 1:26–27, 30–32, 35; BofM, 1 Nephi 11:16–21; Alma 7:10).

   The Holy Spirit cannot be the father of Jesus Christ because *a Spirit* being such as the Holy Ghost or the Holy Spirit cannot procreate flesh and bones. God the Father, who has a body of flesh and bones is He who begat Jesus Christ. The role of the Holy Spirit is to teach, confirm, sanctify, and heal (EofM 2:649–652). The Holy Spirit's role was misconstrued in the Nicene Creed with the Father's bodily role, due to the adopted Trinity doctrine, thus Mary's conception of Jesus was so mysteriously phrased. Members of the Medieval Church would eventually or by the sixth century accept the Nicene Creed with its Trinity doctrine of three beings in one.

President Brigham Young, who succeeded Joseph Smith as President of The Church of Jesus Christ of Latter-day Saints in 1847, clarified the conception and birth of Jesus Christ with this statement in 1861 by saying, "The birth of the Savior was as natural as the births of our children . . . [Jesus Christ] was begotten of his Father, as we were of our fathers." Elder Bruce R. McConkie of the Twelve Apostles expressed the same teaching in his 1966 second edition of *Mormon Doctrine* by saying, "Christ was begotten by an Immortal Father in the same way that mortal men are begotten by mortal fathers" (JD 8:115; MDoc, 546–547).

3. From the third paragraph of the Nicene Creed, "Holy Spirit, the Lord, the giver of life" implies the Holy Spirit or Holy Ghost is the giver of life, which is not accurate. God the Father is the giver of life, and He is both the father of our spirits, and the father of our mortal bodies through Adam. The Son, or Jesus Christ, is the creator of this earth and the author and finisher of our salvation and our eternal lives. Our Heavenly Mother is fully involved in the procreation of spirit children in heaven, or the giving of life, just as Eve was in the flesh with Adam on earth. The Holy Spirit can renew our lives with peace, joy, knowledge, healing, hope, and revelation and other gifts of the Spirit, but the Holy Spirit is not our Heavenly Father, nor is the Holy Ghost the Father of Jesus Christ. The Holy Spirit may dwell in us when we are worthy, but will withdraw from us when we are unworthy (HBJKV,

Luke 3:38; 1 Corinthians 3:17-20; 12–14; Ephesians 3:16–29; D&C 130:22–23; EofM 2:649–651).

4. From the last paragraph of this creed, the concept of "apostolic church" or an implied succession from the original apostles is made, yet history cannot attest to the first Apostles ever giving one bishop or the "Bishop of Rome" superintendency or primacy over all other bishops. No bishop can hold those keys for the whole church unless one of the apostles gives him such keys and authority, which history is vacant of any memory. Once all the early apostles were each martyred without ordination of replacements to that specific office of "apostle" including all keys and authority, then those keys given to Peter by Jesus were lost, and the Early Church no longer held these apostolic powers in the church (HBKJV, Matthew 16:19).

   Joseph Smith learned during his First Vision in 1820 that none of the churches then existing were acceptable to God (PofGP, JS-H 1:19). In other words, the church that Jesus Christ recognizes today as his own must bear his name and its leaders must be true apostles who are able to trace their authority directly to Jesus Christ or through His original apostles (HBJKV, John 15:16; Ephesians 2:20–21; 4:11–14; Hebrews 3:1; 5:4; D&C 27:12; 115:4).

The Prophet Joseph Smith learned by revelation that God our Father is not alone in heaven and exists as a glorified male human being with a body of flesh and bones with his eternal and glorified female human being Companion, His wife, who has a separate body of flesh and bones, after whose express image and being man and woman were created, "Let us make man in our image after our likeness . . . male and female," God told Moses (HBKJV, Genesis 1:26–27; EofM 2:961).

From a recent story in *LDS Living* magazine online, we read a wonderful story that makes this truth about the Godhead and our Mother in Heaven, as taught by the Prophet Joseph Smith, very relevant:

> The prophet Joseph Smith spoke about our Heavenly Mother to the third Relief Society president of the Church, Zina

> D. Young. After losing her mother to "the most trying of circumstances," Zina was speaking to the prophet about her intense grief and asked the question: "Will I know my mother as my mother when I get over to the Other Side?
>
> To which Joseph Smith responded:
>
> Certainly you will. More than that, you will meet and become acquainted with your eternal Mother, the wife of your Father in Heaven (EofM 2:961).[195]

These concepts that mortal men and women living on the earth since the days of Adam and Eve are the children of God and are of the same kind and family as our Heavenly Father and that we have an eternal Mother in Heaven too, are two of the most glorious doctrines of the restored Church of Jesus Christ. These principles of divine truth, which Joseph Smith clearly taught during his lifetime, connect us individually and as families to God. They inspire us to trace our earthly family, parents, and grandparents back to our first parents and to our Heavenly Father and Mother as few other doctrines can (HBKJV, Genesis 1:26–27; Romans 8:16–17).

The word "Trinity" appears in the ante-Nicene father Origen's *De Principiis* or *First Principles* about AD 230 (ANF 4:270). It first appeared officially for the Medieval Church in the Pseudo-Athanasian Creed which was written likely by bishops and theologians in fifth-century France two centuries after Athanasius's death.

This creed was accepted by most Christians of the Medieval Church by the sixth century. The purpose of the Athanasian Creed was to establish the Trinity doctrine and separate it from earlier Arianism or the original teaching that God the Father was a separate being from God the Son or Jesus Christ in both person and body.

Thus, we see how the knowledge of God and the nature of the Godhead understood by ancient prophets was lost to this new amalgamated "Trinity" interpretation to match the thought of the Greek and Roman world. Arius, the priest of Alexandria, valiantly defended his scriptural understanding of the Godhead at the Council of Nicaea, but in the end a single Greek word *homoousios* ("of one substance") won the day and the Christian Councils of 325 and 381 ruled against him and his belief. Arius and his two companions in faith, Theonas and Secundus, were exiled to Illyricum, northeast of the Adriatic Sea in the outer part of the empire, while three other supporters, Theognis of Nicaea, Eusebius of Nicomedia, and Maris of Chalcedon, placed their signatures in deference to the emperor.[196]

The Lord told Joseph Smith in the sacred grove about the creeds of the nineteenth-century churches, saying, "all their creeds were an abomination in his sight" (PofG, JS-H 1:19). The Nicene Creed of AD 325 provides strong evidence that after the original apostles were gone, the Medieval Church could "not endure sound doctrine" nor "come to the knowledge of the truth" regarding the Godhead, and other original teachings of the Early Church of Jesus Christ.

Appendix 2

The Rise of the Medieval Church

The rise of the Medieval Church in secular and religious history is essential knowledge to a fuller understanding of the Prophet Joseph Smith's First Vision. Learning what we can about those first few centuries before the fall of the Roman Empire, the state-churches of the Middle Ages, and the Reformation Era that followed, will tell a very important story. The Church that Christ and His Apostles set up would disappear. This period of time from the end of the Early Church to the Restoration of the gospel beginning in 1820 with Joseph's First Vision is called The Great Apostasy. The Medieval Church was a key part of that evolutionary period.

The fact that there was a Medieval Church that had evolved from the corrupting of the Early Church is the reason why the Father and the Son visited Joseph Smith in the first place. Had the original or Early Church of Christ survived organizationally and doctrinally beyond the first century AD to the present, there would have been no reason for the Savior to come to tell the young Joseph Smith to join none of the churches that existed in 1820, and that none of them were acceptable to Jesus Christ as His Church (PofGP, JS-H 1:19--26; JSP, H1:13).

Prior to the destruction of the Jews at Palestine by the Roman Legions of Titus in AD 70, the Early Church of Christ in Jerusalem, being warned by the Savior before His crucifixion and by revelation to the remaining apostles before the war, these saints then fled to the Greek city of Pella in what is now Jordan (HBKJV, Matthew 24:16; Eusebius, Church History, Book 3, 5:3).

Converts or saints of the Early Church increased in number and expanded into Asia Minor, Greece, Italy, and Northern Africa in the wake of prophetic guidance and successful preaching of the gospel of Jesus Christ by the apostles Peter, Paul, and Barnabas, Mark, and

Thomas. Paul's companion Timothy was the first bishop of Ephesus. Mark, a companion to both Paul and Peter, established the church and became the first bishop of Alexandria, succeeded by Annianus in AD 62 in the eighth year of the Roman Emperor Nero (Eusebius, Church History, Book 2, 24:1).

Their fruits, these early apostolic converts, became the Church of the Gentiles. After more than two centuries of Roman persecutions and many martyrdoms, these "Christians," as the Romans and Greeks called them, became the state church of the Roman Empire under Constantine the Great following the Edict of Milan in AD 313 and the Council of Nicaea in AD 325. These two bodies of Roman and Christian Law changed the Christians' legal status and both Pagans and Christians were unitedly protected as citizens. Unfortunately, for the Christians, their doctrine was also mixed or influenced and redefined with the prevailing philosophies of that day. While Greek Philosophy had a deep impact on the Early Church, the Pagan festivals and sacrifices were ultimately outlawed.

In the Roman Empire the teachings of the Greek Philosophers Plato and Aristotle were introduced to explain Christian doctrines of Deity and exegesis, or the meaning of the scriptures (Barker, 229–235). After the apostles' martyrdoms, what was once a pure Christian religion administered by the holy apostles of Jesus Christ, became doctrinally corrupted by Greek philosophies, then secularized as the state-sanctioned church subject to imperial decrees and compromises. The Apostle Paul had prophesied that "the time will come when they [the saints] will not endure sound doctrine" and would "be turned unto fables," a prophecy which was fulfilled between the first and fourth centuries (HBKJV, 2 Timothy 4:3–4).

As early as the second century, the Christians began to naturally assimilate with the Pagan citizens in the Roman Empire. Tertullian wrote of the Gnostic heresy led by the highly educated Marcion and Valentinus, who waged religious havoc as the Early Church transitioned to the unofficially named Medieval Church. The dualistic sub-deities, reincarnation, carnality, and temple worship imitations of Gnosticism drew many of the early saints from the original teachings of Jesus Christ into this corrupted apostate religion (ANF 3:7, 197–198, 246–520).[197] The bishops of the second- and third-century, pre-Medieval Church recognized many of the Gnostic heresies and condemned them, yet were not able to recognize their own false doctrines that had crept into the state church of the Roman Empire by the early fourth century. These included the unscriptural doctrines of the Trinity which have been addressed.

Beginning early in the Medieval Church of the Gentiles in its largest body called the Roman Catholic Church, the bishop of Rome assumed superintendency over the other churches and bishops. The bishops of Rome claimed authority as Peter's apostolic representative, even though they were bishops, not apostles. Eventually this dominant bishop was given the non-scriptural title of "Pope" who assumed the keys and authorities once held by the Apostle Peter who led the Early Church. The other bishops of the Medieval Church resisted, but over time they eventually bowed.

There is no doubt that Jesus Christ gave the keys of His kingdom to Peter (HBKJV, Matthew 16:19), but there is no evidence in the New Testament or other writings of the ante-Nicene Fathers that any bishops in the Early Church ever held equal authority with the apostles to govern other churches or the whole church. That is where the agreement between different sects tends to end as the Early Church transforms into the medieval period of history. The first three bishops of Rome according to Early Church history were, Linus, Anacletus, and Clement, not Peter.

Professor A. Burt Horsley of Brigham Young University explained this difficult part of Early Church history by quoting church father Irenaeus and then commenting:

> Irenaeus writes, "The blessed apostles, then, having founded and built up the church, committed into the hands of Linus the office of episcopate" (ANF, 1:415) . . . traditionally, in the first lists of the bishops of Rome which we have available (the first one being from Irenaeus), Peter was not listed as the first bishop of Rome, but as the consecrator of the first bishop of Rome who was Linus. In the first list of Irenaeus, with reference to the early pontiffs of Rome, Peter was left out of the lineup. In subsequent references, he began to be included as the first bishop, preceding Linus, Anacletus and Clement

> and Evaristus, etc. It is significant to note, for example, that Eusebius [the fourth-century church historian] says, "Linus was the first to obtain the episcopate [bishopric] of the Church at Rome." (ANF, 1:416)[198]

Because the church in the second and third centuries could not continue an apostolic presence or special witness of the resurrected Lord, nor retain the keys of authority, church fathers who followed after the martyred apostles claimed that the full gospel would be preserved by the "bishops as their successors." Those bishops who were appointed, would continue the "apostolic preaching," which in the words of Irenaeus, "was to be preserved in a continuous line of succession until the end of time."[199]

The problem with this explanation from the church fathers, as Professor Horsley pointed out, is that the first bishops of Rome or any of the bishops in Christendom did not hold apostolic keys and could not function as apostles with authority to govern the entire church and provide the special witness of the resurrected Savior. Preaching from the scriptures and having authority from God are two very different things. Convincingly, the oldest records do not list Peter as the first bishop of Rome. The calling of a true bishop is localized and related to the saints and population who live within a limited geographic area.

The Holy Ghost could bear witness to any righteous man of the love of God and the truths of the scriptures, which are both great blessings. *Yet such witnesses alone do not give the keys and the authority of Jesus Christ to bishops to teach the fullness of the gospel, to conduct the affairs of the Church, and to appoint and ordain other bishops independently.* As Paul so eloquently proclaimed to the Corinthian saints, "For ye may all prophecy one by one, that all may learn, and all may be comforted. And the spirits of the prophets are subject to the prophets. For God is not the author of confusion, but of peace, as in all churches of the saints" (HBKJV, Amos 3:7; 1 Corinthians 12:28; 14:31–33; Ephesians 2:19–21; MDoc, 140, 603–609).

The Early Church's inability to replace the martyred apostles caused a foundational loss of these essential offices and authorities. Their eventual replacement with popes and cardinals centuries later introduced new offices nowhere found in the scriptures. The Bishop of Rome assumed primacy over the other bishops, which was contrary to the original organization of Christ's Early Church where that right belonged solely to the apostles. Bishops held equal authority to each other, they presided only over their local bishopric or episcopate, and they served under the direction of the Apostles and Seventies who were first called and ordained by the voice and hands of the Lord Himself (HBKJV, John 15:16; Luke 10:1).

The Roman Empire collapsed in AD 476 and was overlapped by the Byzantine Empire or Eastern Roman Empire which endured until the middle of the fifteenth century. To the north in Europe a new empire arose which became known as the Holy Roman Empire, which historians have said was neither holy nor Roman, with its first Frankish high king or emperor being Charles I or Charlemagne who was crowned in AD 800. The Medieval Church existed in all three empires.

The Medieval Church by Charlemagne's reign had spread into Europe and the former state-church arrangement between the emperors, kings, and popes remained intact. The teachings of the Early Church of the apostles and their disciples had been changed with edicts, competing bishops and emperors, as well as from councils and creeds, until they were unrecognizable. This was true regarding the Godhead, loss of apostolic authority and the clergy, marriage, and the form of baptism, when compared with Early Church teachings described in the New Testament and in latter-day scripture (HBKJV, Genesis 1:26–28; Daniel 7:13–14; Matthew 10:1–4; 19:14; Luke 10:1–12; Acts 8:38–39; Ephesians 2:19–22; 4:11–14; 1 Timothy 4:1–4; Hebrews 3:1; 5:4; 7:17; James 5:14–16; PofGP, Moses 1:31–33; 8:23–24; Abraham 3:27; BofM, Mosiah 18:14; Moroni 8:9–12; D&C 130:22; 131:1–4; 132:7–19).[200]

Within this new empire, the Medieval Church eventually existed under its new name, the Roman Catholic Church. The word "catholic" means "universal" and is appropriate for the name of the largest and most powerful of all churches since the birth of the Savior. The Medieval Church would divide as a result of the Great Schism of AD 1054, a division over Papal authority and revisions made to the Nicene Creed in AD 381. This created two large denominations of Christianity, the Roman Catholic Church, and the Eastern Orthodox or Orthodox Catholic Church, the latter having about one-fifth the members of the Roman Catholic Church today.

The first church father to mention the word "catholic church" was Ignatius, the bishop of Antioch, in his "Letter to the Smyrnaeans" about AD 107–110. The next reference is in the text of the Nicene Creed, "one, holy, catholic, and apostolic church" which was approved at the Council of Constantinople in AD 381. Both of these uses of the word "catholic" were in the lower-case form and would refer back to the Early Church formed by the Apostles during the first century AD, not to any sect or church using that title as a capitalized name which overtook or branched off from that original Church of Christ and held different doctrines and ordinances.

The first historical use of "Roman Catholic" as a synonym for "Catholic Church" was made in a communication with the Armenian Apostolic Church in 1208. It was not until the Anglican Church was formed in 1534, by Henry the VIII's Act of Supremacy, did the name "Romish [later Roman] Catholic Church" gain usage in the English language.

The Eastern Roman Empire also called the Byzantine Empire possessed territories located in Italy, Greece, the Balkans, Levant, Asia Minor, and North Africa and enjoyed a glorious and worldly existence from 303 until 1453, when the Saracen or Ottoman army stormed Byzantium, first called Constantinople and later Istanbul. The Ottoman leader Mehmed triumphantly entered the Christian Church of Hagia Sophia, which was soon converted into the city's leading mosque.

By AD 380, Christianity had become the state religion of the Roman Empire, and by the fifth century, other religious practices were proscribed. Pagan festivals and sacrifices were banned, as was access to all pagan temples and places of worship.[201] The last Olympic Games were held in 393 at Olympia. As Hellenism declined in Rome, Greek ideas endured in Byzantium via Christians and Muslims.

Pope Gregory of Rome had sent Augustinian of Canterbury in 596 to proselytize the Anglo-Saxon Druids in Britain and the Scot and Irish Celts to Catholicism.[202] The British St. Patrick (386–461) had paved their way in the fifth century as a missionary and as the first bishop in Ireland.

The Lord prophesied in the Book of Isaiah and in the Book of Mormon that the Gentile kings and queens eventually would be "nursing fathers" and "nursing mothers" to the Jews as they gathered back to their lands of inheritance in the latter days. These kings would also support the colonization of America which would become a land of liberty where there would be no kings to rule the people, for Jesus Christ would be their king. However, this would not happen until after the Gentiles had corrupted the holy church of God and committed many crimes and evils (HBKJV, Isaiah 49:23; BofM, 2 Nephi 10:9–16; Mormon 8:23–38; PofGP, Articles of Faith 1:10).

Anciently, apostasy would take place among the House of Israel resulting in their national destruction by the Assyrians, Babylonians, and Romans. The tribes of Israel would in part be lost in the north countries and also mixed with the Gentile nations of ancient Eurasia. The saints of the Early Church of Jesus Christ would escape the slaughter of the Jewish War with the Romans led by Titus as Eusebius has told us, but the Early Church itself would not escape their own falling away or apostasy during the centuries that followed. Before America could be founded, the fullness of the gospel restored, and the Jews could be converted to the Son of Man, something prophetically big had to happen. The prophets Amos, Isaiah, and Paul each predicted by revelations that a *falling away* from the true covenants of the Lord and *a great apostasy* from the Early Church of Christ would take place. The apostasy comes first, then Jesus Christ restores His Church and prepares to come in glory to rule over His Millennial Kingdom on earth. (HBKJV, Isaiah 11:10–12; Amos 8:11–14; Isaiah 29:7–10; 2 Timothy 4:3–4; EofM 1:56–58).

The prophet Nephi during an apocalyptic vision recorded in the Book of Mormon predicted these things about 150 years after Amos and Isaiah prophesied, and about 600 years before Paul's missions and epistles to the Gentiles and the Jews. Nephi wrote:

> And the angel said unto me: Behold the formation of a church which is most abominable above all other churches, which slayeth the saints of God, yea, and tortureth them and bindeth them down, and yoketh them with a yoke of iron, and bringeth them down into captivity.

> And it came to pass that I beheld this great and abominable church; and I saw the devil that he was the founder of it.
>
> And I also saw gold, silver, and silks, and scarlets, and fine-twined linen, and all manner of precious clothing; and I saw many harlots. (1 Nephi 13:5–7)

What does this prophecy of Nephi about "a great and abominable church" mean? From the *Encyclopedia of Mormonism*, Professor Dennis A. Wright explains:

> When Nephi speaks typologically rather than historically, he identifies all the enemies of the Saints with the church of the devil (1 Nephi 14:9–10; 2 Nephi 10:16). They are those from all nations and all time periods who desire "to get gain, and; power over the flesh, and; to become popular in the eyes of the world; who seek the lusts of the flesh and the things of the world, and to do all manner of iniquity (1 Nephi 22:23). [EofM 1:568–569]

What is learned from these scriptures is that no single person, church, or organization can fulfill the prophecy entirely alone, as it applies to all those who fight against God and turn away from His commandments and from His laws. Nephi further explained this when he wrote: "He that fighteth against Zion, both Jew and Gentile, both bond and free, both male and female, shall perish; for they are they who are the whore of all the earth; for they who are not for me are against me, saith our God" (BofM, 2 Nephi 10:16; 22:23–25; 1 Nephi 14:10).

The Holy Roman Empire, existing from AD 800 to 1806 with its many crimes and corruptions, continued the earlier relationship with the state sanctioned Medieval Church, which itself went through a very dark period when many who would be called "saints" were persecuted, tortured, and put to death. The Eastern Orthodox Church to its credit does not have a history of conducting Inquisitions as does the Roman Catholic Church. The Inquisition or Inquisitions did not begin in the thirteenth century as many have thought, but this state-church system of punishing heretics by torture and death went back at least as far as the fourth century (MDoc, 382).[203]

The burning of eighty Waldensians in AD 1211 at Strasbourg is one of several Christian massacres conducted as religious repression. The Spanish Inquisition under Dominican Friar Tomás de Torquemada (AD 1420–1498), the first Grand Inquisitor, led to about 2,000 executions.

The burning at the stake of Joan of Arc in AD 1431 at Rouen is one of the most well-known stories of Christian martyrdom. The victim being a heroine and the liberator of France from England, and a visionary or prophetess, who 489 years after her martyrdom by the state-church, was made a Catholic Saint.

William Tyndale was a leading figure in the Protestant Reformation. As noted in Chapter 2, he produced an English Translation of the New Testament. This he did from original Greek texts. For that, Tyndale was arrested by imperial authorities, tried and condemned for heresy, and strangled and burned at the stake near Brussels in 1536, after being betrayed by his associate Henry Phillips hired by Bishop Stokesley.

The Peasants' Revolt in Germany of 1524–1525 saw large scale battles between the heavily church-taxed and land-poor peasants and the soldiers of the princes, resulting in thousands of lives lost on both sides. The peasants themselves lost 5,000 lives in a single battle at Frankenhausen on May 15, 1525. More than 100,000 lives were lost overall. These peasants were inflamed with religious fervor and devotion by the revolutionary teachings of the reformers Martin Luther and Thomas Müntzer, while Luther, being under the sponsor of the German princes, did not support their rebellion.[204]

History remembers that the massacre of thousands of Waldensians at Mérindol in 1545 France was a combined effort of the church and the state.

Frankish and British Kings were also responsible for noble and good deeds, such as their efforts to liberate the Holy Lands from the Saracens during the Crusades, though this effort was stained by the massacre of the Seljuk Turks at the Siege of Jerusalem in 1099. Ultimately, in numerous military battles that spanned nearly a millennia, these Holy Roman Emperors protected European Christendom and held off of the advancing Arab Muslim armies. The Spanish Moors had already occupied Spain and were first stopped in France at the Battle of Tours in 732. The centuries-long practice of slavery by Viking, Christian, and Saracen nations, the latter often abducting Euro-Slavs, is easily forgotten in the histories written long after Medieval and Byzantine Europe had passed away.[205]

The Protestant Reformation of 1517–1648 created many new churches, made significant changes to previous religious beliefs and practices and broke the single-church option of the Holy Roman Empire in Western Europe. In the centuries following the Protestant Reformation, the five main branches of Protestantism: Lutheranism; Calvinism; Anglicanism; Anabaptism; and Evangelicalism, have produced literally dozens of denominations often named after their national or individual founders. Today, Protestants number close to one billion.

The Catholic Reformation or Counter-Reformation of 1545–1648 ended the gruesome practice of burning people at the stake for heresy, made moderate changes in belief and practice with greater emphasis on training, institutional strengthening, doctrinal apologetics, and defending the Catholic Church against Protestantism as determined in the Council of Trent, 1545–1563. The Catholic Church now numbers about 1.3 billion members. Catholic Relief Services today helps millions of people worldwide in partnership with many nations. The Eastern Orthodox Church has essentially remained doctrinally the same since the eleventh century. Today, there are about 220 million Eastern Orthodox Church members worldwide, notably in Russia, Ethiopia, Ukraine, Romania, Poland, Greece, Serbia, and Bulgaria.[206]

Queen Elizabeth enacted a second Act of Supremacy in 1558 that separated England from the Roman Catholic Church and countered the power of the Pope, making Elizabeth Supreme Governor of the Church of England. The English Reformation, which began in that year, created both Catholic and Protestant martyrs. With the publication of the King James English Bible of 1611, the availability of the scriptures during the next two centuries inspired generations of Christians to seek religious truths and individual freedom. The Church of England became the mother church of the Anglican Church formed in 1867 which today numbers 110 million members.[207] The Anglican Church also followed the state-church pattern of governance.

The Holy Roman Empire endured for a thousand years until Francis II, the last of its European emperors of the Austrian House of the Hapsburgs, who lost several key battles to Napoleon of France, including the Battle of Austerlitz in 1806. The demise of the feudalistic Holy Roman Empire in Europe, the rise of colonial mercantilism which retained slavery, and the future development of Constitutional Republics with individual civil rights among western nations, gradually reduced the number of state-church nations and allowed religious freedom to exist and spread.

The Protestant Reformation would eventually slow the persecutions once received from the Catholic emperors, kings, and princes. However, in some cases, reactionary persecutions were heaped back upon the unsuspecting Catholics, Jews, and unbelievers by the Protestants. The German Peasant Revolt, the English Reformation, and anti-Catholic persecutions in the American Colonies are examples.

The European Protestant and English Reformations were instrumental in creating the Separatists from the Church of England and the Calvinist Puritans or Pilgrims of Europe and others who would first settle in the New England region of Colonial America. They came almost entirely for the purpose of religious freedom.

After the ratification of the US Constitution in 1789 with its Bill of Rights, residents and immigrants to America's thirteen united states would exercise full religious freedom for the first time by any people and nation since the Hebrew Nephites lost their religious liberty about fifteen hundred years earlier (BofM, Mosiah 29:32; Alma 30:7–9). The Prophet Joseph Smith applied this same freedom to ask from God the question of his prayer of faith—"Which of all the sects was right, and which should I join?" Joseph then received an unexpected answer, that he "must join none of them" (PofGP, JS-H 1:18–19). Equally important, Joseph was free and able to act upon what he received from God according to his conscience.

The empires and nations of Great Britain and Europe maintained a state-sponsored requirement in their civil governments, enforcing allegiance to one state and its associated church, for Protestants too, as done for centuries in the Roman Catholic and Orthodox Catholic nations. This state-church principle would continue in each Catholic, Protestant, and Anglican nation outside of the United States until the twentieth century. Ultimately, state-sponsored religion ended—in Britain in 1905, Germany in 1905, France in 1905, Spain in 1978, and Italy in 1984.[208]

In the United States, The Bill of Rights was ratified December 15, 1791 with its First Amendment granting freedom of religion including freedom from any state-run religion. Religious liberty is a treasure inspired by God (D&C 101:77, 80).

Ultimately, none of the Protestant, English, or Catholic Reformations removed the larger presence of unscriptural doctrines from the existing churches. Most notably, the Godhead concept of the Trinity remains a central belief in Catholic, Orthodox, Protestant, and Anglican as well as Evangelical churches, as found in the Nicene-Constantinopolitan Creed which was slowly adopted by the Medieval Church.[209]

This investigation of several of the ante-Nicene fathers including Ignatius, Irenaeus, and Origen, and the fourth-century church historian Eusebius, reveals that none of the branches of the Medieval Church received the original authority and doctrine of the Early Church, i.e., apostles and prophets who hold the keys of the Melchizedek Priesthood. (HBKJV, Matthew 16:19; 17:3; 28:19; John 15:16; Hebrews 7:17).

These apostolic offices and their keys of authority were lost from the Early Church during the early Roman persecutions and "falling away" period that the Apostle Paul had predicted, as *a precondition to the Restoration and Second Coming.* During the Medieval Church Period, the "falling away" continued as the state-run churches established themselves. Then followed the Reformation Period when many new sects arose, each claiming to be the true vine of Christ (HBKJV, 2 Timothy 4:3–4; 2 Thessalonians 2:1–3).

While the Protestant Reformation allowed Christians to read the scriptures, worship God in their own tongues, and inspired the Separatists and Puritans to establish a new colony of their faith in North America in 1620, there was little reconciliation of Protestant doctrine with the Early Church. The Trinity as noted earlier, original sin, infant baptism, and the denial of the need for miracles, apostles, and revelation remained.

The Reformation was a precursor to the Lord's greater plan of a complete *restoration* of the Church of Jesus Christ (D&C 1, 4). Through Joseph Smith's First Vision of Deity in 1820, and his later revelations, he learned that the existing churches were not acceptable to God. The young prophet was commanded by Jesus Christ "to go not after them; and he received a promise that the true doctrine or the fullness of the gospel should at some future time be made known to him" (JSP, H1:523).

Many doctrinal truths of great importance in the restored gospel have been set forth by President Joseph Fielding Smith Jr. (1876–1972), an Apostle and former President of The Church of Jesus Christ of Latter-day Saints. These doctrinal truths included the Great Apostasy of Christendom. Many of these teachings were compiled by the late Elder Bruce R. McConkie and published in three volumes from 1954–1956 entitled, *Doctrines of Salvation.* Elder McConkie, President Smith's son-in-law, was a member of the First Quorum of the Seventy and later called as one of the Twelve Apostles in the latter-day restored Church of Jesus Christ.[210]

It is established that the great apostasy of Christendom was revealed in the First Vision of the Prophet Joseph Smith. In the light of that revelation from Jesus Christ and the scriptures, President Joseph Fielding Smith described the heretical teachings of Christendom from the *falling away* of the Early Church until 1820, that still exist today:

HERESIES OF APOSTATE CHRISTENDOM

Christendom Wholly Apostate in 1820

When Joseph Smith went in the woods to pray, he received a revelation of knowledge, truth, and power, which has been of inestimable value and blessing to the world. What was revealed to him there was given for the overthrow of false creeds and traditions of the ages and led ultimately to the Restoration of the everlasting gospel as revealed by our Redeemer during His ministry.

For hundreds of years the world was wrapped in a veil of spiritual darkness, until there was not one fundamental truth belonging to the plan of salvation that was not, in the year 1820, so obscured by false tradition and ceremonies, borrowed from paganism, as to make it unrecognizable; or else it was entirely denied. By heavenly direction and command of our Lord Jesus Christ, Joseph Smith restored all these principles in their primitive beauty and power.

Doctrine of Apostasy Proved by the First Vision

Joseph Smith declared that in the year 1820 the Lord revealed to him that all the "Christian" churches were in error, teaching for the commandments the doctrines of men. The religious teacher taught that they were in the way of light and truth, notwithstanding their many conflicting creeds.

Amos said, speaking of the latter days: "Behold, the days come, saith the Lord God, that I will send a famine in the land, not a famine of bread, nor a thirst for water, but of hearing the words of the Lord" (HBKJV, Amos 8:11). Paul said, "For the time will come when they will not endure sound doctrine; but after their own lusts shall they heap to themselves teachers, having itching ears; And they shall turn away their ears from the truth and shall be turned unto fables" (HBKJV, 2 Timothy 4:3–4). "Let no man deceive you by any means: for that day [the Second Coming of Christ] shall not come, except there come a falling away first, and that man of sin be revealed, the son of perdition." Again, we find Joseph Smith in harmony with the Bible truth (HBKJV, 2 Thessalonians 2:3; DofS 3:282–283).

Apostate Doctrines Prevailing at Time of First Vision

What was the condition of the religious world, which professed to believe in and practice the doctrines of the Redeemer, when the Father and the Son appeared to Joseph Smith and instructed him? The answer is found in the words of the Lord which are similar to and a fulfilment of the prediction by Isaiah: "They draw near to me with their lips, but their hearts are far from me; they teach for doctrines the commandments of men, having a form of godliness, but they deny the power thereof" (PofGP, JS-H 1:19; HBKJV, Isaiah 29:13). Some of the leading teachings and practices were as follows:

1. That God the Father, the Son, and the Holy Ghost are not three personages, but one ethereal, immaterial God, unknown and unknowable to man, who fills the immensity of space.

2. That the cannon of scripture is full and complete, and since the passing of the apostles there was to be no more revelation, no opening of the heavens, and communications by angels, but the people were left to rely on what was written in the Bible or taught by their priests.
3. That baptism is to cleanse us from "original sin," and that all little children had to be "regenerated" by baptism and if not baptized they will perish [or not have salvation]. The scriptures plainly teach that every man is responsible for his own sins and not for the transgression of Adam and Eve (HBKJV, Jeremiah 31:30).
4. That baptism is an ordinance acceptable to the Lord by sprinkling or pouring water on the heads of unbaptized adults or infants.
5. That men may take upon themselves the authority to be ministers of the word of God, without a divine appointment by one duly authorized by Jesus Christ.
6. That the organization of the Church as established in the days of Jesus Christ and His apostles is no longer necessary; there were to be no more apostles, prophets, and gifts of the Spirit.
7. That man was not created in the image of God in form, for God is not an anthropomorphic being (DofS 3:284).

President Smith taught that it is a heretical belief that someone who has lived an honorable and virtuous life but has not heard of or professed belief in the Lord before death is "forever damned and without means of escape from the torments of hell," denying the mercies of God promised to all (HBKJV, Psalm 89:14; DofS 3:285).

President Smith identified other false religious teachings such as predestination and higher criticism. He also pointed out false philosophies such as evolution, and the radicalized views of those calling themselves progressives (DofS 3:286–291).

Appendix 3

Who Can See God?

Since the Enlightenment Era began, truth seekers have received little encouragement to seek a vision or revelation from God. Honest investigators of the Prophet Joseph Smith will not deny the possibility that Joseph or that a man of righteousness and faith could eventually see and talk to God as Abraham, Moses, and other prophets have experienced (HBKJV, Exodus 33:11; Daniel 10; Acts 7:55–56), that Joseph Smith was telling the truth about his vision, and that there was ample historical evidence of the circumstances that led to Joseph's First Vision. They will also consider the concept of one true church with one Lord, one faith, and one baptism, as the Apostle Paul taught. They will ask God if Joseph Smith organized "the only true and living church upon the face of the whole earth" as Jesus Christ declared to the Prophet by the Holy Spirit during a special conference of elders of the Church on November 1, 1831 (HBKJV, Ephesians 4:5; D&C 1:30).

Who shows Himself and speaks to the prophets when God has a message to convey? President Joseph Fielding Smith said that the Son of God or "Jehovah Gives All Revelation." We have already noted, that until 1820 when the Father and Son appeared to Joseph Smith, that God the Father had not conversed with a man or woman since Adam and Eve spoke with God in the Garden of Eden. The Father only appears or speaks to introduce the Son, who is Jehovah the God of the Old Testament and Jesus Christ of the New Testament who are the same God (HBKJV, Exodus 6:3; Matthew 3:17; BofM, 2 Nephi 31:15; DofS 1:27).

The prophet Moroni wrote, ". . . have angels ceased to appear unto the children of men? Or has he withheld the power of the Holy Ghost from them? Or will he, so long as time shall last, or the earth shall stand, or there shall be one man upon the face thereof to be saved?" (BofM, Moroni 7:36). Of course, Joseph would say, "No."

"DO ALL PROPHETS AND APOSTLES SEE GOD?"

Many probably have wondered about this question. In an excellent blog published in April 2022 by biological engineer and Church history researcher Chad Nielsen, we find the answers from the prophets and apostles themselves. They tell us that they do not have to see God to fulfill their mission on earth. Many have seen the Lord, yet many prophets and apostles have received revelation from the Holy Spirit, through dreams, and other gifts of the Spirit. We can be sure of one thing, that those who are called as prophets, seers, and revelators receive divine revelation regularly and are careful to say and do what the Lord directs. The Prophet Joseph Smith was no different. It was his desire to bring as many souls with him into the presence of God as he could. This has been the mission of every prophet of God, both anciently and in modern times.

Speaking of Abraham, Joseph Smith said:

> This is why Abraham blessed his posterity: He wanted to bring them into the presence of God. They looked for a city, &c. Moses sought to bring the children of Israel into the presence of God, through the power of the Priesthood, but he could not. In the first ages of the world they tried to establish the same thing—& there were Elias's raised up who tried to restore these very glories but did not obtain them. But (Enoch did for himself & those that were with Him, but not for the world) they prophesied of a day when this Glory would be revealed.—Paul spoke of the Dispensation of the fullness of times, when God would gather together all things in one &c &.[211]

Between 1829 and 1842, during the latter-day Restoration of the Church of Jesus Christ, prophets and apostles, seventies, bishops, elders, priests, teachers, and deacons were called. As in the Early Church organized by Jesus Christ, the modern church was built upon the foundation of apostles and prophets with Jesus Christ as its cornerstone, as Paul wrote to the Ephesian saints (HBKJV, John 15:16; Ephesians 2:20). By revelation in June of 1829 the Lord had asked the Three Witnesses to the Book of Mormon, Oliver Cowdery, David Whitmer, and Martin Harris, to select from the Church the first twelve men to be ordained as apostles. Joseph Smith and Oliver Cowdery already held that divine authority as "apostles" from their ordination by the resurrected angels Peter, James, and John in that same month of June 1829 (D&C 18:37; JSP-H 4:242–243).

The twelve men were finally called to be the first latter-day apostles during a Church conference on February 14, 1835. Their names were: Lyman Johnson, age 23; Brigham Young, 33; Heber C. Kimball, 33; Orson Hyde, 30; David W. Patten, 35; Luke Johnson, 27; William E. McLellin, 29; John F. Boynton, 23; Orson Pratt, 23; William Smith, 23; Thomas B. Marsh, 34; and Parley P. Pratt, 27. All had previously served missions. Eight had accompanied Joseph Smith on the Zion's Camp expedition the previous summer (DHC 2:186–189).

In the same Church meeting of February 14, 1835, Oliver Cowdery gave the twelve men, minus Orson Pratt who was out of town, this apostolic charge:

> You have been indebted to other men in the first instance for evidence [of the truth of God's existence, and] on that you have acted. *But it is necessary that you receive a testimony from Heaven for yourselves, so that you can bear testimony to the truth of the Book of Mormon. And that you have seen the face of God; that is more than the testimony of an Angel. When the proper time arrives you shall be able to bear this testimony to the world. When you bear testimony that you have seen God.* This testimony God will never suffer to fall, but will bear you out. Although many will not give heed, yet others will. You will, therefore see the necessity of getting this testimony from heaven. Never cease striving until you have seen God, face to face. Strengthen your faith, cast off your doubts, your sins and all your unbelief and nothing can prevent you from coming to God. Your ordination is not full and complete till God has laid his hand upon you. We require as much to qualify us as did those who have gone before us. God is the same. If the

> Savior in former days laid his hands upon his disciples, why not in the latter Days (DHC 2:194–198, emphasis added).[212]

These apostles had already experienced many revelations and miracles. Between 1831 and 1836 the Savior appeared four times to small groups of the Saints during meetings in Kirtland, Ohio. These divine interludes most notably took place at the School of the Prophets above the Whitney Store and dedication of the Kirtland Temple. This included some of those who would be called as apostles in 1835, when they were not away serving missions to the eastern and southern states.[213]

In the twentieth century, several living prophets or Presidents of the Church, have indicated that they have seen the Savior. Historical records show that President Wilford Woodruff, President Lorenzo Snow, and President Ezra Taft Benson have seen the resurrected Jesus Christ. Other latter-day prophets have acknowledged that they have not seen the Lord, but have heard His voice and have received revelation from the Holy Ghost. Generally, prophets and apostles do not speak of these things openly or in great detail, as they have been commanded not to.[212]

The prophets do not call God and angels down from heaven. As we learned earlier from President Joseph Fielding Smith, all revelation and heavenly manifestations are directed by God through the Lord Jesus Christ. President Gordon B. Hinckley explained the most common revelation given to the prophets and apostles in The Church of Jesus Christ of Latter-day Saints well when he said during two interviews in 1997:

> We have a great, basic reservoir of revelation. But if a problem arises, as it does occasionally, a vexatious thing with which we have to deal, we go to the Lord in prayer. We discuss it as a First Presidency and as a Council of the Twelve Apostles. *We pray about it and then comes the whisperings of a still small voice. And we know the direction we should take and we proceed accordingly* (emphasis added).[215]

We have a great body of revelation, the vast majority of which came from the prophet Joseph Smith. We don't need much revelation. We need to pay more attention to the revelation we've already received. Now, if a problem should arise on which we don't have an answer, we pray about it, we may fast about it, and it comes. Quietly. Usually no voice of any kind, but just a perception in the mind. I liken it to Elijah's experience. When he sought the Lord, there was a great wind, and the Lord was not in the wind. And there was an earthquake, and the Lord was not in the earthquake. And a fire, and the Lord was not in the fire. But in a still, small voice. Now that's the way it works (HBKIV, 1 Kings 19:11–12).[216]

All the prophets and apostles have testified that they have received divine revelation to guide them in their work. President Spencer W. Kimball summed up nicely the reality of revelation among the prophets and apostles in the Church:

> Expecting the spectacular, one may not be fully alerted to the constant flow of revealed communication. I say, in the deepest of humility, but also by the power and force of a burning testimony in my soul, that from the prophet of the Restoration to the prophet of our own year, the communication line is unbroken, the authority is continuous, and light, brilliant and penetrating, continues to shine. The sound of the voice of the Lord is a continuous melody and a thunderous appeal. For nearly a century and a half there has been no interruption. . . . Every faithful person may have the inspiration for his own limited kingdom. But the Lord definitely calls prophets today and reveals his secrets unto them as he did yesterday, he does today, and will do tomorrow: that is the way it is.[217]

No man can see the Son of God or Jehovah who does not hold the Melchizedek Priesthood, except at such times when that priesthood authority does not exist on the earth. In such a case, that person has been foreordained from before the foundations of the earth to see God and to fulfill a great mission of global importance. Such was the time in 1820 when the Father introduced the Son to the young boy Joseph Smith at Palmyra by saying, "This is My Beloved Son. Hear Him." It was the Son or Jehovah who is Jesus Christ who conversed with the Prophet Joseph Smith (D&C 84:19–26; PofGP, JS-H 1:17).[218]

Appendix 4

The Nature of God and Eternal Progression

The truths set forth by the First Vision would eventually unlock to the Prophet Joseph Smith Jr. the mysteries of the Godhead never before explained so clearly.

On April 7, 1844, during the Church's general conference in Nauvoo, Illinois and less than three months before his martyrdom, the Prophet Joseph gave a stirring sermon to more than ten thousand Saints about the nature of God and the Saints' future potential. This knowledge of Deity was the fulfilment of what Joseph Smith had begun to learn as a boy in Palmyra when he experienced his First Vision. This spiritually uplifting sermon lasted nearly two and a half hours. The major elements of the Prophet's sermon were recorded by four clerks, Willard Richards, Wilford Woodruff, Thomas Bullock, and William Clayton. Herein we gain greater knowledge of God, Jesus Christ and our divine relationship to them (TPJS, 342).

In this his greatest sermon, Joseph taught the Saints about eternal progression, explaining that "if men do not comprehend the character of God, they do not comprehend themselves" (TPJS, 343). Joseph taught that God "was once as we are now" and enlarged upon that by saying "all the spirits that God ever sent into the World" or His children were "susceptible of enlargement," and have the capacity to become like God in the eternities ahead (TPJS, 345, 354).

THE KING FOLLETT DISCOURSE[219]

Beloved Saints, I will call the attention of this congregation while I address you on the subject of the dead. The decease of our beloved brother, Elder King Follett, who was crushed in a well by the falling of a tub of rock, has more immediately led me to that subject. I have been requested to speak by his friends and relatives, but inasmuch as there are a great many in this congregation who live in this city as well as elsewhere, who have lost friends, I feel disposed to speak on the subject in general, and offer you my ideas, so far as I have ability, and so far as I shall be inspired by the Holy Spirit to dwell on this subject.

I want your prayers and faith that I may have the instruction of Almighty God and the gift of the Holy Ghost, so that I may set forth things that are true and which can be easily comprehended by you, and that the testimony may carry conviction to your hearts and minds of the truth of what I shall say. Pray that the Lord may strengthen my lungs, stay the winds, and let the prayers of the Saints to heaven appear, that they may enter into the ears of the Lord of Sabaoth, for the effectual prayers of the righteous avail much. There is strength here, and I verily believe that your prayers will be heard.

Before I enter fully into the investigation of the subject which is lying before me, I wish to pave the way and bring up the subject from the beginning, that you may understand it. I will make a few preliminaries, in order that you may understand the subject when I come to it. I do not intend to please your ears with superfluity of words or oratory, or with much learning; but I intend to edify you with the simple truths from heaven.

The Character of God

In the first place, I wish to go back to the beginning -- to the morn of creation. There is the starting point for us to look to, in order to understand and be fully acquainted with the mind, purposes and decrees of the Great Elohim, who sits in yonder heavens as he did at the creation of this world. It is necessary for us to have an understanding of God himself in the beginning. If we start right, it is easy to go right all the time; but if we start wrong, we may go wrong, and it be a hard matter to get right.

There are but a very few beings in the world who understand rightly the character of God. The great majority of mankind do not comprehend anything, either that which is past, or that which is to come, as it respects their relationship to God. They do not know, neither do they understand the nature of that relationship; and consequently they know but little above the brute beast, or more than to eat, drink and sleep. This is all man knows about God or his existence, unless it is given by the inspiration of the Almighty.

If a man learns nothing more than to eat, drink and sleep, and does not comprehend any of the designs of God, the beast comprehends the same things. It eats, drinks, sleeps, and knows nothing more about God; yet it knows as much as we, unless we are able to comprehend by the inspiration of Almighty God. **If men do not comprehend the character of God, they do not comprehend themselves.** I want to go back to the beginning, and so lift your minds into a more lofty sphere and a more exalted understanding than what the human mind generally aspires to.

What Kind of Being Is God?

I want to ask this congregation, every man, woman and child, to answer the question in their own heart, what kind of a being God is? Ask yourselves; turn your thought into your hearts, and say if any of you have seen, heard, or communed with him. This is a question that may occupy your attention for a long time. I again repeat the question -- **What kind of a being is God? Does any man or woman know? Have any of you seen him, heard him, or communed with him? Here is the question that will, peradventure, from this time henceforth occupy your attention. The Scriptures inform us that "This is life eternal that they might know thee, the only true God, and Jesus Christ whom thou hast sent."**

If any man does not know God, and inquires what kind of a being he is, -- if he will search diligently his own heart -- if the declaration of Jesus and the apostles be true, he will realize that he has not eternal life; for there can be eternal life on no other principle.

My first object is to find out the character of the only wise and true God, and what kind of a being he is; and if I am so fortunate as to be the man to comprehend God, and explain or convey the principles to your hearts, so that the Spirit seals them upon you, then let every man and woman henceforth sit in silence, put their hands on their mouths, and never lift their hands or voices, or say anything against the man of God or the servants of God again. But if I fail to do it, it becomes my duty to renounce all further pretensions to revelations and inspirations, or to be a prophet; and I should be like the rest of the world -- a false teacher, be hailed as a friend, and no man would seek my life. But if all religious teachers were honest enough to renounce their pretensions to godliness when their ignorance of the knowledge of God is made manifest, they will all be as badly off as I am, at any rate; and you might as well take the lives of other false teachers as that of mine, if I am false. If any man is authorized to take away my life because he thinks and says I am a false teacher, then, upon the same principle, we should be justified in taking away the life of every false teacher, and where would be the end of blood? And who would not be the sufferer?

The Privilege of Religious Freedom

But meddle not with any man for his religion: and all governments ought to permit every man to enjoy his religion unmolested. No man is authorized to take away life in consequence of difference of religion, which all laws and governments ought to tolerate and protect, right or wrong. Every man has a natural, and, in our country, a constitutional right to be a false prophet, as well as a true prophet. If I show, verily, that I have the truth of God, and show that ninety-nine out of every hundred professing religious ministers are false teachers, having no authority, while they pretend to hold the keys of God's kingdom on earth, and was to kill them because they are false teachers, it would deluge the whole world with blood.

I will prove that the world is wrong, by showing what God is. I am going to enquire after God; for I want you all to know him, and to be familiar with him; and if I am bringing you to a knowledge of him, all persecutions against me ought to cease. You will then know that I am his servant; for I speak as one having authority.

God an Exalted Man

I will go back to the beginning before the world was, to show what kind of being God is. What sort of a being was God in the beginning? Open your ears and hear, all ye ends of the earth, for I am going to prove it to you by the Bible, and to tell you the designs of God in relation to the human race, and why He interferes with the affairs of man.

God himself was once as we are now, and is an exalted man, and sits enthroned in yonder heavens! That is the great secret. If the veil were rent today, and the great God who holds this world in its orbit, and who upholds all worlds and all things by his power, was to make himself visible, I say, if you were to see him today, you would see him like a man in form—like yourselves in all the person, image, and very form as a man; for Adam was created in the very fashion, image and likeness of God, and received instruction from, and walked, talked and conversed with him, as one man talks and communes with another.

In order to understand the subject of the dead, for consolation of those who mourn for the loss of their friends, it is necessary we should understand the character and being of God and how he came to be so; for I am going to tell you how God came to be God. We have imagined and supposed that God was God from all eternity. I will refute that idea, and take away the veil, so that you may see.

These are incomprehensible ideas to some, but they are simple. *It is the first principle of the Gospel to know for a certainty the Character of God, and to know that we may converse with him as one man converses with another, and that he was once a man like us; yea, that God himself, the Father of us all, dwelt on an earth, the same as Jesus Christ himself did; and I will show it from the Bible* [HBKJV, Luke 24:39; Rev. 1:6].

Power of the Father and the Son

I wish I was in a suitable place to tell it, and that I had the trump of an archangel, so that I could tell the story in such a manner that persecution would cease for ever. What did Jesus say? (Mark it, Elder Rigdon!) The Scriptures inform us that Jesus said, As the Father hath power in Himself, even so hath the Son power -- to do what? Why, what the Father did. The answer is obvious -- in a manner to lay down His body and take it up again. Jesus, what are you going to do? To lay down my life as my Father did, and take it up again. Do we believe it? If you do not believe it, you do not believe the Bible. The Scriptures say it, and I defy all the learning and wisdom and all the combined powers of earth and hell together to refute it.

Here, then, is eternal life -- to know the only wise and true God; and you have got to learn how to be Gods yourselves, and to be kings and priests to God, the same as all Gods have done before you, namely, by going from one small degree to another, and from a small capacity to a great one; from grace to grace, from exaltation to exaltation, until you attain to the resurrection of the dead, and are able to dwell in everlasting burnings, and to sit in glory, as do those who sit enthroned in everlasting power. And I want you to know that God, in the last days, while certain individuals are proclaiming his name, is not trifling with you or me.

The Righteous to Dwell in Everlasting Burnings

These are the first principles of consolation. How consoling to the mourners when they are called to part with a husband, wife, father, mother, child, or dear relative, to know that, although the earthly tabernacle is laid down and dissolved, they shall rise again to dwell in everlasting burnings in immortal glory, not to sorrow, suffer, or die any more; but they shall be heirs of God and joint heirs with Jesus Christ. What is it? To inherit the same power, the same glory and the same exaltation, until you arrive at the station of a God, and ascend the throne of eternal power, the same as those who have gone before. What did Jesus do? Why; I do the things I saw my Father do when worlds come rolling into existence. My Father worked out his kingdom with fear and trembling, and I must do the same; and when I get my kingdom, I shall present it to my Father, so that he may obtain kingdom upon kingdom, and it will exalt him in glory. He will then take a higher exaltation, and I will take his place, and thereby become exalted myself. So that Jesus treads in the tracks of his Father, and inherits what God did before; and God is thus glorified and exalted in the salvation and exaltation of all his children. It is plain beyond disputation, and you thus learn some of the first principles of the Gospel, about which so much hath been said.

When you climb up a ladder, you must begin at the bottom, and ascend step by step, until you arrive at the top; and so it is with the principles of the Gospel -- you must begin with the first, and go on until you learn all the principles of exaltation. But it will be a great while after you have passed through the veil before you will have learned them. It is not all to be comprehended in this world; it will be a great work to learn our salvation *and exaltation even beyond the grave.* I suppose I am not allowed to go into an investigation of anything that is not contained in the Bible. If I do, I think there are so many over-wise men here, that they would cry "treason" and put me to death. So I will go to the old Bible and turn commentator today.

Meaning of the Hebrew Scriptures

I shall comment on the very first Hebrew word in the Bible; I will make a comment on the very first sentence of the history of the creation in the Bible -- *Berosheit.* I want to analyze the word. *Baith* -- in, by through, and everything else. Rosh--the head. *Sheit* -- grammatical termination. When the inspired man wrote it, he did not put the baith there. An old Jew without any authority added the word; he thought it too bad to begin to talk about the head! It read first, "The head one of the Gods brought forth the Gods." That is the true meaning of the words. Baurau signifies to bring forth. If you do not believe it, you do not believe the learned man of God. Learned men can teach you no more than what I have told you. *Thus the head God brought forth the Gods in the grand council.*

I will transpose and simplify it in the English language. Oh, ye lawyers, ye doctors, and ye priests, who have persecuted me, I want to let you know that the Holy Ghost knows something as well as you do. The head God called together the Gods and sat in grand council to bring forth the world. The grand councilors sat at the head in yonder heavens and contemplated the creation of the worlds which were created at the time. When I say doctors and lawyers, I mean the doctors and lawyers of the Scriptures. I have done so hitherto without explanation, to let the lawyers flutter and everybody laugh at them. Some learned doctors might take a notion to say the Scriptures say thus and so; and we might believe the Scriptures; they are not to be altered. But I am going to show you an error in them.

I have an old edition of the New Testament in the Latin, Hebrew, German and Greek languages. I have been reading the German, and find it to be the most [nearly] correct translation, and to correspond nearest to the revelations which God has given to me for the last fourteen years. It tells about Jacobus, the son of Zebedee. It means Jacob. In the English New Testament it is translated James. Now, if Jacob had the keys, you might talk about James through all eternity and never get the keys. In the 21st of the fourth chapter of Matthew, my old German edition gives the word Jacob instead of James.

The doctors (I mean doctors of law, not physic) say, "If you preach anything not according to the Bible, we will cry treason." How can we escape the damnation of hell, except God be with us and reveal to us? Men bind us with chains. The Latin says Jacob and the German says Jacob; here we have the testimony of four against one. I thank God that I have got this old book; but I thank him more for the gift of the Holy Ghost. I have got the oldest book in the world; but I [also] have the oldest book in my heart, even the gift of the Holy Ghost. I have all the four Testaments. Come here, ye learned men, and read, if you can. I should not have introduced this testimony, were it not to back up the word rosh -- the head, the Father of the Gods. I should not have brought it up, only to show that I am right.

A Council of the Gods

In the beginning, the head of the Gods called a council of the Gods; and they came together and concocted a plan to create the world and people it. When we begin to learn this way, we begin to learn the only true God, and what kind of a being we have got to worship. Having a knowledge of God, we begin to know how to approach him, and how to ask so as to receive an answer. When we understand the character of God, and how to come to him, he begins to unfold the heavens to us, and to tell us all about it. When we are ready to come to him, he is ready to come to us.

Now, I ask all who hear me, why the learned men who are preaching salvation, say that God created the heavens and the earth out of nothing? The reason is, that they are unlearned in the things of God, and have not the gift of the Holy Ghost; they account it blasphemy in any one to contradict their idea. If you tell them that God made the world out of something, they will call you a fool. But I am learned, and know more than all the world put together. The Holy Ghost does, anyhow, and He is within me, and comprehends more than all the world: and I will associate myself with Him.

Meaning of the Word Create

You ask the learned doctors why they say the world was made out of nothing; and they will answer, "Doesn't the Bible say He *created* the world?" And they infer, from the word create, that it must have been made out of nothing. Now, the word create came from the baurau which does not mean to create out of nothing; it means to organize; the same as a man would organize materials and build a ship. Hence, we infer that God had materials to organize the world out of chaos -- chaotic matter, which is element, and in which dwells all the glory. Element had an existence from the time he had. The pure principles of element are principles which can never be destroyed; they may be organized and reorganized, but not destroyed. They had no beginning, and can have no end.

The Immortal Spirit

I have another subject to dwell upon, which is calculated to exalt man; but it is impossible for me to say much on this subject. I shall therefore just touch upon it, for time will not permit me to say all. It is associated with the subject of the resurrection of the dead, -- namely, the soul -- the mind of man -- the immortal spirit. Where did it come from? All learned men and doctors of divinity say that God created it in the beginning; but it is not so: the very idea lessens man in my estimation. I do not believe the doctrine; I know better. Hear it, all ye ends of the world; for God has told me so; and if you don't believe me, it will not make the truth without effect. I will make a man appear a fool before I get through; if he does not believe it. I am going to tell of things more noble.

We say that God himself is a self-existent being. Who told you so? It is correct enough; but how did it get into you heads? Who told you that man did not exist in like manner upon the same principles? Man does exist upon the same principles. God made a tabernacle and put a spirit into it, and it became a living soul. (Refers to the old Bible.) How does it read in the Hebrew? It does not say in the Hebrew that God created the spirit of man. It says "God made man out of the earth and put into him Adam's spirit, and so became a living body."

The mind or the intelligence which man possesses is co-equal with God himself. I know that my testimony is true; hence, when I talk to these mourners, what have they lost? Their relatives and friends are only separated from their bodies for a short season: their spirits which existed with God have left the tabernacle of clay only for a little moment, as it were; and they now exist in a place where they converse together the same as we do on the earth.

I am dwelling on the immortality of the spirit of man. Is it logical to say that the intelligence of spirits is immortal, and yet that it had a beginning? The intelligence of spirits had not beginning, neither will it have an end. That is good logic. That which has a beginning may have an end. There never was a time when there were not spirits; for they are co-equal [co-eternal] with our Father in heaven.

I want to reason more on the spirit of man; for I am dwelling on the body and spirit of man -- on the subject of the dead. I take my ring from my finger and liken it unto the mind of man -- the immortal part, because it has no beginning. Suppose you cut it in two; then it has a beginning and an end; but join it again, and it continues one eternal round. So with the spirit of man. As the Lord liveth, if it had a beginning, it will have an end. All the fools and learned and wise men from the beginning of creation, who say that the spirit of man had a beginning, prove that it must have an end; and if that doctrine is true, then the doctrine of annihilation would be true. But if I am right, I might with boldness proclaim from the house-tops that God never had the power to create the spirit of man at all. God himself could not create himself.

Intelligence is eternal and exists upon a self-existent principle. It is a spirit from age to age, and there is no creation about it. All the minds and spirits that God ever sent into the world are susceptible of enlargement.

The Power to Advance in Knowledge

The first principles of man are self-existent with God. God himself, finding he was in the midst of spirits and glory, because he was more intelligent, saw proper to institute laws whereby the rest could have a privilege to advance like himself. The relationship we have with God places us in a situation to advance in knowledge.

He has power to institute laws to instruct the weaker intelligences, that they may be exalted with himself, so that they might have one glory upon another, and all that knowledge, power, glory, and intelligence, which is requisite in order to save them in the world of spirits.

This is good doctrine. It tastes good. I can taste the principles of eternal life, and so can you. They are given to me by the revelations of Jesus Christ; and I know that when I tell you these words of eternal life as they are given to me, you taste them, and I know that you believe them. You say honey is sweet, and so do I. I can also taste the spirit of eternal life. I know it is good; and when I tell you of these things which were given my by inspiration of the Holy Spirit, you are bound to receive them as sweet, and rejoice more and more.

The Relation of Man to God

I want to talk more of the relation of man to God. I will open your eyes in relation to your dead. All things whatsoever God in his infinite wisdom has seen fit and proper to reveal to us, while we are dwelling in mortality, in regard to our mortal bodies, are revealed to us in the abstract, and independent of affinity of this mortal tabernacle, but are revealed to our spirits precisely as though we had no bodies at all; and those revelations which will save our spirits will save our bodies. God reveals them to us in view of no eternal dissolution of the body, or tabernacle. Hence the responsibility, the awful responsibility, that rests upon us in relation to our dead; for all the spirits who have not obeyed the Gospel in the flesh must either obey it in the spirit or be damned. Solemn thought! -- dreadful thought! Is there nothing to be done? -- no preparation -- no salvation for our fathers and friends who have died without having had the opportunity to obey the decrees of the Son of Man? Would to God that I had forty days and nights in which to tell you all! I would let you know that I am not a "fallen prophet."

Our Greatest Responsibility

What promises are made in relation to the subject of the salvation of the dead? and what kind of characters are those who can be saved, although their bodies are mouldering and decaying in the grave? When his commandments teach us, it is in view of eternity; for we are looked upon by God as though we were in eternity. God dwells in eternity, and does not view things as we do.

The greatest responsibility in this world that God has laid upon us is to seek after our dead. The Apostle says, "They without us cannot be made perfect;" (Hebrews 11:40) for it is necessary that the sealing power should be in our hands to seal our children and our dead for the fullness of the dispensation of times -- a dispensation to meet the promises made by Jesus Christ before the foundation of the world for the salvation of man.

Now, I will speak of them. I will meet Paul half way. I say to you, Paul, you cannot be perfect without us. It is necessary that those who are going before and those who come after us should have salvation in common with us; and thus hath God made it obligatory upon man. Hence, God said, "I will send you Elijah the prophet before the coming of the great and dreadful day of the Lord; and he shall turn the heart of the fathers to the children, and the heart of the children to their fathers, lest I come and smite the earth with a curse." (Malachi 4:5–6.)

A Salvation for Men

I have a declaration to make as to the provisions which God hath made to suit the conditions of man -- made from before the foundation of the world. What has Jesus said? **All sin, and all blasphemies, and every transgression, except one, that man can be guilty of, may be forgiven; and there is a salvation for all men, either in this world or the world to come, who have not committed the unpardonable sin, there being a provision either in this world or the world of spirits.** Hence God hath made a provision that every spirit in the eternal world can be ferreted out and saved unless he has committed that unpardonable sin which cannot be remitted to him either in this world or the world of spirits. God has wrought out a salvation for all men, unless they have committed a certain sin; and every man who has a friend in the eternal world can save him, unless he has committed the unpardonable sin. And so you can see how far you can be a savior.

The Unpardonable Sin

A man cannot commit the unpardonable sin after the dissolution of the body, and there is a way possible for escape. Knowledge saves a man; and in the world of spirits no man can be exalted but by knowledge. So long as a man will not give heed to the commandments, he must abide without salvation. If a man has knowledge, he can be saved; although, if he has been guilty of great sins, he will be punished for them. But when he consents to obey the Gospel, whether here or in the world of spirits, he is saved.

A man is his own tormenter and his own condemner. Hence the saying, They shall go into the lake that burns with fire and brimstone. The torment of disappointment in the mind of man is as exquisite as a lake burning with fire and brimstone. I say, so is the torment of man.

I know the Scriptures and understand them. I said, no man can commit the unpardonable sin after the dissolution of the body, nor in this life, until he receives the Holy Ghost but they must do it in this world. Hence the salvation of Jesus Christ was wrought out for all men, in order to triumph over the devil; for if it did not catch him in one place, it would in another; for he stood up as a Savior. All will suffer until they obey Christ himself.

The contention in heaven was -- Jesus said there would be certain souls that would not be saved; and the devil said he could save them all, and laid his plans before the grand council, who gave their vote in favor of Jesus Christ. So the devil rose up in rebellion against God, and was cast down, with all who put up their heads for him. (Book of Moses

-- Pearl of Great Price, Chap. 4:1–4; Book of Abraham, Chap. 3:23–28.)

The Forgiveness of Sins

All sins shall be forgiven, except the sin against the Holy Ghost; for Jesus will save all except the sons of perdition. What must a man do to commit the unpardonable sin? He must receive the Holy Ghost, have the heavens opened unto him, and know God, and then sin against Him. **After a man has sinned against the Holy Ghost, there is no repentance for him. He has got to say that the sun does not shine while he sees it; he has got to deny Jesus Christ when the heavens have been opened unto him, and to deny the plan of salvation with his eyes open to the truth of it; and from that time he begins to be an enemy.** This is the case with many apostates of the Church of Jesus Christ of Latter-day Saints.

When a man begins to be an enemy to this work, he hunts me, he seeks to kill me, and never ceases to thirst for my blood. He gets the spirit of the devil -- the same spirit that they had who crucified the Lord of Life -- the same spirit that sins against the Holy Ghost. You cannot save such persons; you cannot bring them to repentance; they make open war, like the devil, and awful is the consequence.

I advise all of you to be careful what you do, or you may by-and-by find out that you have been deceived. Stay yourselves; do not give way; don't make any hasty moves, you may be saved. If a spirit of bitterness is in you, don't be in haste. You may say, that man is a sinner. Well, if he repents, he shall be forgiven. Be cautious: await. When you find a spirit that wants bloodshed -- murder, the same is not of God, but is of the devil. Out of the abundance of the heart of man the mouth speaketh.

"In My Father's House"

The best men bring forth the best works. The man who tells you words of life is the man who can save you. I warn you against all evil characters who sin against the Holy Ghost; for there is no redemption for them in this world nor in the world to come.

I could go back and trace every subject of interest concerning the relationship of man to God, if I had time. I can enter into the mysteries; I can enter largely into the eternal worlds; for Jesus said, "In my Father's house are many mansions; if it were not so, I would have told you. I go to prepare a place for you" (John 14:2). Paul says, "There is one glory of the sun, and another glory of the moon, and another glory of the stars; for one star differeth from another star in glory. So also is the resurrection of the dead" (1 Cor. 15:41). What have we to console us in relation to the dead? We have reason to have the greatest hope and consolations for our dead of any people on the earth; for we have seen them walk worthily in our midst, and seen them sink asleep in the arms of Jesus; and **those who have died in the faith are now in the celestial kingdom of God.** And hence is the glory of the sun.

Righteous Mourners Rejoice

You mourners have occasion to rejoice, speaking of the death of Elder King Follett; for your husband and father is gone to wait until the resurrection of the dead--until the perfection of the remainder; for at the resurrection your friend will rise in perfect felicity and go to celestial glory, while many must wait myriads of years before they can receive the like blessings; and your expectations and hopes are far above what man can conceive; for why has God revealed it to us?

I am authorized to say, by the authority of the Holy Ghost, that you have no occasion to fear; for he is gone to the home of the just. Don't mourn, don't weep. I know it by the testimony of the Holy Ghost that is within me; and you may wait for your friends to come forth to meet you in the morn of the celestial world.

Rejoice, O Israel! Your friends who have been murdered for the truth's sake in the persecutions shall triumph gloriously in the celestial world, while their murderers shall welter for ages in torment, even until they shall have paid the uttermost farthing. I say this for the benefit of strangers.

I have a father, brothers, children, and friends who have gone to a world of spirits. They are only absent for a moment. They are in the spirit, and we shall soon meet again. The time will soon arrive when the trumpet shall sound. When we depart, we shall hail our mothers, fathers, friends, and all whom we love, who have fallen asleep in Jesus. There will be no fear of mobs, persecutions, or malicious lawsuits and arrests; but it will be an eternity of felicity.

Baptism

I will leave this subject here, and make a few remarks on the subject of baptism. The baptism of water, without the baptism of fire and the Holy Ghost attending it, is of no use; they are necessarily and inseparably connected. An individual must be born of water and the Spirit in order to get into the kingdom of God. In the German, the text bears me out the same as the revelations which I have given and taught for the last fourteen years on that subject. I have the testimony to put in their teeth. My testimony has been true all the time. You will find it in the declaration of John the Baptist. (Reads from the German.) John says, "I baptize you with water, but when Jesus comes, who has the power (or keys), he shall administer the baptism of fire and the Holy Ghost." Where is now all the sectarian world? And if this testimony is true, they are all damned as clearly as anathema can do it. I know the text is true. I call upon all you Germans who know that it is true to say, Aye. (Loud shouts of "Aye.")

Alexander Campbell, how are you going to save people with water alone? For John said his baptism was good for nothing without the baptism of Jesus Christ. "Therefore, not leaving the principles of the doctrine of Christ, let us go on unto perfection; not laying again the foundation of repentance from dead works, and of faith toward God, of the doctrine of baptisms, and of laying on of hands, and of resurrection of the dead, and of eternal judgment. And this will we do, if God permit." (Heb. 6:1-3).

There is one God, one Father, one Jesus, one hope of our calling, one baptism. * * * Many talk of baptism not being essential to salvation; but this kind of teaching would lay the foundation of their damnation. I have the truth, and am at the defiance of the world to contradict me, if they can.

I have now preached a little Latin, a little Hebrew, Greek, and German; and I have fulfilled all. I am not so big a fool as many have taken me to be. The Germans know that I read the German correctly.

A Call to Repentance

Hear it, all ye ends of the earth -- all ye priests, all ye sinners, and all men. Repent! repent! Obey the Gospel. Turn to God; for your religion won't save you, and you will be damned. I do not say how long. **There have been remarks made concerning all men being redeemed from hell; but I say that those who sin against the Holy Ghost cannot be forgiven in this world or in the world to come; they shall die the second death**. Those who commit the unpardonable sin are doomed to Gnolom -- to dwell in hell, worlds without end. As they concoct scenes of bloodshed in this world, so they shall rise to that resurrection which is as the lake of fire and brimstone. Some shall rise to the everlasting burnings of God; for God dwells in everlasting burnings, and some shall rise to the damnation of their own filthiness, which is as exquisite a torment as the lake of fire and brimstone.

I have intended my remarks for all, both rich and poor, bond and free, great and small. I have no enmity against any man. I love you all; but I hate some of your deeds. I am your best friend, and if persons miss their mark it is their own fault. If I reprove a man, and he hates me, he is a fool; for I love all men, especially these my brethren and sisters.

I rejoice in hearing the testimony of my aged friends. You don't know me; you never knew my heart. No man knows my history. I cannot tell it: I shall never undertake it. I don't blame any one for not believing my history. If I had not experienced what I have, I could not have believed it myself. I never did harm any man since I was born in the world. My voice is always for peace.

I cannot lie down until all my work is finished. I never think any evil, nor do anything to the harm of my fellowman. When I am called by the trump of the archangel and weighed in the balance, you will all know me then. I add no more. God bless you all. Amen.

(Bold emphasis added; TPJS, 342–362)

Notes

Notes to Acknowledgments

1. Paul R. Cheesman, "An Analysis of the Accounts Relating to Joseph Smith's Early Visions," Master's thesis, College of Religious Instruction, Brigham Young University, 1965, Appendix D.
2. Milton V. Backman, Jr., "Awakenings in the Burned-over District: New Light on the Historical Setting of the first Vision," *BYU Studies*, volume 9, number 3 (Spring, 1969): pp. 301-321; Anderson, Richard L. "Circumstantial Confirmation of the First Vision through Reminiscences," *BYU Studies Quarterly*. Provo: Brigham Young Univ., volume 9, number 3 (1969): pp. 376–81.
3. James B. Allen, "Eight Contemporary Accounts of Joseph Smith's First Vision What Do We Learn from Them," *Improvement Era*. April 1970, pp. 4-13; See also note 6 in this article for reference to Section 20 account of the First Vision; Dean C. Jessee, *The Papers of Joseph Smith*, Salt Lake City: Deseret Book, 2 vols.1989, 1992.
4. Michael Hubbard MacKay and Nicholas J. Frederick, *Joseph Smith's Seer Stones*. Salt Lake City: Brigham Young University and Deseret Book. 2016, 243 pp. Christopher Cannon Jones, *Journal of Book of Mormon Studies*, volume 26, Provo: BYU Press, (2017): p. 230.

Notes to Introduction

5. Richard Lyman Bushman, "A Joseph Smith for the Twenty-First Century," *Brigham Young University Studies*, volume 40, issue 3, article 5 (July 1, 2001): pp. 155–171.

Notes to Chapter 1

6. Steven C. Walker, "Seer," *Encyclopedia of Mormonism*, New York: Macmillan Publishing Company, 1992, 3:1292-1293; Richard E. Turley, Jr., "Seer Stones," *Encyclopedia of Mormonism*, 3:1293. Accessed July 15, 2020 at: https://contentdm.lib. byu.edu/digital/collection/EoM/id/4184.

7. Joseph Smith, Jr., author, Ronald K. Esplin and Larry E. Morris, editors, "PREFACE" to *Book of Mormon*, ca. August 1829, *Documents* series of *The Joseph Smith Papers*, Salt Lake City, Utah: The Church Historian's Press, 2013, volume 1, p. 93.

8. Richard E. Turley, Jr., "Joseph the Seer," *Ensign*, October, 2015, pp. 49–50.

9. Turley, "Joseph the Seer," p. 50.

10. Birdsall Richard D. "The Second Great Awakening and the New England Social Order." *Church History*, volume 39, 1970, pp. 345-364.

11. Paul E. Johnson, *A Shopkeeper's Millennium: Society and Revivals in Rochester,* New York, 1815–1837, New York: Hill & Wang, 1978, pp. 4–5, 136–141.

12. Grant Underwood, *The Millenarian World of Early Mormonism*, Urbana: The University of Illinois Press, 1993, pp. 20–23. Joseph Smith, Jr., et. al., *The Doctrine And Covenants* 21:2, 1989; *Doctrine And Covenants*, XLVI:1, 1835, JSP, R2:301–593; *Book of Commandments* XXII:2, 1833, JSP, R2:3–172; *The Joseph Smith Papers* on-line, http:// www.josephsmith papers.org.

Notes to Chapter 2

13. Quoted in Robert D. Hales, "Preparations for the Restoration and the Second Coming: "My Hand Shall Be over Thee," *Ensign*, November, 2005, pp. 88-92; Elder Hales quoted from S. Michael Wilcox, *Fire in the Bones: William Tyndale— Martyr, Father of the English Bible* (2004), p. 47. Matzko, John "The Encounter of the Young Joseph Smith with Presbyterianism." *Dialogue: A Journal of Mormon Thought.* (2007, Volume 40, Number 3), pp. 68–70. Matzko notes that "Lucy Mack Smith had been reared by a devout Congregationalist mother through a childhood that can truly be described as 'a series of losses.' Thus, not surprisingly, when Lucy reached Palmyra, she developed a connection with the Presbyterian church, even though she held aloof from membership."

14. William A. Morton, *From Plowboy To Prophet…*, SLC: Deseret Book Co., 1952, pp. 4-6; George A. Smith and Elias Smith, editors, *History of the Prophet Joseph By His Mother Lucy Smith,* SLC: Improvement Era, 1902, pp. 72-80; Scot Facer Proctor and Maurine Jensen Proctor,

editors. *The Revised and Enhanced History of Joseph Smith By His Mother*, SLC: Bookcraft. 1996, p. 90, note 4. For the original record of Joseph Smith's employment as a young man with Josiah Stowell, Sr. looking for a lost Spanish silver mine, see JS History / Smith, Joseph, et al. History, 1838–1856, vols. A-1–F-1 (original), A-2–E-2 (fair copy). Historian's Office, History of the Church, 1839–ca. 1882. CHL. CR 100 102, boxes 1–7. The history for the period after 5 Aug. 1838 was composed after the death of Joseph Smith. Josiah Stowell also gave a character reference for the young Joseph Smith Jr. during a trial in South Bainbridge, Chenango County, New York, 1826, 1830, see "The Original Prophet. By a Visitor to Salt Lake City." *Fraser's Magazine* 7, no. 28 (Feb. 1873) 225–235. For Lucy Mack Smith and her three children, Hyrum, Samuel and Sophronia being members of the Presbyterian Church for ten years (1820-1830) see Proctor, *The Revised and Enhanced History*... p. 212, or the original manuscript in Lucy Mack Smith, History, rough draft or preliminary manuscript, 1844–1845, book 9, p. 8, The Joseph Smith Papers, accessed June 2, 2018, http://www. josephsmithpapers.org/paper-summary/lucy-mack- smith-history-1844-1845/212. The 1902 edition of George A. Smith and Elias Smith left out this paragraph about Lucy's Presbyterian membership. Preston Nibley's 1958 edition of Lucy's history, p. 161 included and referred to Lucy's Presbyterian membership with the words of Deacon Beckwith, "you and most of your children have belonged to our [Presbyterian] church for some time," based on the revised manuscript or "fair copy" made by Howard and Martha Coray under the direction of Lucy Mack Smith and the Twelve Apostles in Nauvoo, Illinois (Letter of Lucy Mack Smith to her son William Smith, January 23, 1845). P. Nibley left out the names of the children which were included in Lucy's preliminary manuscript cited above, book 9, p. 8.

One should not be concerned with Lucy's Presbyterian membership as opposed to her solemn faith in her son Joseph Smith's divine mission to establish the Lord's kingdom on earth. Joseph's mother Lucy Mack Smith confirms the persecutions which Joseph received as a result of his 1820 First Vision prior to September 1823 when the angel Moroni first visited Joseph. (See notes 48, 52–55 below).

The above quotation of Deacon Beckwith from Lucy's history came in 1828 during the translation of the Book of Mormon, the same year Lucy and her three siblings quit attending the Presbyterian Church. It is apparent from the historical records available that Joseph Smith's family did not get involved in Joseph's mission until September 22, 1827 when Joseph actually received the gold plates from the angel Moroni. In September 1823 after Moroni's first visit to Joseph, Moroni commanded Joseph to go tell his father about the vision and commandments he was given. When Joseph told his father Joseph later recorded that his father said that the visitation of Moroni "was of God" (JS-H 1:49–50). We have no record of such a conversation after Joseph's 1820 First Vision. Prior to 1827 Joseph spoke very little about his First Vision after being reprimanded and persecuted harshly by the local ministers, one in particular whom Joseph mentions in his history (JS-H 1:21). Regarding Lucy's date of joining with the Presbyterians before or after 1820 and Joseph Smith's First Vision, see Richard L. Bushman, *Joseph Smith and the Beginnings of Mormonism* (Urbana and Chicago, Illinois: University of Illinois Press; Reprint edition, 1987), p. 53, note 32. ISBN 0252060121. Dr. Bushman preferred the early 1820 date, though some have tried to make a case as late as 1824 during one of many revival events in Palmyra. For Lucy's and her two son's suspension from the Presbyterian Church on March 10, 1830, see Milton V. Backman and James B. Allen, "Membership of Certain of Joseph Smith's Family in the Western Presbyterian Church of Palmyra," *Brigham Young University Studies*, 10 no. 4 (1970): p. 482–484 and Wesley P. Waters quoted in Fawn M. Brodie, *No Man Knows My History: The Life of Joseph Smith*, Second Edition, 1971, New York: Vintage Books, 1995, p. 24.

15. Scot Facer Proctor and Maurine Jensen Proctor, editors, Lucy Mack Smith, *The Revised and Enhanced History of Joseph Smith by his Mother*, Salt Lake City: Bookcraft. 1996, pp. 3–11, 479.

16. Schmuhl, Albert F., *The Royal Line*, a chart prepared for the New York Stake Genealogical Board, Church of Jesus Christ of Latter-day Saints centennial exhibition, chart and microfilm, LDS Family History Library, SLC, Utah, March, 1936. A copy of this chart is in my possession (S. Wilden); Michael De Groote, "DNA shows Joseph Smith was Irish," *Deseret News*, August 8, 2006: Uga A. Perego, "Joseph Smith DNA Revealed: New Clues from the Prophet's Genes," August 7, 2008 FAIRMORMON Conference; *Jeremiah* 43:6,7 and 11; *Jeremiah* 44:28; *Jeremiah* 45:1, 5; F. Rev. R. A. Glover, *England the Remnant of Judah*, Rivington Press, 1881. Joseph Smith, Jr. was Scottish, Irish and English according to Perego's DNA report and the Smith family tree prepared by Albert Schmuhl.

17. Richard L. Bushman, Joseph Smith And The Beginnings Of Mormonism, Urbana and Chicago, University of Illinois Press, 1984, pp. 47-48, 64-65; Conover, George S., ed. History of Ontario County, New York: With Illustrations and Family Sketches of Some of the Prominent Men and Families. Syracuse, NY: D. Mason, 1893, p. 330; Joseph Smith---History 1:29–59.

18. Joseph Fielding Smith, Jr., "A Peculiar People: Modern Revelation—The Coming of Moroni," *Deseret News,* June 6, 1931, Church section, p. 8; see also *Doctrines of Salvation,* volume 3, pp. 3-4; Joseph Fielding Smith, Jr., "A Peculiar People: Prophecy Being Fulfilled," *Deseret News,* Sept. 19, 1931, Church section, p. 6; both citations are quoted in Joseph Fielding Smith, Jr., "Chapter 26: Preparing for the Coming of Our Lord," *Teachings of Presidents of the Church: Joseph Fielding Smith,* SLC, Utah: The Church of Jesus Christ of Latter-day Saints, 2013, pp. 319–32.

Notes to Chapter 3

19. Donna Hill, *Joseph Smith: The First Mormon*, Garden City, NY: Doubleday, 1977, pp. 22–25, 45. An important work and very fair, even with the acknowledged typos in its notes and bibliography.

20. George Albert Smith, "History of George Albert Smith," MS, Church History Library, and BYU Special Collections; and Rex C. Reeve, "Joseph Smith, the Chosen Instrument," *Ensign*, October, 1985.

21. Mary Audentia Smith Anderson, *Ancestry and Posterity of Joseph Smith and Emma Hale,* Independence, Missouri, 1929, p. 52, a facsimile of the Asael Smith's January 14, 1796 letter to Jacob Towne is included, as quoted in Donna Hill, *Joseph Smith, The First Mormon,* New York: Doubleday, 1977, p. 21–22.

22. Lorenzo Dow, quoted in Donna Hill, *Joseph Smith, The First Mormon,* New York: Doubleday, 1977, p. 44.

23. Preston Nibley, *History of Joseph Smith by His Mother Lucy Mack Smith,* SLC: Bookcraft, 1958, pp. 46–58.

24. Lucy Mack Smith, *History, 1845,* Church History Library, SLC, Utah, "fair copy" or "revised manuscript," p. 73.

Notes to Chapter 4

25. Smith, Lucy Mack, Biographical Sketches of Joseph Smith the Prophet, and His Progenitors for Many Generations, Liverpool: S.W. Richards, 1853, pp. 55–59, 70-74; See also, Bushman, Richard Lyman (2005), *Joseph Smith: Rough Stone Rolling*, New York: Knopf, ISBN 1-4000-4270-4m, 2005, p. 26.

26. Paul E. Johnson, A Shopkeeper's Millennium: Society and Revivals in Rochester, New York, 1815–1837, New York: Hill & Wang, 1978, p. 4.

27. Ronald G. Walters, *American Reformers, 1815–1860*, American. Century Series. New York: Hill and Wang, 1978; Paul E. Johnson, A *Shopkeeper's Millennium*, pp.152–157.

28. Michael D. Quinn, "JOSEPH SMITH'S EXPERIENCE OF A METHODIST "CAMP-MEETING" IN 1820." *Dialogue* Internet E-Paper #3, July 12, 2006. Enlarged December 20, 2006. p. 19, notes 70 and 71. https://www.dialogue journal.com/wpcontent/uploads/2010/04/QuinnPaperless.Pdf. Joseph Smith's Religious Camp Meeting," *Dialogue Internet*, July 12, 2006. Enlarged December 20, 2006, p. 19, note 70; Milton W. Hamilton, *The Country Printer: New York State*, 1785-1830, 1964, p.139; for lack of local revival publications see, *Palmyra Register*, Palmyra, Wayne County, N.Y., 1817–1821, weekly; *Palmyra Herald and Canal Advertiser*, Palmyra, Wayne County, 1822–1823, weekly; New York State Newspapers List, which provide newspaper subject matter.

29. Milton V. Backman, Jr., "Awakenings in the Burned-over District: New Light on the Historical Setting of the first Vision," *BYU Studies*, volume 9, number 3 (1969): p. 11.

30. Steven C. Harper, "History Is People, Places, Sources, and Stories: An Interview with Milton V. Backman, Jr.," *Mormon Historical Studies* 6 (2005): pp. 110–11.

31. Methodist Minutes (1821) pp. 27–28 quoted in Milton V. Backman, Jr., Awakenings in the Burned Over District: New Light on the Historical Setting of the First Vision," *BYU Studies*, volume 9, number 3 (1969): pp. 301–320.

Notes to Chapter 5

32. *Joseph Smith--History* 1:5, *The Pearl Of Great Price*, SLC: The Church of Jesus Christ of Latter-day Saints, 1989, p. 47.

33. Richard Lyman Bushman, *Joseph Smith: Rough Stone Rolling*, 2005, New York: Knopf, p. 37.

34. Blakeslee, "Notes for a History of Methodism in Phelps, 1886," manuscript, page 7; Milton V. Backman, Jr., *Joseph Smith's First Vision*, p. 74, note 34; see also Quinn, "Camp Meeting," p 11, note 35 who refers to Backman. A copy of this document is in the Brigham Young University Library. Milton Backman reports that Blakeslee wrote in his manuscript history of "a camp meeting held near Palmyra in 1818, in which twenty were baptized and forty converted to the Methodist society, and which was not reported in the newspapers and the religious journals of that age" (Backman, p. 74, note 34). Phelps, New York is 13 miles from Palmyra, or within walking or an hour's horse riding distance in the early 19th century. In contrast, Joseph and several companions walked 250 miles from St. Louis, Missouri to Independence, Missouri in July of 1831 (Donna Hill *Joseph Smith, The First Mormon*, Garden City: Doubleday, New York: 1977, pp. 135).

35. E. Latimer, *The Three Brothers: Sketches of the Lives of Rev. Aurora Seager, Rev. Micah Seager, Rev. Schuyler Seager, D.D.*, New York: Phillips & Hunt, 1880,p. 12 (for Aurora's death in 1819, pp. 21-22, for quotations, including his 1818 "diary"; see Quinn, "Joseph Smith and "Camp-Meeting," Dialogue Internet Article, 20 Dec 2006, pp. 2, 57, notes 4 and 5.

36. D. Michael Quinn, "JOSEPH SMITH'S EXPERIENCE OF A METHODIST 'CAMP-MEETING' IN 1820," *Dialogue* Internet E-Paper #3, December 20, 2006, p. 3; Grant H. Palmer, *An Insider's View of Mormon Origins*, Salt Lake City: Signature Books, 2002, pp. 240–44.

37. Dean C. Jessee, *The Papers of Joseph Smith,* Salt Lake City: Deseret Book, 1989, Volume 1 of 2, p. 5, Joseph's 1832 account. Dean C. Jessee's previous work *The Personal Writings of Joseph Smith* in one volume was published in 1984, revised in 2002 and preceded *The Papers of Joseph Smith* (PJS) cited above and *The Joseph Smith Papers* (JSP), which JSP began being published in 2008 in more than two dozen volumes; Quinn, "JOSEPH SMITH'S EXPERIENCE OF A

METHODIST "CAMP-MEETING" IN 1820," *Dialogue* Internet E-Paper #3, Dec. 2006, p. 4.

38. D. Michael Quinn, "JOSEPH SMITH'S EXPERIENCE OF A METHODIST "CAMP-MEETING" IN 1820." Joseph Smith's Religious Camp Meeting," *Dialogue Internet*, E-Paper #3, 20 Dec. 2006, p. 18, note 68.

39. Richard Lloyd Anderson, "Probing the Lives of Christ and Joseph Smith," *FARMS Review*, volume 21, issue 2.

40. Milton V. Backman, Jr., "Awakenings in the Burned-Over District: New Light on the Historical Setting of the First Vision," BYU Studies volume 9, number 3 (1969): p. 309 and note 19. Dr. Backman reports that the Irishman James Couser died at the Methodist Camp meeting in Palmyra as reported by the Palmyra Register, June 28, and July 5, 1820.

41. D. Michael Quinn, "JOSEPH SMITH'S EXPERIENCE OF A METHODIST 'CAMP-MEETING' IN 1820." Joseph Smith's Religious Camp Meeting," *Dialogue* Internet E-Paper #3, 2006, p. 38; *JS-H* 1:7-14. For Rev. Walters' Ontario Circuit Methodist net loss of 6 members See Wesley P. Walters, "New Light on Mormon Origins," *Dialogue*, volume 4, no. 1, 1969, pp. 66, 76, note 21.

42. Benaijah Williams diary, July 15, 1820, copy in Church History Library, Salt Lake City; spelling regularized, quoted from "First Vision Accounts," lds.org. The Reverend Benaijah Williams, was born on 24 Aug 1789 and died on 22 Jan 1864. Rev. Williams was a Methodist preacher and circuit rider in western New York who wrote five volumes of diaries or journals of his daily life.

43. D. Michael Quinn, "JOSEPH SMITH'S EXPERIENCE OF A METHODIST "CAMP-MEETING" IN 1820," *Dialogue* Internet E-Paper #3, 2006, p. 12. See also, Donald L. Enders, "A Snug Log House," *Ensign*, August, 1985, lds.org; "Palmyra-Manchester 1820-31," Map 2, *CHURCH HISTORY CHRONOLOGY, MAPS AND PHOTOGRAPHS,* SLC: Intellectual Reserve, Inc., 1999.

Notes to Chapter 6

44. Elder Bruce R. McConkie, "The Morning Breaks; the Shadows Flee," General Conference Address, in the Tabernacle, Salt Lake City, Utah, April 6, 1978. See also, *Ensign*, May 1978.

45. John P. Pratt, "Enoch Calendar Testifies of Christ," *Meridian Magazine*, Sept. 11, 2001; John P. Pratt, Review of *Mapping Time: The Calendar and Its History*, by E. G. Richards, *American Mathematical Monthly*, volume 107, number 1, January, 2000; Wikipedia, "Enoch Calendar." Accessed June 15, 2020 at https://en.wikipedia. org/wiki/ Enoch_calendar.

Notes to Chapter 7

46. Joseph Smith, Sr., Blessing, to JS, Kirtland, OH, 9 Dec. 1834; in *Patriarchal Blessing Book 1*, pp. 3–4; handwriting of Oliver Cowdery; Church History Library, Salt Lake City, Utah; Martha J. Coray, "Biographical Sketches of the Mack Family and Autobiography of Lucy Mack Smith," manuscript, c. 1845, LDS Church History Library, SLC, UT; Enders, "A Snug Log House," *Ensign*, August, 1985, https://www. lds.org/ensign/1985/08/a-snug-log-house, note 4.

47. Jean B. Bingham, General Primary President, "United in Accomplishing God's Work," General Conference Talk given Saturday evening, April 4, 2020, Accessed June21, 2020. https://www. churchofjesuschrist.org/study/general-conference/2020/04/34bingham. Gospel Top-ics, "Joseph Smith's Teachings about Priesthood, Temple, and Women," (an official Church essay) topics.ChurchofJesusChrist. org; See also, Jean B. Bingham, "united in Accomplishing God's Work," *Ensign*, May 2020, "https://www.churchofjesuschrist.org/study/ ensign/2020/05/34 bingham.

48. Lucy Mack Smith, Biographical Sketches of Joseph Smith the Prophet, and His Progenitors for Many Generations, Liverpool: S.W. Richards, 1853, p. 140.

49. Scot and Maurine Proctor, "The 19th Century Controversy about Lucy Mack Smith's History of Her Son, Joseph" *Meridian Magazine*, internet, January 2, 2001; Richard Lloyd Anderson, "His Mother's Manuscript: An Intimate View of Joseph Smith," *Brigham Young University Forum* address, January 27, 1976; Scot Facer Proctor and

Maurine Jensen Proctor, editors. *The Revised and Enhanced History of Joseph Smith by his Mother*, Salt Lake City: Bookcraft. 1996, p. 94.

50. *Joseph Smith---History* 1:1-25, in *The Pearl of Great Price*, 1981,1989, pp. 47-51. Joseph Smith, first person account, April 30, 1838, Manuscript History of the Church, six large handwritten volumes, 1838–1856, vol. A-1, pp. 2–3 in the handwriting of George Robinson; "Draft" copied by James Mulholland in 1841; and a revised Draft 2 copy was made by Howard Coray, 1841, presumably under Joseph Smith's direction and used for "Extracts from the History of Joseph Smith." in the *Pearl of Great Price*, 1851 published by Franklin D. Richards, apostle and President of the British Mission.

51. Pres. Gordon B. Hinckley (1910–2008), "Inspirational Thoughts," *Ensign*, August, 1997, p. 3.

Notes to Chapter 8

52. Lucy Mack Smith, Biographical Sketches of Joseph Smith the Prophet, and His Progenitors for Many Generations, by Lucy Smith, Mother of the Prophet. Liverpool: S.W. Richards for Orson Pratt. 1853; Scot and Maurine Proctor, "The 19th Century Controversy about Lucy Mack Smith's History of Her Son, Joseph" Meridian Magazine, internet, January 2, 2001; Richard Lloyd Anderson, "His Mother's Manuscript: An Intimate View of Joseph Smith," Brigham Young University Forum address, January 27, 1976; Scot Facer Proctor and Maurine Jensen Proctor, editors. The Revised and Enhanced History of Joseph Smith by his Mother, Salt Lake City: Bookcraft. 1996, p. 94.

53. Scot Proctor and Maurine Proctor, editors, *The Revised and Enhanced History of Joseph Smith By His Mother*, 1996, pp. 100-101. This gives the record of Joseph's mother confirming his religious persecutions before 1822 and corresponds with the earlier "fair copy" written in early 1845, a 337 page manuscript of Lucy's dictated history recorded by Howard and Martha Coray in the Church History Library in Salt Lake City, Utah. See "Lucy Mack Smith, History, 1845," The Joseph Smith Papers, accessed June 3, 2018, http://www.josephsmith papers.org/paper-summary/lucy-mack-smith-history-1845/1, pp. 77–78.

    Further historical notes on Lucy's history: From the "Historical Introduction" of Lucy's history online with the original manuscripts in the Church History Library in Salt Lake City we read, "Writing to her only surviving son, William, on 23 January 1845, Smith informed him, "I have by the council of the 12 [Apostles] undertaken a history of the family, that is my Fathers Family and my own." She added: People are often enquiring of me the particulars of Joseph's getting the plates *seeing the angels at first* and many other things which Joseph never wrote or published. I have told over many things pertaining to these matters to different persons to gratify their curiosity indeed have almost destroyed my lungs giving these recitals to those who felt anxious to hear them I have now concluded to write down every particular as far as possible and if those who wish to read them will help me a little they can have it all in one piece to read at their leasure—" (spelling retained and italics added).

"To help defray the cost of publication she asked William to start a subscription to raise about $100 to buy paper to print her history (Lucy Mack Smith, Nauvoo, IL, to William Smith, 23 Jan. 1845, CHL)."

"Later that year on 8 October, at a general conference of the church being held in the Nauvoo temple, [Lucy] Smith spoke of the completion of her project. According to the conference minutes she "gave notice that she had written her history, and wished it printed before we leave this place" ("Conference Minutes," Times and Seasons, 1 Nov. 1845, 6:1014). However, arrangements could not be made for its publication prior to the saints' departure from Nauvoo. It was eventually printed by Orson Pratt in 1853 in Liverpool, England."

"Years later, Martha Jane Knowlton Coray, writing from Provo, Utah, in June 1865, responded to a request from Brigham Young for information regarding her role in the drafting and publication of Mother Smith's history. Regarding Smith, Coray wrote, "I was her amanuensis at the time the Book was written." She then cited her own practice of "noting down everything, I heard and read which possessed 140 [pages or items of] any peculiar interest to me...I was occupied, from time to time as occasion offered, in making notes of sermons, and other things which I thought reliable such as: discourses by yourself, the twelve, and other responsible men." She then related that this practice "made it an easy task for me to transmit to paper" what Smith dictated to her. She added, "Hyrum and Joseph were dead, and thus without their aid, she [Lucy] attempted to prosecute the work, relying chiefly upon her memory There were two [337 page "fair copy"] Manuscripts prepared, one copy was given to Mother Smith, and the other retained in the Church" (Martha Jane Knowlton Coray, Provo,

UT, to Brigham Young, 13 June 1865, Brigham Young Office Files, CHL)."

"The two completed manuscripts Coray referenced in her letter to Young were preceded by a draft, sometimes referred to as the [240 page] "rough draft manuscript." Martha Jane Coray and her husband, Howard, composed this draft as they met with Smith during the fall and winter 1844–1845. Then, in early 1845, utilizing the rough draft and other notes and sources, the Corays apparently penned two revised, or "fair," [337 page] copies. The sole extant fair version is titled "The History of Lucy Smith Mother of the Prophet." Miscellaneous fragments included with the rough draft copy suggest that the Corays may also have produced an intermediate draft prior to transcribing the two fair copies. Assuming an intermediate draft once existed in some form, most of it has been lost."

54. Proctor and Proctor, editors, Lucy Mack Smith, *History of Joseph Smith By His Mother*, 1996, pp. 135, 145. It was not until Joseph obtained the plates in September of 1827 that his parents and siblings began to understand and believe in the great mission in front of Joseph Smith.

55. Richard L. Bushman, *Joseph Smith and the Beginnings of Mormonism*, Urbana and Chicago, Illinois: University of Illinois Press; Reprint edition, 1987, pp. 204-205. Dr. Bushman discusses evidence of revivals in Palmyra and neighboring towns in relation to Joseph's First Vision of 1820. Bushman confirms that both secular and sectarian history confirms that Joseph could experience religious excitement in Palmyra Village which resulted from revivals in nearby towns in 1820 and during a period from 1818 to 1824 both before and after his First Vision.

56. Scott Proctor and Maurine Proctor, editors, Lucy Mack Smith, *The Revised and Enhanced History of Joseph Smith By His Mother*, 1996, p. 144 and note 14, p. 147; Backman, *Eyewitness Accounts*, p. 70; Andrew H. Hedges, "'All My Endeavors to Preserve Them,'" *Journal of Book of Mormon Studies* 8, no. 2 (1999): pp. 14–23.

57. Dean C. Jessee, Editor, *The Papers Of Joseph Smith*, Volume 1, SLC: Deseret Book, 1989, p. 430. This reference comes from Joseph Smith's 1842 letter to John Wentworth which included a First Vision account as well as the Articles of Faith, the coming forth of the *Book of Mormon* and information about the origin of the American Indians. It was first

published in the *Times and Seasons*, March 1, 1842 in Nauvoo, Illinois; *Times and Seasons, March 1, 1842*. p. 141.

58. Joseph Smith, Jr., et al, *History of the Church (DHC)*, 4:535–41; B. H. Roberts, *A Comprehensive History Of The Church of Jesus Christ of Latter-day Saints (CHC)*, Salt Lake City: Utah, Deseret News Press, 1930, First Edition, 1:55.

Notes to Chapter 9

59. Dean C. Jessee quoted in John W. Welch, editor, *Opening The Heavens, Accounts of Divine Manifestations, 1820-1844*, SLC/Provo: BYU Press/ Desert Book, 2005, p. 49-52; four of these five accounts, save Levi Richard's account, are found also in Dean C. Jessee, *The Papers of Joseph Smith,* Salt Lake City: Deseret Book, 1989, Volume 1, pp. 387–470; These latter pages also include the Israel Daniel Rupp account.

60. Dean C. Jessee, James B. Allen and John W. Welch, quoted in John W. Welch, editor, *Opening The Heavens, Accounts of Divine Manifestations, 1820- 1844*, SLC/Provo: BYU Press/Desert Book, 2005, pp. 1–75. These pages include thirteen accounts of the First Vision.

61. This primary reference or account of Joseph Smith's First Vision was presented to me by Dr. Mark E. Mitchell in February 2018 during a telephone discussion about the subject. This account was also noted in a 1970 *Improvement Era* article by James B. Allen referenced below. See *Doctrine And Covenants* 20:5-8, revelation from the Lord given through Joseph Smith in April 1830. See also *Book of Commandments*, Independence, Missouri, 1833, Section XXIV, verse 6; *History of the Church (DHC)*, volume 1, pp. 64-70; for original manuscript source see Robin Scott, Robert J. Woodford, Steven C. Harper, editors, 1830 revelation to Joseph Smith, "Articles and Covenants," *The Joseph Smith Papers, Revelations And Translations*, Volume 2, The Church Historians Press: Salt Lake City, Utah, 2009, pp. 195, 202; Section 20 was first published by Oliver Cowdery in, "Revelations" entitled "THE ARTICLES AND COVENANTS OF THE CHURCH OF CHRIST" on the first page of the first issue of the *Evening and Morning Star* in June of 1832 (January 1835), p. 1. See also James B. Allen, "Eight Contemporary Accounts of Joseph Smith's First Vision What Do We Learn from Them," *Improvement Era*, April 1970, pp. 12, note 6. This article gives reference to the Section 20 account

of the First Vision. For facsimile of original publication, "Book of Commandments, 1833," p. 48, The Joseph Smith Papers, accessed July 31, 2020 at https://www.josephsmithpapers.org/paper-summary/book-of-commandments-1833/52.

62. Dean C. Jessee, "History [1832]," *The Papers of Joseph Smith*, Volume 1, SLC: Deseret Book, 1989, pp. 3-7; for the same record see Dean C. Jessee, *The Personal Writings of Joseph Smith*, SLC: Deseret Book, Revised Edition, 2002, pp.9-11. See also facsimile manuscript, "History, circa Summer 1832," pp. 1-2, The Joseph Smith Papers, accessed July 31, 2020 at https://www.josephsmithpapers.org/paper-summary/history-circa-summer-1832/1.

63. Dean C. Jessee, *The Papers of Joseph Smith*, Volume 2, SLC: Deseret Book, 1992, pp. 68-69. This is Joseph's "Ohio Journal 1835-1836," November 9, 1835. See also facsimile manuscript, "Journal, 1835–1836," The Joseph Smith Papers, pp. 22-23, accessed July 31, 2020 at https://www.josephsmithpapers.org/paper-summary/journal-1835-1836/1.

64. Dean C. Jessee, *The Papers of Joseph Smith*, Volume 1, SLC: Deseret Book, 1989, pp. 124-127. This is Joseph's "History 1834-1836," November 9, 1835. See also facsimile manuscript, "History, 1834–1836," The Joseph Smith Papers, pp. 120-21. Accessed August 1, 2020 at https://www.josephsmithpapers. org/paper-summary/history-1834-1836/.1

65. Dean C. Jessee, *The Papers of Joseph Smith*, volume 2, SLC: Deseret Book, 1992, pp. 78-79. This is Joseph's "Ohio Journal 1835-1836," November 14, 1835. See also Dean C. Jessee, Mark Ashurst-McGee and Richard L. Jensen, editors, *The Joseph Smith Papers, Journals, Volume 1: 1832-1839*, Salt Lake City: The Church Historian's Press, 2008, p. 100.

66. Dean C. Jessee, *The Papers of Joseph Smith*, Volume 1, SLC: Deseret Book, 1989, pp. 136-137. This is Joseph's "History 1834-1836," November 14, 1835. See also facsimile manuscript, "History, 1834–1836," The Joseph Smith Papers, p. 128. Accessed August 1, 2020 at https://www.josephsmithpapers. org/paper-summary/history-1834-1836/.1

67. Joseph Smith, History, [ca. June 1839–ca. 1841]; handwriting of George Robinson, "Draft" copied by James Mulholland; in JS History, 1838–1856, six large volumes, vol. A-1, CHL, SLC, Utah;

same account presumably revised by Joseph Smith and copied by Howard Coray in 1841. For the Coray copy see Steven C. Harper, *Joseph Smith's First Vision*, 2012, SLC: Deseret Book, pp. 32-33. *Times and Seasons*, 15 Mar. 1842, volume 3, number 10, pp. 726–728, 748-749; Lucy Mack Smith's "History of Joseph Smith," 1845 final manuscript revised by Howard Coray and approved by Lucy Mack Smith based on her desire to copyright and have the Church print the book; and *The Pearl of Great Price* published in 1851 in England. In the twentieth-century 1981 edition of The Pearl of Great Price it is found in Joseph Smith—History 1:1-26; Dean C. Jessee, *The Personal Writings of Joseph Smith*, SLC: Deseret Book, 1984, 2002, pp. 226–232; *History of the Church*, SLC: Deseret Book, 1948, volume 1, pp. 1–8. See also, "History, 1838–1856, volume A-1 [23 December 1805–30 August 1834]," p. 1, The Joseph Smith Papers, accessed August 1, 2020 at https://www.josephsmithpapers.org/paper-summary/history-1838-1856-volume-a-1-23-december-1805-30-august-1834/1.

68. Joseph Smith, "Church History," in *Times and Seasons* (Nauvoo, IL), 1 Mar. 1842, vol. 3, no. 9 (no. 45), pp. 706–710; Joseph Smith's letter replying to John Wentworth, editor of the Chicago Democrat newspaper, 1842, see Dean C. Jessee, *The Personal Writings of Joseph Smith*, SLC: Deseret Book, Revised Edition, 2002, p. 241-248. See also, "Church History," 1 March 1842," p. 706–710, The Joseph Smith Papers, accessed August 1, 2020 at https://www.josephsmith papers.orgpaper-summary/church-history-1-march-1842/1.

69. Israel Daniel Rupp, *An Original History of the Religious Denominations at Present Existing in the United States*, Philadelphia, 1844, pp. 404-410. See also John Welch, et al., editors, Dean C. Jessee, "The Earliest Documented Accounts of Joseph Smith's First Vision," in *Opening the Heavens, Accounts of Divine Manifestations, 1820-1844*. Provo and Salt Lake City: Brigham Young University Press and Deseret Book. 2005, pp. 17-19. Israel Daniel Rupp (1803-1878) of Lancaster County, Pennsylvania and a Swiss Mennonite, wrote a letter to Joseph Smith in July 1843 requesting a chapter on Mormonism for his book on American religions. Joseph promptly replied and after it was published in 1844 a copy of Rupp's book was given to Joseph Smith while he was living in Nauvoo, Illinois. See also Joseph's follow up or second "Letter to Israel Daniel Rupp, 5 June 1844," pp. 1–2, The Joseph Smith Papers, accessed August 1, 2020 at https://www.josephsmithpapers.org/paper-summary/letter-to-israel-daniel-rupp-5-june-1844/1.

70. Orson Pratt, one of the original apostles of the 1835 quorum, "A[n] Interesting Account of Several Remarkable Visions…," Edinburgh, Scotland, September 1840, Appendix, pp. 2-5; See also, "Appendix: Orson Pratt, A[n] Interesting Account of Several Remarkable Visions, 1840," pp. 2–5, *The Joseph Smith Papers*, accessed July 26, 2018, http://www.Josephsmithpapers. org/paper-summary/appendix-orson-pratt-an-interesting-account-of-several-remarkable-visions -1840/1. Unlike the other nine accounts referenced above, this account was not written by nor was its writing supervised by Joseph Smith. It was wholly Elder Orson Pratt's record of what he heard the Joseph say during his personal life experiences with the Prophet beginning in early October 1830. Orson Pratt was baptized on September 19, 1830, his nineteenth birthday, and is mentioned in a record of the early conversations of several notable early Latter-day Saints (see "Covenant of Oliver Cowdery and Others, 17 October 1830," 1, josephsmithpapers.org). On February 14, 1835, Orson Pratt was among the first twelve men ordained in the latter days to the Quorum of Twelve Apostles under the hands of Oliver Cowdery and David Whitmer, two of the Three Witnesses of the Book of Mormon (see John A. Widtsoe, *Priesthood And Church Government*, Deseret Book Co., 1954, p. 363). In the above referenced pamphlet of 1840 under "faith and doctrine," Elder Pratt's gave thirteen statements which are in part comparable to what would become the thirteen "Articles of Faith" written by Joseph Smith two years later. However, overall, they are very different and much longer and more verbose than the succinct "Thirteen Articles of Faith" found in the Wentworth Letter published in the *Times and Seasons* of March 1, 1842 at Nauvoo, Illinois.

71. Orson Hyde, one of the original apostles of the 1835 quorum, pamphlet entitled, Ein Ruf aus der Wüste" (A Cry out of the Wilderness) printed in Frankfurt, Germany, 1842, pp 13-15. Original publication in LDS Church Archives, Church History Library, Salt Lake City, Utah; Discussed and referenced in John W. Welch, ed., *Opening the Heavens, Accounts of Divine Manifestations, 1820-1844*, 2005, pp. 21–22, 51. See also, Jessee, *Papers of Joseph Smith*, 1:402–25.

72. Levi Richards, Journal, June 11, 1843, LDS Church History Library, discussed referenced in John W. Welch, ed., *Opening the Heavens, Accounts of Divine Manifestations, 1820-1844*, 2005, pp. 23-24, 49; Thomsonian physician to Joseph Smith and member of the Council of Fifty or Anointed Quorum. See Matthew J. Grow, Ronald K.

Esplin, Mark Ashurst McGee, et al, editors, *The Joseph Smith Papers, Administrative Records, Council of Fifty, March 1844 – January 1846*, Salt Lake City: The Church Historian's Press, 2016, p. 187, name listed as "20 Levi Richards" [born] April 14, 1799." Andrew F. Ehat and Lyndon W. Cook, eds., *The Words of Joseph Smith, (*Provo, Utah: Brigham Young University Religious Studies Center, 1980), p. 215.

73. David Nye White interview of Joseph Smith at Nauvoo, Illinois on August 28, 1843. White's article was entitled, "The Prairies, Nauvoo, Joe Smith, the Temple, the Mormons, &c" and was published in the September 15, 1843 issue of the *Pittsburg Weekly Gazette* and later in the *New York Spectator*, September 23, 1843; Joseph Smith is quoted by White and referenced in John W. Welch, ed., *Opening the Heavens, Accounts of Divine Manifestations, 1820–1844*, 2005, pp. 24–25, 33, note 30. See also Jessee, *Papers of Joseph Smith*, 1:438–44.

74. 1844, Alexander Neibaur, Journal, May 24, 1844, MS, LDS Church History Library, a German dentist and the first Jewish convert to Mormonism; Quoted and referenced in John W. Welch, ed., *Opening the Heavens, Accounts of Divine Manifestations, 1820-1844*, 2005, pp. 25–26, 50. See also, "Alexander Neibaur, Journal, 24 May 1844, extract," p. [23–24], The Joseph Smith Papers, accessed August 7, 2020, https://www.josephsmithpapers.org/paper-summary/alexander-neibaur-journal-24-may-1844-extract/2.

75. Robin Scott, Robert J. Woodford, Steven C. Harper, editors, 1830 revelation to Joseph Smith, "Articles and Covenants," *The Joseph Smith Papers, Revelations And Translations*, The Church Historians Press: Salt Lake City, Utah, 2009, pp. 74-77; Oliver Cowdery, "Revelations" circa April 1830 [D&C 20], entitled "THE ARTICLES AND COVENANTS OF THE CHURCH OF CHRIST" on page one of the first issue of *The Evening and Morning Star* in June of 1832, (*E&MS*, 1832, p. 1); *The Joseph Smith Papers*, p. [4], accessed July 14, 2018, http://www.Josephsmith papers.org/paper-summary/articles-and-covenants-circa-april-1830-dc-20/1; The same is found in the *Book of Commandments*, 1833, Section XXIV, verse 6, pp. 3-4; and in *Doctrine And Covenants*, 1835, Section 2, verse 2, pp. 76–77; The Joseph Smith Papers, accessed July 14, 2018, http://www.josephsmithpapers.org/paper- summary/ doctrine-and-covenant s-1835/210.

76. "THE ARTICLES AND COVENANTS OF THE CHURCH OF CHRIST" [*Doctrine And Covenants 20*], *The Evening and Morning Star,*

June, 1832, volume 1, number 1, Independence, Missouri, republished by Eugene Wagner of Basel, Switzerland and printed by F. Wochner K.G., Mühringen, Germany, 1969, p. 1; "Book of Commandments, Section [Chapter XXIV:6-7], 1833," p. 48, The Joseph Smith Papers, accessed March 16, 2018, http://www.josephsmithpapers.org/ paper-summary/book-of-commandments-1833/52; "Doctrine and Covenants, [Section II:2,] 1835," p. 77, The Joseph Smith Papers, accessed March 16, 2018, http://www.josephsmithpapers.org/paper-summary/doctrine-and-covenants-1835/85 "Section 20, The Articles and Covenants of the Church," *Doctrine and Covenants Student Manual*, SLC: The Church of Jesus Christ of Latter-day Saints, 2002, pp. 39–43.

77. John W. Welch, editor, *Opening The Heavens, Accounts of Divine Manifestations, 1820-1844*, SLC/Provo: BYU Press/Desert Book, 2005, pp. 1-75; The first chapter in this book by Dean C. Jessee and the second chapter by James B. Allen and John W. Welch together cover the contemporary accounts of the First Vision; See also Dean C. Jessee, *The Personal Writings of Joseph Smith*, SLC: Deseret Book, revised edition, 2002, pp. 9–20, 104–105, 112–113, 226–232, 241--243; Dean C. Jessee, *The Papers of Joseph Smith*, Volume 1, SLC: Deseret Book, 1989, pp. 124–127, 132.

78. Dean C. Jessee, *The Personal Writings of Joseph Smith*, SLC: Deseret Book, Revised Edition, 2002, pp.3, 5. The 1832 First Vision account. Crossed out words in the original omitted.

79. Dean C. Jessee, Editor, *The Papers of Joseph Smith*, Volume 1, SLC: Deseret Book, 1989, pp. 5–7, original spelling retained; JS—H 1:6–7. See also Luke 2:19.

80. Dean C. Jessee, *The Papers of Joseph Smith*, Volume 2, 1992, pp. 68–69.

81. Ibid, pp. 78–79.

82. Joseph Smith, History, [ca. June 1839–ca. 1841]; handwriting of George Robinson, "Draft" made by James Mulholland and Robert B. Thompson; sixty-one pages; in JS History, 1838–1856, vol. A-1, CHL, SLC, Utah; *Times and Seasons*, 15 March 1842, pp. 726–28; 1 April 1842, pp. 748–49; Lucy Mack Smith's "History of Joseph Smith;" 1845 final manuscript revised by Howard Coray and approved by Lucy Mack Smith based on her desire to copyright and have the Church print the book; and The Pearl of Great Price published in 1851 in England. In the twentieth-century 1981 edition of The Pearl of Great Price it is found in Joseph Smith—History 1:1–26; Dean C. Jessee, *The*

Personal Writings of Joseph Smith, SLC: Deseret Book, 1984, 2002, pp. 226–232; *History of the Church*, SLC: Deseret Book, 1948, volume 1, pp. 1–8.

83. Joseph Smith, "Church History," in *Times and Seasons* (Nauvoo, IL), 1 Mar. 1842, vol. 3, no. 9 (no. 45), pp. 706–710; Joseph Smith identified these two personages as God the Father and Jesus Christ. JS History, vol. A-1, 3; see also JS History, ca. Summer 1832, 3; JS, Journal, 9–11 Nov. 1835; and JS, "Latter Day Saints," p. 405; This quotation from the Wentworth letter is also found in, Dean C. Jessee, *The Personal Writings of Joseph Smith*, SLC: Deseret Book, Revised Edition, 2002, p. 242; K. L. Davidson, D. J. Whittaker, M. Ashurst-McGee, R. L. Jensen, editors, *The Joseph Smith Papers, Histories*, Volume 1, The Church Historian's Press, 2012, pp. 489–501; See also the Savior's similar counsel given to Joseph Smith by the Lord in *Luke* 17:23.

84. Israel Daniel Rupp, An Original History of the Religious Denominations at Present Existing in the United States, Philadelphia, 1844, pp. 404–410.

85. Milton V. Bachman, *Eyewitness Accounts of the Restoration*, Salt Lake City: Deseret Book, 1986, p. 18.

86. Carter, Kate, "The Jews in Early Utah, Alexander Neibaur, The Mormon," in Carter, Kate (ed.), *Treasures of Pioneer History*, 1, Salt Lake City, Utah: Daughters of Utah Pioneers, 1952, pp. 333–340; Ogden, D. Kelly, "Two From Judah Minister to Joseph" in Porter, Larry C., ed., *Regional Studies in LDS History: Illinois* (Provo, Utah: Brigham Young University, Religious Studies Center, 1995) pp. 232–237, accessed August 11, 2020 at: https://en.wikipedia. org/wiki/ Alexander_Neibaur; FamilySearch for Alexander Neibaur at: https://ancestors.familysearch. org/en/KWJC-PZR/ alexander-neibaur-1808-1883,

Notes to Chapter 10

87. Gordon B. Hinckley, "God Hath Not Given Us the Spirit of Fear," *Ensign*, October, 1984, An edited version of an address given 5 November 1983 at the Salt Lake Institute of Religion. From lds.org accessed March 2018.

88. Richard Lloyd Anderson, "Joseph Smith's Testimony of the First Vision," *Ensign*, April, 1996, lds.org accessed March 2018.

89. Stephen Prothero, *American Jesus: How the Son of God Became a National Icon*, New York: Farrar, Straus and Giroux, 2003, p. 171.

90. Steven C. Harper, "A Seeker's Guide to the Historical Accounts of Joseph Smith's First Vision," *Religious Educator*, 12, no. 1, 2011, pp. 165–176.

Notes to Chapter 11

91. Milton V. Bachman, "Harmony of Eight Contemporary Accounts of the First Vision," Appendix A, *Eyewitness Accounts of the Restoration*, SLC: Deseret Book, 1986, p. 201–203.

Notes to Chapter 12

92. "History of Orson Pratt," Brigham Young, Editor, *The Latter-Day Saints Millennial Star*, Liverpool: The Church of Jesus Christ of Latter-day Saints, vol. 27, 11 February 1865, p. 88.

93. Orson Pratt, A[n] *Interesting Account of Several Remarkable Visions*, Edinburgh, Scotland, 1840 (missionary pamphlet), quoted in Milton Backman, Jr., Confirming Witnesses of the First Vision, *Ensign*, January, 1986. Accessed online June 25, 2018, https://www.churchofjesuschrist.org/ensign/1986/01/confirming-witnesses-of-the-first-vision.

94. Orson Pratt, "Are the Father and the Son Two Distinct Persons," *Millennial Star*, volume 11, 15 September 1849, pp. 281–84; 15 October 1849, pp. 309–312.

95. John Taylor, "Three Nights' Public Discussion," Liverpool: John Taylor, 1850, pp. 23–24; John Taylor, *Deseret News: Semi-Weekly*, SLC, Utah, 18 April 1882; John Taylor, auth., G. Homer Durham, ed., *The Gospel Kingdom*, SLC: Deseret Book Co., 2002, (1st Edition 1887) p. 355.

96. John Taylor, *Journal of Discourses*, London: George D. Watt, Publisher, 1879, volume 21, pp. 161.

97. Milton V. Backman, Jr., "Confirming Witnesses of the First Vision" *Ensign*, January, 1986.

98. Wilford Woodruff, *The Latter-Day Saints Millennial Star*, Liverpool, England: The Church of Jesus Christ of Latter-day Saints, volume 52, April 28, 1890, p. 258.

Notes to Chapter 13

99. William B. Smith, William Smith on Mormonism, Lamoni, IA: Herald Steam Book and Job Office, 1883], p. 9. Published in Dan Vogel, editor, *Early Mormon Documents,* Salt Lake City, Signature Books, 1996–2003, 5 volumes, 1:494–495.

100. Lucy Mack Smith, author, Preston Nibley, editor, *The History of Joseph Smith By His Mother Lucy Mack Smith,* Bookcraft, 1958, p. 342.

101. Oliver Cowdery to W. W. Phelps, October 1834, *Messenger and Advocate,* Volume 1, Number 1, p. 13. Here Oliver Cowdery promises the saints he will share the history of the church; Oliver Cowdery to W. W. Phelps, December, 1834, "Letter III," *Messenger and Advocate,* Volume 1, Number 3, pp. 41–43. Oliver Cowdery begins to lay the historical foundation of religious excitement in Palmyra before Joseph Smith's First Vision.

102. Oliver Cowdery to W.W. Phelps, February, 1835, "Letter IV," *Messenger and Advocate,* Volume 1, Number 5, pp. 77–80. Counseled by Joseph Smith, Oliver Cowdery shifts from his history of the First Vision in Joseph's "15th" year to Joseph's "17th" year and his history of the visitation of the angel Moroni, the ancient record *The Book of Mormon* to be translated.

103. Roger Nicholson, "The Cowdery Conundrum: Oliver's, Aborted Attempt to Describe Joseph Smith's First Vision in 1834 and 1835," *Interpreter, A Journal Of Mormon Scripture,* volume 8, 2014, pp. 27–44. Accessed online at: https://journal.interpreterfoundation.org/the-cowdery-conundrum-olivers-aborted-attempt-to-describe-joseph-smiths-first-vision-in-1834-and-1835/.

104. The reminiscent claim that Joseph joined the Methodist Church: Joseph and Hiel Lewis, "Mormon History. A New Chapter, About to Be Published," *Amboy Journal* [Illinois] 24 (30 April 1879): 1; reproduced in Vogel, *Early Mormon Documents* 4:300–306;

   The reminiscent claim that Joseph joined the Baptists: Fayette Lapham, "Interview with the Father of Joseph Smith, the Mormon Prophet, Forty Years Ago. His Account of the Finding of the Sacred Plates," *Historical Magazine* [second series] 7 (May 1870): 305–309; reproduced in Vogel, *Early Mormon Documents* 1:456–466;

   The reminiscent claim that Joseph joined the Presbyterians: Mrs. S.F. Anderick affidavit of 24 June 1887, cited in Arthur B.

Deming, *Naked Truths About Mormonism* newspaper (January 1888), 2.; reproduced in Dan Vogel, *Early Mormon Documents* 2:207–211;

A contemporary statement that Joseph didn't join the Methodists: Pomeroy Tucker, *Origin, Rise, and Progress of Mormonism* New York: D. Appleton and Co., 1867, 17–18. The four references above accessed on November 16, 2020 at: https://www.fairmormon.org/answers/Joseph_Smith%27s_First_Vision/Joining_other_churches.

105. Joseph's expressions about the local churches: Lucy Mack Smith, author, Preston Nibley, editor, *The History of Joseph Smith By His Mother Lucy Mack Smith*, Bookcraft, 1958, pp. 90–91; see an earlier publication: Lucy Mack Smith, *History of Joseph Smith by His Mother* Salt Lake City: Stevens and Wallis, 1945, p. 90–91.

106. Contemporary statements that Joseph didn't join any church prior to 1830: Lucy Mack Smith, *History of Joseph Smith by His Mother*, Salt Lake City: Stevens and Wallis, 1945, p. 90; Letter, Josiah Stowell Jr. to John S. Fullmer, 17 February 1843; "The Golden Bible, or, Campbellism Improved." *Observer and Telegraph*, 18 November 1830 [Hudson, Ohio], no page nos.; "Gold Bible, No. 3," *The Reflector* (Palmyra, New York) 2, no. 12 (1 February 1831), no page nos.; Orson Pratt, *Journal of Discourses* 14:140–141.

107. Lucy Mack Smith, *Biographical Sketches Of Joseph Smith The Prophet...*, Liverpool: S. W. Richards, 1853, pp. 48-49; Richard L. Bushman, *Joseph Smith and the Beginnings of Mormonism*, Urbana and Chicago, Illinois: University of Illinois Press; Reprint edition, 1987, p. 53, note 32; Scot F. Proctor, *The History of Joseph Smith By His Mother*, Bookcraft, 1996, p. 50.

108. Lucy Mack Smith, *Biographical Sketches*, 1853, pp. 48–49; https://www.fairmormon.org/answers/Joseph_Smith%27s_First_Vision/Lucy_Mack_Smith_and_the_Presbyterians#Question:_Did_Lucy_Mack_Smith_state_when_she_joined_the_Presbyterians.3F. Accessed in March of 2018.

109. Lucy Mack Smith, *Biographical Sketches*, 1853, pp. 83–84. Accessed November 17, 2020 online at: https://contentdm.lib.byu.edu/digital/collection/NCMP1820-1846/id/16442.

110. Russell R. Rich, "The Dogberry papers and the Book of Mormon," *BYU Studies* 10 (Spring 1970), p. 316; Lucy Mack Smith, *Biographical Sketches*, pp. 143–144, 146-147; Milton V. Backman, Joseph Smith's First Vision, SLC, UT: Deseret Book Co., 1981, pp. 182–183; Richard

L. Bushman, *Joseph Smith and the Beginnings of Mormonism*, Urbana: Illini Books, 1988, pp. 108–110, 227 note 106; Proctor, *History of Joseph Smith By His Mother*, p. 214, note 3.

111. Lucy Mack Smith, The History of Joseph Smith By His Mother Lucy Mack Smith, Bookcraft, 1958, pp. 72–74.

112. William Smith, *On Mormonism, 1883*; "J. S. Peterson interview with William Smith," 1893, *Zion's Ensign*, January 13, 1894; reprinted in *Latter-day Saints' Millennial Star*, February 26, 1894, pp. 133; Guy L. Dorius, "'Now This Caused Us to Marvel': The Breadth of God's Heaven and the Depth of His Mercy" in *Joseph Smith and the Doctrinal Restoration*, Provo: Brigham Young University, Religious Studies Center, 2005, pp. 144–56; William Smith, *The Saints' Herald*, vol. 30, no. 23, 9 June 1883, p. 388; William Smith, *On Mormonism, 1883*, Dan Vogel editor, *Early Mormon Documents* (Salt Lake City, Signature Books, 1996–2003), 5 vols, 1:494–495; Accessed at: https://www.fairlatterdaysaints.org and http://www.sidneyrigdon.com.

Notes to Chapter 14

113. Michael H. MacKay and Nicholas J. Frederick, *Joseph Smith's Seer Stones*, Salt Lake City: Brigham Young University and Deseret Book, 2016, p. 128. The Urim and Thummim the Prophet Joseph Smith used was the same received by the brother of Jared upon the mount (D&C 17:1). For further history on Joseph Smith's use of the URIM AND THUMMIM: The Prophet's mother, Lucy Mack Smith, recorded in her history of Joseph Smith, completed in Nauvoo, Illinois in 1845, that Joseph used the instrument called "a Urim and Thummim; and it was by this that the angel [Moroni] showed him those things which he saw in vision [during 1827–1829]: he could also ascertain at any time, the approach of danger, either to himself or the Record [the gold plates of the Book of Mormon]. On account of which he always kept it about his person." "Lucy Mack Smith, History, 1845," known as the "fair copy" or "revised manuscript," Chapter 23, p. 113, CHL; "Lucy Mack Smith, History 1844-1845" preliminary or "rough draft" version, Book 5, inserted page after page 10 and Book 6, page 1, CHL. The Joseph Smith Papers, accessed August 20, 2021, https://www.josephsmithpapers.org/paper-summary/lucy-mack-smith-history-1845/1.

114. Andrew Jenson, editor, "William Clayton's Testimony," Historical Record, volume 6, pp. 225–226; William Clayton, Journal, July 12, 1843, quoted in MacKay and Fredericks, *Joseph Smith's Seer Stones*, SLC: Deseret Book, 2016, p. 130.

Notes to Chapter 15

115. Eric A. Eliason, "Seer Stones, Salamanders, and Early Mormon 'Folk Magic' in the Light of Folklore Studies and Bible Scholarship," *BYU Studies Quarterly*, vol. 55, No. 1 (2016): pp. 90–91.

116. Eric A. Eliason, "Seer Stones…," *BYU Studies Quarterly*, vol. 55, No. 1 (*2016*): pp. 75, 80, 84, 88–89.

117. Wesley P. Walters, Joseph Smith's Bainbridge, N.Y., *Court Trials and from Occult to Cult with Joseph Smith*, Jr., Pamphlet, 1977; D. Michael Quinn, *Early Mormonism and the Magic World View*, Salt Lake City, Utah: Signature Books, Second Edition 1998, pp. 30-65; Mark Ashurst-McGee, "A Pathway to Prophethood: Joseph Smith Junior as Rodsman, Seer, and Judeo-Christian Prophet," Master's thesis, Utah State University, 2000.

Notes to Chapter 16

118. Paul Y. Hoskisson, "Urim and Thummim," Daniel H. Ludlow, general editor, *The Encyclopedia of Mormonism*, New York: Macmillan Publishing Company, 1992, 4:1499-1500; accessed online at: https://contentdm.lib.byu.edu/digital/collection/EoM/id/4184 March 19, 2018.

119. Joseph Smith III, "Last Testimony of Sister Emma," *Saints' Herald* 26, Oct. 1, 1879, p. 289.

120. a) Joseph Smith had two seer stones by 1826: Mackay and Frederick, *Joseph Smith's Seer Stones*, 2016, p. 77; b) A seer stone (brown or white) dug up in 1822: Willard Chase, in Howe, Mormonism Unveiled, 1834, pp. 240–248; c) Emma Smith stated in an 1870 letter that a "dark" or brown seer stone was used in translation of *Book of Mormon* when she was acting as scribe and this brown stone was later given to Oliver Cowdery: Emma Smith Bidamon to Emma Pilgrim, March 27, 1870, Community of Christ Library-Archives, in Dan Vogel, *Early Mormon Documents*, 1996, 1:532; David Whitmer, *An Address to All Believers in Christ*, 1887, p. 32; David Whitmer, Interview in *Omaha Herald*, 17

Oct. 1886; *Saints' Herald* 33 (Nov. 1886): p. 706, quoted in Mackay and Frederick, p. 227; d) Wilford Woodruff recorded in his journal in 1841 that the Lord showed Joseph Smith the location of the white seer stone called "Gazelem": Pomeroy Tucker spoke of Joseph's stone as "whitish, glassy . . . opaque resembling quartz" in his *Origin, Rise and Progress of Mormonism* in 1867, pp. 129–130, Michael H. MacKay and Nicholas J. Frederick, *Joseph Smith's Seer Stones*, SLC: Deseret Book, 2016, pp. 77–78, 107; e) Confusion among scholars as to whether the white or brown seer stone is "Gazelem" referred to in Alma 37:23 used to translate the *Book of Mormon*: Quinn, Van Wagoner, Walker and Vogel believe that the brown seer stone is "Gazelem" and was used for most of the translation of the *Book of Mormon*. Ashurst-McGee, Mackay and Frederickson seem to favor the white stone being "Gazelem", Mackay and Fredericks pp. 105–109; 39–44, 66–77, 167. Perhaps both the brown and white seer stones were used during the translation of the Book of Mormon after the Urim and Thummim were taken away as suggested by Gerrit J. Dirkmaat and Michael Hubbard MacKay, "Firsthand Witness Accounts of the Translation Process," Religious Studies Center, BYU, Winter, 2021, note 32. Accessed June 19, 2022 at: https://rsc.byu.edu/coming-forth-book-mormon/firsthand-witness-accounts-translation-process.

121. "Mormonism—No. II," Tiffany's Monthly, (July 1859), p. 164, cited in, Matthew B. Brown, *All Things Restored*, American Fork: UT, Covenant Books, 2000, p. 53–54 and in Turley, Jensen, and Ashurst-McGee, "Joseph the Seer," *Ensign*. October 2015. See also Matthew B. Brown, *All Things Restored Confirming the Authenticity of LDS Beliefs*, American Fork, UT, 2000, p. 53–54.

122. Wilford Woodruff, Journal, February 19, 1842, Church History Library; D. Michael Quinn, *Early Mormonism and the Magic World View*, Salt Lake City: Signature Books, 1998, pp. 242, 244. Michael H. MacKay and Nicholas J. Frederick, *Joseph Smith's Seer Stones*, SLC: Deseret Book, 2016, pp. 127–128.

123. David Whitmer, *An Address to All Believers in Christ*, 1887, pp. 30–33, 53–61.

124. D. Michael Quinn, *Early Mormonism and the Magic World View*, Salt Lake City: Signature Books, 1998, pp. 246. "According to Brigham Young, 'Joseph found two small ones on the beach in Nauvoo—a little larger than a black walnut without the shock on.'" For descriptions

and provenance of the hollow green and sandy Nauvoo seer stones see Mackay and Frederickson, pp.145–150. Both D. Michael Quinn and Brigham Young are cited in http://research.omicsgroup.org/index.php/Seerstone(Latter_Day_Saints), accessed 3-19-2018; General Church Minutes, 30 Sept. 1855, CHL, CR 100 318.

125. Orson Pratt, "Two Days' Meeting at Brigham City, June 27, 1874," *Millennial Star*, August 11, 1874, pp. 498-499, quoted in MacKay and Frederick, *Joseph Smith's Seer Stones*, p. 126.

126. Michael Hubbard MacKay and Nicholas J. Frederick, *Joseph Smith's Seer Stones*, BYU-Deseret Book, 2016, pp. 129–130. This book is essential for studying Joseph Smith's seer stones.

127. MacKay, p. 126–127; Richard E. Turley Jr., "Joseph the Seer," *Ensign*, October, 2015.

128. MacKay and Fredericks, p. 79; D. Michael Quinn, *Early Mormonism and the Magic World View*, 1998, p. 250; *DHC* 7:285; Wilford Woodruff's Journal, Dec. 27, 1841.

Notes to Chapter 17

129. Email correspondence from Mark E. Mitchell to Steven A. Wilden, May 23, 2018. Several emails were shared between Brother Mark Mitchell and myself on the subject of "The Book of Mormon and the Godhead in the Light of Joseph Smith's First Vision."

130. Woodruff, Wilford. *The Discourses of Wilford Woodruff*, ed. G. Homer Durham. Salt Lake City, 1968, p. 62, quoted in Cannon, Elaine Anderson, "Mother in Heaven," *Encyclopedia of Mormonism*, New York: Macmillan, 1992, 2:961, accessed May 29, 2018 online at: https://contentdm.lib.byu.edu/digital/collection/EoM/id/3962.

131. Baugh, Alexander L. "Parting the Veil: Joseph Smith's Seventy-six Documented Visionary Experiences, " *BYU Studies*, volume 38, no. 1 (Provo, UT: BYU Press, 1999): pp. 22-69; enlarged and reprinted in Welch, John W., editor, *Opening The Heavens, Accounts of Divine Manifestations,* Provo: Brigham Young University Press, 2005, pp. 265–326; See Welch, pp. 280-283 where Joseph Smith and other witnesses saw the Father and the Son four more times between 1831–1836, after his First Vision of 1820; See visionary experiences, numbers 33,

36, 37 and 41, in Welch, pp. 311–312; See D&C 76:19–23 and D&C 137.

In another account, it is reported that Joseph Smith, Sidney Rigdon and Zebedee Coltrin saw together a vision of our Heavenly Father and Heavenly Mother, seated together on thrones, which was recorded in the journal of late nineteenth-century apostle Abraham H. Cannon, the son of George Q. Cannon, the Prophet Joseph Smith's cousin, as follows:

> One day the Prophet Joseph Smith asked him (Zebedee Coltrin) and Sidney Rigdon to accompany him into the woods to pray. When they had reached a secluded spot Joseph laid down on his back and stretched out his arms. He told the brethren to lie one on each arm and then shut their eyes. After they had prayed he told them to open their eyes. They did so and they saw a brilliant light surrounding a pedestal which seemed to rest on the ground. They closed their eyes and again prayed. They then saw, on opening them, the Father seated upon a throne; they prayed again and on looking saw the Mother also; after praying and looking the fourth time they saw the Savior added to the group. He had auburn brown, rather long, wavy hair and appeared quite young. (*Journal of Abraham H. Cannon*, 25 Aug. 1880, LDS archives, Church History Library, Salt Lake City, Utah)

132. Jessee, Ashurst-McGee and Jensen, *The Joseph Smith Papers, Journals, Volume 1*, 1832–1839, SLC: The Church Historian's Press, 2008, pp. 87–89; *Acts* 7:55–56.

133. Dean C. Jessee, *The Papers of Joseph Smith*, Salt Lake City: Deseret Book, Volume 1, 1989, pp. 3–7, 124–127, 429–431; Dean C. Jessee, *The Papers of Joseph Smith*, SLC: Deseret Book, Volume 2, 1992, pp. 69, 79; Dean C. Jessee, *Personal Writings of Joseph Smith*, SLC: Deseret Book, 2002, pp. 226–232; Doctrine and Covenants, Section 2.

134. Doctrine and Covenants, Sections 6, 11, 14–16 were given by the use of the Urim and Thummim. https://www.churchofjesuschrist.org/study/scriptures/gs/urim-and-thummim.

135. Brodie, *No Man Knows My History…*, Alfred A. Knopf, 1945, p. 25, or an "evolutionary fantasy" in Brodie, "Supplement," *No Man Knows My History…*, Fawn Brodie, 1971, 1973 and Vintage Books, 1995, pp. 409, 405–425. All of these theories and misstatements of history have been shown to be inadequate or have been overturned by historians in recent

years. Other critics, such as the Rev. Wesley P. Walters, claimed in 1967 there were "no revivals" in Palmyra in 1820, nor from 1817 until 1824. See Wesley P. Walters, *Bulletin of the Evangelical Theological Society* 10, Fall 1967; Wesley P. Walters, "New Light on Mormon Origins From the Palmyra Revival," *Dialogue: A Journal of Mormon Thought,* 4, Spring 1969: pp. 61, 67, 77 note 44; See rebuttal to Walters claims by D. Michael Quinn, "Joseph Smith's Religious Camp Meeting," *Dialogue Internet,* July 12, 2006. Enlarged December 20, 2006. pp. 2–3 and note 2.

136. Dean C. Jessee, *The Papers of Joseph Smith*, Salt Lake City: Deseret Book, Volume 1, 1989, p. 127.

137. John W. Welch, ed., *Opening The Heavens, Accounts of Divine Manifestations, 1820–1844*, SLC/Provo: Brigham Young University Press/Desert Book, 2005, p. 1.

138. Ibid, p. 1–2.

139. MS, 1-2, Church *Archives; Compare History of the Church,* 2:198–99; quoted in John W. Welch, ed., *Opening the Heavens: Accounts of Divine Manifestations, 1820–1844,* Provo, UT: Brigham Young University Press, 2005, p. 30, note 8.

140. Andrew Marshall, "What's missing in Joseph Smith's historical record?" *Deseret News*, Salt Lake City, Utah, February 5, 2009. Bruce Van Orden, "I have a Question: What do we know about the location of the Garden of Eden?" Ensign, (Jan. 1994). Accessed November 1, 2020 at: https://www.churchofjesuschrist.org/study/ensign/1994/01/i-have-a-question/what--do-we-know-about-the-location-of-the-garden-of-eden.

141. Marshall, *Deseret News*, February 5, 2009.

142. Ibid.

143. Elder Richard J. Maynes, "The First Vision: Key to Truth," *Ensign*, June 2017.

Notes to Chapter 18

144. Wesley P. Walters, "New Light on Mormon Origins from Palmyra Revival," *Bulletin of the Evangelical Theological Society*, no. 4 (fall 1967), pp. 227-244; reprinted, Wesley P. Walters, "New Light on Mormon Origins," *Dialogue*, volume 4, no. 1, 1969; Rev. Walters

shared his views with the Presbyterian Church in: Walters, Wesley P. 1980. "Joseph Smith's First Vision Story Revisited." *Journal of Pastoral Practice* 4; Steven C. Harper, "Evaluating Three Arguments against Joseph Smith's First Vision," in *Exploring the First Vision*, ed. Samuel Alonzo Dodge and Steven C. Harper, Provo, UT: Religious Studies Center, 2012, pp. 307–308; Steven C. Harper, *Joseph Smith's First Vision, A Guide to the Historical Accounts*, Provo: Deseret Book, 2012, pp. 67-83. Wesley Walters claimed that because there was a gap in the reported revivals at Palmyra between 1819- 1823, therefore Joseph could not of had any vision during that time. Wesley P. Walters, "New Light on Mormon Origins from Palmyra (N. Y.) Revival," *Bulletin of the Evangelical Theological Society*, Vol. 10, no. 4 (Fall 1967), p. 228.

145. Dan Vogel, *Joseph Smith: The Making of a Prophet*, Salt Lake City: Signature Books, 2004, p. xv.

146. Oliver Cowdery to William W. Phelps, December 1834, "Letter III," *The Latter Day Saints' Messenger and Advocate*, Volume 1, Number 3, Kirtland, Ohio, pp. 42-43; William Smith, *William Smith on Mormonism*, Lamoni, IA: 1883, p. 6; *Deseret Evening News*, January 20, 1894, p. 11. Larry C. Porter, "Reverend George Lane—Good 'Gifts,' Much 'Grace,' Marked 'Usefullness,'" *Exploring the First Vision*, ed. Samuel Alonzo Dodge and Steven C. Harper, Provo, UT: Religious Studies Center, 2012, pp. 199–226.

147. John Wesley, "Thoughts upon Methodism," in *The Methodist Societies: History, Nature, and Design*, ed. Rupert E. Davies, vol. 9 of *The Bicentennial Edition of the Works of John Wesley*, ed. W. Reginald Ward and Richard P. Heitzenrater (Nashville: Abingdon, 1976–), pp. 527.

148. Eber D. Howe, *Mormonism Unveiled*, Painesville, Ohio, 1834, pp. 11, 57, 278.

149. Lucy Mack Smith, author, Scot and Maurine Proctor, editors, *History of Joseph Smith By His Mother*, SLC: Bookcraft, 1996, p. 131; Richard Lloyd Anderson, "Joseph Smith's New York Reputation Reappraised," *Brigham Young University Studies*, volume 10, no. 3 (Summer 1970): p. 285. For more details, see Richard Lloyd Anderson, "The Reliability of the Early History of Lucy and Joseph Smith," *Dialogue: A Journal of Mormon Thought*, vol. 4, no. 2, Summer 1969, pp.16, 19.

150. Fawn Brodie, *No Man Knows My History The Life of Joseph Smith*, Knopf, first edition, 1945, Vintage Books, 1995, pp. 1–15, 24; J. Spencer Fluhman, "Anti-Mormonism and the Question of Religious

Authenticity" in *Antebellum America: Journal of Religion & Society*, Volume 7, 2005, pp. 1-9; Hugh Nibley, *No, Ma'am, That's Not History*, Salt Lake City: Bookcraft, 1960, p. 5; *The New York Times Book Review*, November 25, 1945, p. 5, quoted in Fawn M. Brodie, Wikipedia. https://en.wikipedia.org/wiki/Fawn_M._Brodie. Accessed on internet March 18, 2018.

151. Jan Shipps, *Sojourner in the Promised Land: Forty Years among the Mormons*, University of Illinois Press, 2000, p. 165. Other secular twentieth-century historians praised Fawn Brodie's biography of Joseph Smith including Bernard DeVoto, Wallace Stegner, and Carl Sandburg. Fawn's uncle, Elder David O. McKay, a member of the Quorum of the Twelve Apostles said publicly several months after *No Man Knows My History* was published: "My heart aches this morning because one who was pretty close to me has failed. She has violated conventions in childhood and broken through the fence of consideration and decency. She found the poison grain of unbelief and now languishes in spiritual apathy and decay." Vardis Fisher, the noted Utah novelist, stated in a review for the *New York Times* that the book was, "almost more of a novel than a biography because she rarely hesitates to give the content of a mind or to explain motives which at best can only be surmised." Newell G. Bringhurst, Editor, *Reconsidering No Man Knows My History*, Logan: Utah State University, 1996, pp. 46, 49.

152. Fawn Brodie, *No Man Knows My History…*, 1945 edition, p. 84; Fawn Brodie, *No Man Knows My History: The Life of Joseph Smith,* New York: Alfred A. Knopf, 2nd ed., 1971, p. 403. According to Fawn Brodie, Joseph Smith was a "genius of improvisation."

153. Fawn Brodie, *No Man Knows My History…*, 1945 edition, p. 410; PofGP, *Joseph Smith--History*, 1:19; Milton V. Backman, Jr., and James B. Allen, "Membership of Certain of Joseph Smith's Family in the Western Presbyterian Church of Palmyra," *Brigham Young University Studies*, volume 10 number 4 (1970): pp. 482–484.

154. Orson Pratt, *Interesting Account of Several Remarkable Visions*, Edinburgh, Scotland, 1840 (missionary pamphlet), quoted in Milton V. Backman, Jr., Confirming Witnesses of the First Vision, *Ensign*, January, 1986. Available online at lds.org.

155. Fawn M. Brodie, *No Man Knows My History…*, 1945 edition, p. 84.

156. Fawn M. Brodie, *No Man Knows My History*, 1945, pp. 1–15, 24, 83–87; Joseph Smith and Martin Harris begin translating the gold

plates in April 1828, *Joseph Smith Papers, History*, Volume 1, 2012, p. 244; Scot Facer Proctor and Maurine Jensen Proctor, editors, *The Revised and Enhance History of Joseph Smith By His Mother*, SLC: Bookcraft, 1996, p. 223; Larry C. Porter, "A Study of the Origins of the Church of Jesus Christ of Latter-day Saints in the States of New York and Pennsylvania, 1816–1831." PhD diss., Brigham Young University, pp. 251–252.

157. Fawn M. Brodie, *No Man Knows My History…*, 1945 edition, p. 85.

158. Founder of the Mormon History Association, Professor of History at Utah State University and later LDS Church Historian, Leonard J. Arrington's provided well-conceived criticisms of *No Man Knows My History* in "Scholarly Studies of Mormonism in the Twentieth Century" published in *Dialogue: A Journal of Mormon Thought* in 1966, which Fawn Brodie dismissed without a reply; see Fawn M. Brodie's Letter to Dean Brimhall, dated 18 November 1967 where Brodie wrote that Arrington "was of the school that was so emotionally committed to the church that the truth will always elude them"; see Bringhurst cite following, pp. 179, 301, note 80; Newell G. Bringhurst, *Fawn McKay Brodie: A Biographer's Life* pp 35-37, Norman: University of Oklahoma Press, 1999, p. 289, note 17; Louis Midgley, "The Legend and Legacy of Fawn M. Brodie," abstract, Review of *Fawn McKay Brodie: A Biographer's Life* (1999), by Newell G. Bringhurst., *FARMS Review of Books*, volume 13, number 1, 2001, pp. 21–71., pp. 25, 28, 38; Louis Midgley, "F. M.Brodie—The Fasting Hermit and Very Saint of Ignorance: A Biographer and Her Legend," *FARMS Review of Books*, volume 8, number 2, 1996, pp. 171–75, 190–210.

159. Letters of William H. Reeder to Fawn M. Brodie, May 23, 1946 and June 19, 1946. William Reeder was President of the New England States Mission and issued Fawn Brodie's invitation or summons to a priesthood council for heresy related to her biography of Joseph Smith that Fawn Brodie did not attend. President Reeder later wrote her excommunication letter cited above. A PDF "copy" of both letters are in the possession of the author which were published by the Salamander Society, http://www.salamandersociety.com/x-files/460523brodie_excom.pdf. Fawn Brodie's attitudes about Joseph Smith, Mormonism and her excommunication were also chronicled by Newell G. Bringhurst, *Fawn McKay Brodie: A Biographer's Life*. Norman: University of Oklahoma Press, 1999, p. 289, note 17.

160. Shirley E. Stephenson, "FAWN McKAY BRODIE: AN ORAL HISTORY INTERVIEW," *Dialogue A Journal of Mormon Thought*, Arlington: Virginia, Summer 1981, volume 14, number 2, p. 106. Center for Oral and Public History, California State University at Fullerton, Shirley E. Stephenson's interview with Fawn M. Brodie, November 30, 1975.

161. Shirley E. Stephenson, "FAWN McKAY BRODIE: AN ORAL HISTORY INTERVIEW," *Dialogue A Journal of Mormon Thought*, Arlington: Virginia, Summer 1981, volume 14, number 2, p. 103.

162. Steven C. Harper, "Evaluating Three Arguments against Joseph Smith's First Vision," in *Exploring the First Vision*, ed. Samuel Alonzo Dodge and Steven C. Harper, Provo, UT: Religious Studies Center, 2012, pp. 307–23; Fawn Brodie, *No Man Knows My History…*, 1995, pp. 24, 405, Supplement.

163. Shirley E. Stephenson, "FAWN McKAY BRODIE: AN ORAL HISTORY INTERVIEW," *Dialogue A Journal of Mormon Thought*, Arlington: Virginia, Summer 1981, volume 14, number 2, p. 105; "Biography of Fawn McKay Brodie," interview with Shirley E. Stephenson, 30 November 1975, Oral History Collection, Fullerton State University, Fullerton, CA, p. 10; Fawn Brodie, *No Man Knows My History…*, 1995 edition, p. 418; Charles L. Cohen, "No Man Knows My Psychology...," *Brigham Young University Studies*, volume 44, number 1, (2005): pp. 55–78.

164. Louis Midgley, "The Legend and Legacy of Fawn Brodie." *FARMS Review of Books*. Neal A. Maxwell Institute. Provo: BYU. volume 13, number 1, 2001, pp. 21–71. ISSN: 2168-3123 (online) Review of *Fawn McKay Brodie: A Biographer's Life* (1999), by Newell G. Bringhurst.

165. Shirley E. Stephenson, "FAWN McKAY BRODIE: AN ORAL HISTORY INTERVIEW," *Dialogue A Journal of Mormon Thought*, Summer 1989, volume 14, number 2, p. 104.

166. Fawn Brodie, *No Man Knows My History…*, 1971, 1995 edition, p. 25.

167. Steven C. Harper, "Evaluating Three Arguments against Joseph Smith's First Vision," in *Exploring the First Vision*, ed. Samuel Alonzo Dodge and Steven C. Harper, Provo, UT: Religious Studies Center, 2012, pp. 307–323; Bringhurst, *Fawn McKay Brodie*, p.106.

168. Richard L. Bushman, interview by Samuel Dodge, July 31, 2009, Provo, UT, quoted in Steven C. Harper, Steven C. Harper, "Evaluating

Three Arguments against Joseph Smith's First Vision," in *Exploring the First Vision*, pp. 307-323; Dean C. Jessee, James B. Allen (July 27, 2009), Richard L. Anderson (July 29, 2009), Larry C. Porter (July 30, 2009), Richard L. Bushman (July 31, 2009), Milton V. Backman Jr. (August 12, 2009), interviews by Samuel A. Dodge, transcriptions in possession of Steven C. Harper.

169. Prof. Marvin S Hill writes on "unusual excitement" with Richard L. Bushman and Milton V. Backman comments over Rev. Wesley Walters 1967 and 1969 Dialogue articles. see "The First Vision Controversy. . ."Dialogue: A Journal of Mormon Thought, (Summer 1982):31-46.

170. Steven C. Harper, "Evaluating Three Arguments against Joseph Smith's First Vision, "in *Exploring the First Vision*, pp. 307-323; Quinn, D. Michael, "JOSEPH SMITH'S EXPERIENCE OF A METHODIST "CAMP-MEETING" IN 1820." Dialogue Internet E-Paper #3 July 12, 2006. Enlarged December 20, 2006. p. 19, notes 70 and 71. https://www.dialoguejournal.com/wpcontent/uploads/2010/04/QuinnPaperless.Pdf.

171. Benaijah Williams, diaries, in possession of Michael Brown, Philadelphia, PA, quoted in Steven C. Harper, "Evaluating Three Arguments against Joseph Smith's First Vision," in *Exploring the First Vision*, pp. 307–323.

172. Marvin S. Hill, "The First Vision Controversy: A Critique and Reconciliation," *Dialogue: A Journal of Mormon Thought*, (Summer 1982), volume 15, no. 2, p. 43.

173. Marvin S. Hill, "The First Vision Controversy: A Critique and Reconciliation," *Dialogue: A Journal of Mormon Thought*, 1982, volume 15, no. 2, p. 43, continued.

174. Richard L. Bushman, *Joseph Smith And The Beginnings Of Mormonism*, Urbana and Chicago: University of Illinois Press, 1984, pp. 43-188. Professor Bushman gives a fine scripturally predicted and historically verified account of the four great achievements of the Prophet Joseph Smith: the First Vision; the Translation of the Book of Mormon; the establishment of the Church of Christ which included receiving priesthood authority by divine visitations from angels or resurrected former prophets; and the Restoration of All Things. Dr. Bushman shows that unlike Alexander Campbell who was a child of the Enlightenment, as shown by his Christian theological writings, Joseph Smith on the other hand was more like a prophet and seer, bringing forth new revelations,

doctrines, and ordinances whose writings both in the Book of Mormon and in the Doctrine and Covenants were more like the Bible.

175. Shirley E. Stephenson, "FAWN McKAY BRODIE: AN ORAL HISTORY INTERVIEW," *Dialogue A Journal of Mormon Thought*, Arlington: Virginia, Summer 1981, volume 14, number 2, p. 107.

Notes on Chapter 19

176. Elder Bruce R. McConkie, "Joseph Smith---The Mighty Prophet of the Restoration," *Ensign*, April 1976; Elder Bruce R. McConkie, "Once or Twice in a Thousand Years," *Conference Report*, October 1967, p. 43.

177. Louis Ginzberg, *The Legends of the Jews*, Philadelphia: The Jewish Publication Society of America, 1948, 2:7, 5:299, note 201; Raphael Patai, *The Messiah Texts*, New York: Avon Books, 1979, p. 165; Charles C. Torrey, "The Messiah Son of Ephraim, *Journal of Biblical Literature*, Volume 66, 1947, p. 253; Quoted in Matthew B. Brown, *All Things Restored*, American Fork, UT: Covenant Communications, 2000, p. 34.

Notes to Chapter 20

178. Israel Daniel Rupp, *An Original History of the Religious Denominations at Present Existing in the United States*, Philadelphia, 1844, pp. 404-410; using the [July?]1843 letter of Joseph Smith to Daniel Rupp and its almost identical account of the First Vision as found in the Wentworth letter.

179. Joseph Smith, Jr., "Church History," *Times And Seasons*, Nauvoo, IL: The Church of Jesus Christ of Latter-day Saints, (Volume 3, Number 9, March 1, 1842), p. 707. See also the Wentworth Letter, 1842 (JSP, H1:494).

180. David Whitmer, *An Address to All Believers in Christ,* Richmond, Mo.: n.p., 1887, p. 12, quoted in Elder Russell M. Nelson, "A Treasured Testament," *Ensign*, July 1993, p. 61). In David Whitmer's own words he describes Joseph's translation of part of the plates of the Book of Mormon using the seer stone.

> Joseph Smith would put the seer stone into a hat, and put his face in the hat, drawing it closely around his face to exclude the light; and in the darkness the spiritual light would shine. A piece of something resembling parchment would appear, and on that

appeared the writing. One character at a time would appear, and under it was the interpretation in English. Brother Joseph would read off the English to Oliver Cowdery, who was his principal scribe, and when it was written down and repeated to Brother Joseph to see if it was correct, then it would disappear, and another character with the interpretation would appear. Thus the Book of Mormon was translated by the gift and power of God, and not by any power of man. (David Whitmer, "An Address to All Believers in Christ," Richmond, Mo.: n.p., 1887, p. 12)

Two pictures: "The manner of translation was as wonderful as the discovery. By putting his finger on one of the characters and imploring divine aid, then looking through the Urim and Thummim, he would see the import written in plain English on a screen placed before him. After delivering this to his emanuensi,[sic] he would again proceed in the same manner and obtain the meaning of the next character, and so on till he came to the part of the plates which were sealed up." (Truman Coe, Presbyterian Minister living among the Saints in Kirtland, 1836.)

"I cheerfully certify that I was familiar with the manner of Joseph Smith's translating the book of Mormon. He translated the most of it at my Father's house. And I often sat by and saw and heard them translate and write for hours together. Joseph never had a curtain drawn between him and his scribe while he was translating. He would place the director in his hat, and then place his [face in his] hat, so as to exclude the light, and then [read] to his scribe the words as they appeared before him." (Elizabeth Ann Whitmer Cowdery, Oliver Cowdery's wife, 1870. Fair Mormon, accessed December 30, 2020 at: https://www.fairmormon.org /answers/Joseph_Smith/Seer_stones/%22Rock_in_hat%22_used_for_Book_of_Mormon_translation#Question:_Did_Joseph_Fielding_Smith_say_that_it_was_not_reasonable_for_Joseph_Smith_to_use_a_seer_stone_to_translate_the_Book_of_Mormon.3F.)

181. Oliver Cowdery to W. W. Phelps, Letter 8, undated, ca. September–October 1835, printed in *Messenger and Advocate*, 2 October 1835: p. 199; quoted in Scott H. Faulring, "An Examination of the 1829 "Articles of the Church of Christ" in Relation to Section 20 of the Doctrine and Covenants, *BYU Studies Journal*, volume 43, number 4 (2004): pp. 64–67.

182. Oliver Cowdery's 1829 Manuscript, "A Commandment from God or Articles of the Church of Christ," LDS Church Archives, quoted in Robert J. Woodford, "The Historical Development of the Doctrine and Covenants," 3 vols., Ph.D. Dissertation, Brigham Young University, 1974, 1:288; Hiram Page to William [?], a letter of March 4, 1848, Fishing River, photocopy of original archives, Reorganized Church of Jesus Christ of Latter Day Saints Independence, Missouri; Brian Q. Cannon and *BYU Studies* Staff, "Priesthood Restoration Documents," *BYU Studies*, volume 35, number 4 (1995-1996): pp. 163–207, notes 25 and 94.

183. Elder Dallin H. Oaks, "Elder Oaks Testifies before US Congressional Subcommittee," May 13, 1992, Accessed online on October 29, 2020 at: https://www.churchofjesuschrist.org/study/ensign/1992/07/news-of-the-church/elder-oaks-testifies-before-u-s-congressional-subcommittee; Congressional Record, House: Hearings Before The Subcommittee On Civil And Constitutional Rights Of The Committee On The Judiciary, House Of Representatives, One Hundred Second Congress, Second Session, On H.R. 2797, Religious Freedom Restoration Act Of 1991, May 13 And 14, 1992, Serial No. 99, Accessed online October 29, 2020 at: https://www.justice.gov/sites/default/files/jmd/legacy/2014/07/13/hear-99-1992.pdf; Senate: The Religious Freedom Restoration Act, Hearing Before The Committee On The Judiciary, United States Senate, One Hundred Second Congress, Second Session, On S. 2969, A Bill To Protect The Free Exercise Of Religion, September 18, 1992, Serial No. J 102-82, Washington, D.C., Accessed online on October 29, 2020 at: https://www.justice. gov/sites/default/files/jmd/legacy/2014/02/13/hear-j-102-82-1992.pdf.

184. Spencer W. Kimball, *The Teachings of Spencer W. Kimball*, ed. Edward L. Kimball, Salt Lake City: Bookcraft, 1982, pp. 428–30, quoted in Milton V. Backman, Jr., "Confirming Witnesses of the First Vision," *Ensign*, Jan. 1986, pp. 32–37.

185. President Russell M. Nelson, "Come Follow Me," 189th Annual General Conference of The Church of Jesus Christ of Latter-day Saints in the Conference Center in Salt Lake City, Sunday Morning Session, April 7, 2019, *Ensign* magazine, May, 2019. Accessedhttps://www. churchofjesuschrist.org/study/ ensign/2019/05/46 nelson.

Notes to Appendix 1

186. 1 Enoch 39:2, 7; 40:1-7; 46:1-5; 48:2-4, 11, Richard Laurence trans., reprinted 1821, 1882 editions, Thousand Oaks, CA: Artisan Sales, 1980; "Trinity," Stanford Encyclopedia of Philosophy, Nov. 20, 2020. Accessed at: https://plato.stanford.edu/entries/trinity/ Dec. 26, 2020.

187. Richard R. Hopkins. *How Greek Philosophy Corrupted the Christian Concept of God*, 1998, 2009, pp. 11, 413, 441; Origen, *De Principiis* 1:32, in ANF 4:377; Tertullian in *Elucidations*, ANF 3:63.

188. James L. Barker, *Apostasy From The Divine Church*, Kate Montgomery Barker, Printed by Deseret News Press, Salt Lake City, Utah, 1960, pp. 230-231; Alfred Weber, *History of Philosophy*, New York: Charles Scribner's Sons, 1896, 1904, translated from the Fifth French Edition, pp. 20, 75–76, 84–85, 88–89, 116–117, 174 on *immaterialism*, cited in J. Barker's book.

189. Kenneth S. Latourette, *A History of Christianity: Volume I: Beginnings to 1500*, Revised New York: HarperCollins, 1975, pp.144–146.

190. Ted A. Campbell, *Christian Confessions: A Historical Introduction*, Louisville, KY: Westminster John Knox Press, 1st edition (March 1, 1996) 1996, p. 41.

191. John Burnaby, *The Belief of Christendom: A Commentary on the Nicene Creed*, London: National Society, S.P.C.K., 1959, p. 70.

192. "Council of Nicaea" *Encyclopedia Britannica* https://www.britannica.com/event/ Council-of-Nicaea-Christianity-325. Accessed July 7, 2019. "Homoousios," *Encycl. Britannica*, 30 Jul. 2019.

193. Roman Rite, Order of Mass, "What We Believe," US Catholic Council of Bishops. Accessed online at: www.usccb.org on September 20, 2020. Source for the text of the Nicene Creed.

194. Steven D. Cone, *Theology from the Great Tradition*, Bloomsbury Publishing; 22 February 2018. ISBN 978-0-567-67002-1. p. 417; "Homoousios," *Encyclopedia Britannica*, 30 Jul. 2019.

195. Katie Lambert and Danielle Wagner, "11 Powerful Truths About Our Heavenly Mother from Prophets and Apostles," LDS Living (online), May 9, 2012; Susa Young Gates, *History of the Young Ladies' Mutual Improvement Association*, No. 16. Truths-About-Heavenly-Mother-from-Prophets-and-Apostles/s/85272. Accessed 9-20-2020. For more

historical teachings about "Mother in Heaven" see, Daniel H. Ludlow, editor, *Encyclopedia of Mormonism*, 1992, Volume 2, p. 961; David L. Paulson and Martin Polido, "A Mother There: A Survey of Historical Teachings about Mouther in Heaven," *BYU Studies*, 2011, Volume 50: Issue 1, pp. 70–97. "Mother in Heaven," Gospel Topics, topics.lds.org. Topic: Mother in Heaven.

196. Warren H. Carroll, *The Building of Christendom: A History of the Christian Church*, Volume 2, West Chester, PA: Christendom Press, 1987, p. 12.

Notes to Appendix 2

197. George R. S. Meade, *Pistis Sophia*, London, 1896, pp. 1-3, 10-12, 15-19, 278-281; Steven A. Wilden, "A Gnostic Presence...", *Ancient* American, December 2014, volume 18, issue105, pp. 35–39.

198. A. Burt Horsley, *Peter And The Popes*, S.L.C., Utah: Bookcraft Inc., 1989, pp. 36.

199. *Catechism of the Catholic Church,* Second Edition, 1997, p. 30; Irenaeus, *Against Heresies*, 3, 3:1; *Patrologia Graeca* 7:848. Irenaeus can "reckon up" bishops called by apostles, ANF 1:415.

200. a) Greek influence and changes to the Godhead: James L. Barker, *Apostasy From The Devine Church*, 1960, pp. 222, 230–231; Richard R. Hopkins, *How Greek Philosophy Corrupted the Christian Concept of God*, 1998, 2009, pp. 11, 413, 441; Origen, *De Principiis* 2:9:6, in *ANF* 4:292; b) Loss of the office of Apostle in the Church: A. Burt Horsley, *Peter And The Popes*, S.L.C., Utah: Bookcraft, Inc., 1989, pp. 33-41; c) Celibacy of the Clergy: Diderot, Denis. "Celibacy." *The Encyclopedia of Diderot & d'Alembert*, 1752, volume 2, pp. 801-806, Transl. by Siân Reynolds, University of Michigan Press, 2013; d) Form of baptism changed: Origen mentions infant baptism in 3rd century in his *Homilies on Leviticus* 8.3.11, *Commentary on Romans* 5.9, and *Homily on Luke* 14.5; e) No record of apostolic succession from Peter, Irenaeus, ANF 1:415.

201. "Byzantine Empire," Wikipedia, accessed September 20, 2020 at: https://en.wikipedia.org/ wiki/Byzantine_Empire. Koch, Carl (1994). *The Catholic Church: Journey, Wisdom, and Mission. Early Middle Ages*: St. Mary's Press. Wikipedia, accessed on September 19, 2021.

202. Gregorian Mission, Wikipedia, Sept. 20, 2020 at: https://en.wikipedia.org/wiki/Gregorian_ mission.

203. *Encyclopedia Britannica*, 1946 ed., 12:377, quoted in McConkie, *Mormon Doctrine*, 1966, p. 274.

204. a) Waldensian Massacre: https://en.wikipedia.org/wiki/M%C3%A9rindol_massacre; b) Spanish Inquisition: https://www.britannica.com/topic/Spanish-Inquisition; c)` Joan of Arc: Andrew Lang, *The Story of Joan of Arc*, London, 1906; d) William Tyndale: David Daniell, *William Tyndale A Biography*, Yale University Press, 2001; d) The German Peasants Revolt: https://www.thoughtco. com/german-peasants-war-4150166.

205. Joseph Strayer, "Slavery, Slave Trade," *Dictionary of the Middle Ages*, Vol. 11. New York: Scribner, 1982.

206. a) Catholic Church Membership: "Pubblicazione dell'Annuario Pontificio e dell'Annuario Statistico della Chiesa, 25.03.2020" (in Italian). Holy See Press Office. 25 March 2020; b) Eastern Orthodox Church membership: Brien and Palmer, *The Atlas of Religion*, 2007, University of California Berkeley, p. 22. "Counter-Reformation"; Wikipedia.

207. *World Christian Trends*, William Carey Library, 2001. p. 272. "List of Christian Denominations," Wikipedia, accessed September 29, 2020. https://en.wikipedia.org/wiki/List_of_Christian_denominations_by_number_of_members. "Act of Supremacy"; "Church of England," Wikipedia.

208. "Separation of Church and State," Wikipedia. https://en.wikipedia.org/wiki/Separation_of_church_and_state. Accessed September 29, 2020.

209. "Nicene Creed, Christianity," Wikipedia accessed Sept. 29, 2020. https://www. britannica.com/topic/Nicene-Creed.

210. In his preface to volume three of *Doctrines of Salvation*, Elder McConkie recorded a tribute to President Smith given to him on the 80th anniversary of this birth (July 19, 1956) by his associates in the Quorum of the Twelve Apostles:

> In his vigorous denunciation of the theories of men which would negate the truths of the restored gospel, he has often drawn the criticisms of some of the exponents of the theories he has assailed, but seldom has he failed to win the admiration and respect of his severest critics because of his scholarship and the

> consistency of his course, which is as undeviating as the stars of heaven. No one ever has had occasion to question where he stood on any controversial issue...In his profound gospel writings and in his theological dissertations, he has given to his associates and to the Church a rich legacy which will immortalize his name among the faithful... (Improvement Era, July 1956, vol. 59, No. 7:495; DofS 3:v-vi)

Notes to Appendix 3

211. Cook, Lyndon W. (2009-09-03). *The Words of Joseph Smith* (Kindle Locations 524-529). Deseret Book Company. Kindle Edition, quoted in Chad Nielsen, "Do all Prophets and Apostles See God?", *TIMES AND SEASONS*, April 30, 2022,https://www.timesandseasons.org/index.php/2022/04/do-all-prophets-and-apostles-see-god/, accessed June 8, 2022.
212. "Kirtland Council Minutes," 21 February 1835, CHL, Salt Lake City, Utah, quoted in Chad Nielsen, *TIMES AND SEASONS*, April 30, 2022.
213. Karl Ricks Anderson, *Joseph Smith's Kirtland: Eyewitness Accounts* (Salt Lake City: Deseret Book Company, 1989), pp. 107-113, quoted in Chad Nielsen, *TIMES AND SEASONS*, April 30, 2022.
214. Lorenzo Snow, Teachings of the Presidents of the Church: Lorenzo Snow (Salt Lake City: Church of Jesus Christ of Latter-day Saints, 2012), 238-239; Wilford Woodruff, in Collected Discourses Delivered by: President Wilford Woodruff, His Two Counselors, the Twelve Apostles, and Others, edited by Brian H. Stuy, 5 vol. (BHS Publishing, 1987–1992), 5:225.; citing John Lee Jones biography (no date) and Minutes of Salt Lake Temple dedication on 6–24 April 1893, 16th session, 13 April 1893.Ezra Taft Benson, "Five Marks of the Divinity of Jesus Christ," University of Utah fireside, 9 December 1979. Published in New Era 10 (December 1980): 48 and Ensign (December 2001); Boyd K. Packer, Conference Report, April 1971: 122–25, Boyd K. Packer, "The Witness," General Conference (webpage), accessed June 9, 2022, https://www.lds.org/ general-conference/print/2014/04/the-witness?lang=eng&clang=eng, quoted in Chad Nielsen, "Do all Prophets and Apostles See God?", *TIMES AND SEASONS*, April 30,

2022, https://www.timesandseasons.org/index.php/2022/04/do-all-prophets-and-apostles-see-god/ accessed June 8, 2022.

215. Interview with President Gordon B. Hinckley, ABC News Australia: Compass, November 9, 1997. http://www.lds-mormon.com/hinckley.shtml, quoted in Chad Nielsen, TIMES AND SEASONS, April 30, 2022.

216. Don Lattin, "Interview with President Gordon B. Hinckley," SF Gate, 13 April 1997. http://www.sfgate.com/news/article/SUNDAY-INTERVIEW-Musings-of-the-Main-Mormon-2846138.php#page-1, quoted in Chad Nielsen, TIMES AND SEASONS, April 30, 2022.

217. Spencer W. Kimball, "Revelation: The Word of the Lord to His Prophets," *CR*, April 1977.

218. GENERAL REFERENCES OF FIRST VISION ACCOUNTS: James B. Allen, "Eight Contemporary Accounts of the First Vision—What Do We Learn from Them?" *Improvement Era*, volume 73, April, 1970, pp. 4-13; For Levi Richards's report of the 1843 speech, see Andrew F. Ehat and Lyndon W. Cook, eds., *The Words of Joseph Smith,* (Provo, Utah: Brigham Young University Religious Studies Center, 1980), p. 215; Milton V. Bachman, *Eyewitness Accounts of the Restoration*, 1986, 239 pp.; Richard Lloyd Anderson, "Joseph Smith's Testimony of the First Vision," *Ensign*, April, 1996; Text and full historical introductions of eleven First Vision reports are found in Dean C. Jessee, *The Papers of Joseph Smith*, Volume 1, (SLC: Deseret Book, 1989), pp. 1--7, 124–27, 136-137, 265–67, 387–470 and Volume 2, pp. 68-69. Eight accounts are also found in Milton R. Backman, Jr., *Joseph Smith's First Vision*, 2d ed. (Salt Lake City: Bookcraft, 1980), p. 155–177; Thirteen First Vision accounts are included in John W. Welch, ed., *Opening The Heavens, Accounts of Divine Manifestations, 1820-1844*, (SLC/Provo: BYU Press/Desert Book, 2005), p. 1-75; Steven C. Harper, *Joseph Smith's First Vision: A Guide to the Historical Accounts*, (Salt Lake City: Deseret Book, 2012), p. 32–33; for the 1838 account in the *PofGP*, 1841 [*Draft 2*] written by Howard Coray of the 1838 original manuscript of *JS History* in George Robinson's handwriting, see *1838-1856, Volume A-1* recopied in June of 1839 to August 1843 by James Mulholland which includes the 1838 account of the First Vision, see original printed histories in, Karen Lynn Davidson, David J. Whittaker, Mark Ashurst-McGee, and Richard L. Jensen, editors, *The Joseph Smith Papers, Volume 1: Histories, 1832–1844* [these histories written or

directed by Joseph Smith], The Church Historians Press: Salt Lake City, Utah, 2012; Joseph Smith to John Wentworth, letter, "Church History"1842, *Times and Seasons*, volume 3, number. 9, March 1, 1842, pp. 706–710, T&S signed by JS, CHL; "Joseph Smith's History" [1838 account], *Times and Seasons*, volume 3, number. 10, March 15, 1842, pp. 726–728, 748-49; Joseph Smith, first person, to Israel Daniel Rupp, [July], 1843, letter written by W. W. Phelps for J. Smith; follows T&S, "Church History"; published in, Israel Daniel Rupp, *An Original History of the Religious Denominations at Present Existing in the United States*, 1844, CHL. For a good introduction to how the six volume Manuscript History of the Church was written, see Dean C. Jessee, "The Writing of Joseph Smith's History," *Brigham University Studies Quarterly*, volume 10, issue 4, (October 1, 1971). Accessed on-line at: https://scholarsarchive.byu.edu/byusq/vol11/iss4/8. For a more recent introduction of the same see, https://www.josephsmithpapers.org/doc/introduction-to-history-1838-1856-manuscript-history-of-the-church.

Notes to Appendix 4

219. Joseph Fielding Smith, *Teachings Of The Prophet Joseph Smith*, S.L.C., Utah: Deseret Book Company, 1938, 1977, pp. 342–362. Accessed online June 11, 2022 at: www. http:// boap.org/LDS/Joseph-Smith/Teachings/T6.html. This discourse was delivered on April 7, 1844 at Nauvoo, Illinois during a church conference and as the funeral sermon for friends and family of Elder King Follett. An early convert to the Church of Christ, later called The Church of Jesus Christ of Latter-day Saints, in 1831, he was a police constable and was notably the last prisoner released in the 1838 Mormon War in Missouri. Elder Follett died while building stone walls inside a well in Nauvoo when a tub of rocks fell on his head. As the men were lowering the bucket of rocks into the well the rope snapped. King Follett was buried with full Masonic honors. Joseph's sermon is not verbatim, but the notes taken by the four clerks make it one of the best recorded sermons of the Prophet. T&S, August 15, 1844; DHC 6:302-317. See also, "The King Follett Discourse" accessed June 10, 2022 at: https://www.churchofjesuschrist.org/study/history/topics/king-follett-discourse?lang=eng.

Abbreviations

HBKJV ...... *The Holy Bible*, King James Version, 1611, 1988; churchofjesuschrist.org.

BofM .... *The Book of Mormon*, trans. by Joseph Smith Jr., 1830, 1988; churchofjesuschrist.org.

D&C .... *The Doctrine and Covenants*, 1835, 1988; churchofjesuschrist.org.

PofGP .... *The Pearl of Great Price*, 1851, 1989; churchofjesuschrist.org.

JST .... Joseph Smith's New Translation of the Bible, 1867, 1970; Joseph Smith Translation, 1979.

PSDP .... *Pseudepigrapha* (and Apocryphal), *The Book of Enoch* or 1 Enoch, translated from the Ethiopic by Richard Laurence, 1821, John Thompson 1882 edition, Artisan reprint, 1983.

APCR ...... *Apocrypha, 2 Esdras*, Anchor Bible, vol. 42, 1982, trans. by J. M. Myers, Lutheran Theological Seminary.

ANF .... *The Ante-Nicene Fathers, Translations of the Writings of the Fathers Down to A.D. 325*. Edited by Alexander Roberts and James Donaldson. 10 vols. 1885–1887, Repr. 1968.

JS-H .... Joseph Smith—History from The Pearl of Great Price, 1838, 1851, 1989.

JD .... *Journal of Discourses*, George D. Watt, General Editor, 1854-1886, 26 volumes.

E&MS........*The Evening and Morning Star*, Newspaper, W. W. Phelps, Editor, Independence, MO, 1832–1833 and Oliver Cowdery, Editor, Kirtland, OH, 1833–1834.

MS............*The Latter-Day Saints Millennial Star*, Parley P. Pratt, first Editor, Manchester, England, 1840-1970, 130 volumes. MS is also an abbreviation for Manuscript in chapter 9.

PJS............*The Papers of Joseph Smith,* Dean C. Jessee, Editor, (1832-1844), 2 volumes. 1989, 1992.

TPJS..........*Teachings of The Prophet Joseph Smith*, comp. Joseph Fielding Smith, Jr., 1938, 1977.

WJS..........*The Words of Joseph Smith* (Nauvoo Discourses), Andrew F. Ehat and Lyndon W. Cook, 1980.

DBY..........*Discourses of Brigham Young*, compiled by John A. Widtsoe, 1954.

JSP............*The Joseph Smith Papers,* Ronald K. Esplin, Editor, (1828-1844), 2008–2021, 24 vols.

DHC.........Documentary History of The Church Of Jesus Christ Of Latter-Day Saints, Period 1 History of Joseph Smith the Prophet, (1805–1844), 1912, 1970, 6 of 8 volumes, incl. Volume 7 about Period 2 Manuscript History of Brigham Young and Volume 8 Index.

CHC.........*Comprehensive History of the Church* (1638–1930), B. H. Roberts, 1930, 6 volumes.

CHL..........Church History Library, The Church of Jesus Christ of Latter-day Saints, SLC, Utah.

DofS..........*Doctrines of Salvation*, Joseph Fielding Smith Jr., comp. Bruce R. McConkie, 1954–1956, 3 volumes.

EofM ....*Encyclopedia of Mormonism*, Daniel H. Ludlow, Editor, 1992, 2007, 4 volumes.

MDoc.......*Mormon Doctrine*, Bruce R. McConkie, Second Edition, 1st Printing, 1966.

SLSP.........*Salt Lake School of the Prophets Minute Book*, Salt Lake City, Utah, 1883.

T&S..........*Times and Seasons*, Newspaper, Nauvoo, Illinois, Joseph Smith, Editor, 1839–1846.

Sources

Allen, James B. "Eight Contemporary Accounts of Joseph Smith's First Vision—What Do We Learn from Them," *Improvement Era*. April 1970.

Allen, James B. Book Review of Grant H. Palmer's, "An Insider's View of Mormon Origins," *BYU Studies Quarterly*. Provo: Brigham Young University, 43:2, (April-June, 2002): pp. 175–190.

Allen, James B. and Leonard, Glen M. *The Story of the Latter-day Saints*. SLC: Deseret Book. 1976.

Anderson, Mary Audentia Smith. *Ancestry and Posterity of Joseph Smith and Emma Hale*, Independence, Missouri, 1929.

Anderson, Richard Lloyd. "Probing the Lives of Christ and Joseph Smith" *Review of Books on the Book of Mormon 1989–2011*, Provo: FARMS, vol. 21, issue 2, (2009): 1-29. https://scholarsarchive.byu.edu/msr/vol21/iss2/3.

Anderson, Richard Lloyd. "The Reliability of the Early History of Lucy and Joseph Smith," *Dialogue: A Journal of Mormon Thought*. Vol. 4 no. 2, (Summer 1969): 13–28.

Anderson, Richard L. (1969) "Circumstantial Confirmation of the First Vision through Reminiscences," *BYU Studies Quarterly*. Provo: Brigham Young University, Volume 9: Issue 3, (Spring), pp. 376–81.

Anderson, Richard Lloyd. "His Mother's Manuscript: An Intimate View of Joseph Smith," *Brigham Young University Forum,* address, (January 27, 1976).

Anderson, Richard L. "Joseph Smith's Testimony of the First Vision," *Ensign*. Salt Lake City, UT: The Church of Jesus Christ of Latter-day Saints, April 1996.

Ashurst-McGee, Mark. "A Pathway to Prophethood: Joseph Smith Junior as Rodsman, Village Seer, and Judeo-Christian Prophet," Master's thesis, Utah State University, 2000.

Backman, Milton V. Jr. (1969) "Awakenings in the Burned-over District: New Light on the Historic al Setting of the First Vision," *BYU Studies*, Provo: Brigham Young University, Volume 9: Issue 3 (Spring), pp. 1–15.

Backman, Milton V. Jr. "Confirming Witnesses of the First Vision," *Ensign*, January, 1986, accessed online, June 25, 2018, https://www.lds.org/ensign/ 1986/01/confirming-witnesses-of-the-first-vision?

Backman, Milton V. Jr. *Eyewitness Accounts of the Restoration*, Salt Lake City: Deseret Book, 1983, 1986, 239 pages.

Backman, Milton V. Jr. *Joseph Smith's First Vision: Confirming Evidences and Contemporary Accounts*, 2nd ed. Salt Lake City: Bookcraft, 1971, 1980. The quotation noted here comes from the second edition published in 1980.

Backman, Milton V. Jr. "Joseph Smith's Recitals of the First Vision," *Ensign*, January 1985, pp. 8–17.

Barker, James L., *Apostasy From The Divine Church*, SLC, UT: Kate Montgomery Barker, Publisher, 1960, 813 pages.

Bickmore, Barry Robert. Restoring The Ancient Church: Joseph Smith and Early Christianity, Ben Lomond, CA: FAIR, 1999. 391 pages.

Birdsall Richard D. "The Second Great Awakening and the New England Social Order." *Church History*, Minneapolis, MN: American Society of Church History, volume 39, Issue 3 (September, 1970; Reprinted: Cambridge University Press: 28 July 2009): 345–364.

Bringhurst, Newell G. *Fawn McKay Brodie: A Biographer's Life*. Norman: University of Oklahoma Press, 1999. xviii + 350 pages.

Brodie, Fawn McKay. *No Man Knows My History The Life of Joseph Smith*. New York: Alfred A. Knopf, 1945; Fawn M. Brodie, Second Edition, 1971, 1973, Vintage Books, 1995. 519 pages.

Brown and Holzapfel. *The Lost 500 Years*, SLC: Deseret Book, 2006, pp. 112–114.

Brown, Matthew B., *All Things Restored: Confirming the Authenticity of LDS Beliefs*, American Fork, UT: Covenant Communications, 2000, 274 pages.

Brown, S. Kent. "Biblical Egypt: Land of Refuge, Land of Bondage," *Ensign*, Sept. 1980.

Burnaby John, *The Belief of Christendom: A Commentary on the Nicene Creed*, London: National Society, S.P.C.K., 1959, 224 pages.

Bushman, Richard L. "A Joseph Smith for the Twenty-First Century." *Brigham Young University Studies*, volume 40, no. 3. (July 1, 2001): pp. 155–171.

Bushman, Richard L. Joseph Smith and the Beginnings of Mormonism. Urbana and Chicago: University of Illinois Press. Reprint edition, 1987.

Bushman, Richard Lyman. *Joseph Smith: Rough Stone Rolling.* New York: Knopf, 2005.

Campbell, Ted A., Christian Confessions: A Historical Introduction, Louisville, KY: Westminster John Knox Press, 1st edition (March 1, 1996)1996, 360 pages.

Cannon, Brian Q. and BYU Studies Staff. (1995-1996) "Priesthood Restoration Documents," *BYU Studies.* Volume 35: Issue 4, pp. 163-207, notes 25, 94.

Carroll, Warren H. *The Building of Christendom: A History of the Christian Church Volume 2*, West Chester, PA: Christendom Press, 1987, 618 pages.

Cheesman, Paul R. "An Analysis of the Accounts Relating to Joseph Smith's Early Visions." Master's thesis. College of Religious Instruction. Brigham Young University, 1965. Appendix D.

Clayton, William. *Journal*. July 12, 1843, William Clayton Letterbooks. Special Collections, J. Willard Marriott Library. University of Utah, Salt Lake City.

Cowdery, Oliver. October, 1834. *Messenger and Advocate.* Kirtland, Ohio: The Church of Jesus Christ of Latter-day Saints, volume 1, number 1. Oliver Cowdery to W. W. Phelps. Cowdery, Oliver. February 1835. *Messenger and Advocate*, volume 1, number 5. Oliver Cowdery to W.W. Phelps.

Crowther, Duane S. *The Prophecies of Joseph Smith.* Bountiful, UT: Horizon, 1983, Sixteenth Printing, 1997, 413 pages.

Curley, Edwin, Editor, Thomas Hobbes. *Leviathan*, Indianapolis, IN: Hackett Publishing Company; Notations and Selected Variants from 1668 Latin edition (March 1, 1994), 532 pages.

Davidson, Karen Lynn, Whittaker, David J., Ashurst-McGee, Mark, and Jensen, Richard L., editors. *The Joseph Smith Papers, Volume 1: Histories, 1832–1844.* The Church Historians Press: Salt Lake City, Utah, 2012.

Deseret News. Various editors and authors. Salt Lake City, Utah. 1931-2009.

Dorius, Guy L. "'Now This Caused Us to Marvel': The Breadth of God's Heaven and the Depth of His Mercy." *Joseph Smith and the Doctrinal Restoration.* Provo: Brigham Young University. Religious Studies Center, 2005.

Dow, Lorenzo. The Dealings of God, Man and the Devil, as Exemplified in the Life, Experience and Travels of Lorenzo Dow, In a Period of More than Half a Century. Norwich: William Faulkner, 1833.

Ehat, Andrew F. and Cook, Lyndon W. eds. *The Words of Joseph Smith.* Provo, Utah: Brigham Young University Religious Studies Center. 1980.

Eliason, Eric A. (2016) "Seer Stones, Salamanders, and Early Mormon 'Folk Magic' in the Light of Folklore Studies and Bible Scholarship," *BYU Studies Quarterly.* Provo: Brigham Young University. Volume 55: Issue 1, pp. 73–93.

Ehat, Andrew F. and Lyndon W. Cook, eds. *The Words of Joseph Smith.* Provo, UT: Bookcraft and Brigham Young University Religious Studies Center, 1980.

Enders, Donald L. "'A Snug Log House' A Historical Look at the Joseph Smith, Sr., Family Home in Palmyra, New York," *Ensign*, August 1985. https://www.lds.org/ensign/1985/08/a-snug-log-house.

Evans, Charles, D., "The Vision of Patriarch Charles D. Evans," *The Contributor*, S.L.C., Utah: Pub. Co. August, 1894, Vol. 15: No. 10, pp. 638–641.

Faulring, Scott H., editor. *An American Prophet's Record: The Diaries and Journals of Joseph Smith.* Salt Lake City: Signature Books in association with Smith Research Associates. 1987. pp. 3–8.

Faulring, Scott H. (2004) "An Examination of the 1829 "Articles of the Church of Christ" in Relation to Section 20 of the Doctrine and Covenants. *BYU Studies Quarterly.* Provo, UT: Brigham Young University. Volume 43: Issue 4, pp. 57–91.

Fluhman, J. Spencer. "Anti-Mormonism and the Question of Religious Authenticity," *Antebellum America: Journal of Religion & Society*. Provo, Utah: Brigham Young University, volume 7 (2005):1-9. Accessed at https://www. academia.edu/8184965/Anti-Mormonism_and_the_Question_of_Religious_Auth enticity_in_Antebellum_America.

Hamilton, Milton W. *The Country Printer: New York State*. 1785-1830. 2nd ed. Port Washington, Long Island, NY: Ira J. Friedman. 1964, p. 139 for quotation, p. 143 Cayuga's newspaper in 1827, as quoted in Norton, "Comparative Images," p. 249.

Harper, Steven C. 2005. "History Is People, Places, Sources, and Stories: An Interview with Milton V. Backman, Jr." *Mormon Historical Studies* 6, (Salt Lake City, UT: Mormon Historical Sites Foundation, Spring 2005): pp. 110–11.

Harper, Steven C. "Evaluating Three Arguments against Joseph Smith's First Vision," in *Exploring the First Vision*, ed. Samuel Alonzo Dodge and Steven C. Harper, Provo, UT: Religious Studies Center, 2012, pp. 307–323.

Harper, Steven C., *Joseph Smith's First Vision: A Guide to the Historical Accounts*, Salt Lake City: Deseret Book, 2012, 128 pages.

Hill, Donna. *Joseph Smith: The First Mormon*, New York: Doubleday, 1977. 527 pages.

Hinckley, President Gordon B. "God Hath Not Given Us the Spirit of Fear," *Ensign*, October, 1984.

Hinckley, President Gordon B. "Inspirational Thoughts," *Ensign*, August 1997.

Hopkins Richard R. *How Greek Philosophy Corrupted the Christian Concept of God*, Springville, UT: Horizon Publishers 1998, Cedar Fort, Inc., 2009, 464 pages.

Horsley, A. Burt. *Peter And The Popes*, Salt Lake City: Brigham University Religious Studies Center and Bookcraft, 1989, 152 pages.

Howe, Eber D. *Mormonism Unveiled*, Painsville, Ohio. 1834, 290 pages.

Hyde, Orson, Ein Ruf aus der Wüste, eine Stimme aus dem Schoose der Erde: Kurzer Ueberblick des Ursprungs und der Lehre der Kirche "Jesus Christ of Latter Day Saints" in Amerika, gekannt von Manchen unter der Benennung: "Die Mormonen" (A Cry out of the Wilderness: A Voice from the Bowels of the Earth: A Short Summary of the Origin and Teaching of the Church [of] "Jesus Christ of Latter Day Saints" in America, Known by Many Under the Name "the Mormons"), 115 pages. Im Selbstverlage des Verfassers (Self Published by the Author), Frankfurt, Germany, 1842. See also "Orson Hyde, Ein Ruf aus der Wüste, 1842," pp. 13-30, The Joseph Smith Papers, accessed July 26, 2018, http://www.joseph smithpapers.org/paper-summary/orson-hyde-ein-ruf-aus-der-wste-1842.

Jenson, Andrew, editor. *Historical Record,* 1886–1890. Salt Lake City: Deseret News, multi-volumes. Available at LDS Archives, Church History Library, SLC.

Jessee, Dean C., editor (1969) "The Early Accounts of Joseph Smith's First Vision," *BYU Studies Quarterly.* Provo, UT: BYU. Volume 9: Issue 3, pp. 275–94.

Jesse, Dean C., Ashurst-McGee, Mark and Jensen, Richard L., editors. *The Joseph Smith Papers,* Journals, Volume 1: 1832-1839, Salt Lake City: The Church Historian's Press, 2008, 506 pp. For references to other volumes of The Joseph Smith Papers, Documents, Histories, Journals, Revelations, Translations...see pp. 249–252ff.

Jessee, Dean C., editor. *The Papers of Joseph Smith,* 2 vols. Salt Lake City: Deseret Book, 1989–1992.

Jessee, Dean C., Compiler and Editor. *Personal Writings of Joseph Smith,* revised. Salt Lake City: Deseret Book; Provo, UT: Brigham Young University Press, 2002.

Jessee, Dean C. "The Earliest Documented Accounts of Joseph Smith's First Vision," and James B. Allen and John W. Welch, "The Appearance of the Father and the Son to Joseph Smith in 1820," in *Opening the Heavens.* Salt Lake City: Deseret Book, 2005.

Jessee, Dean C. (1971) "The Writing of Joseph Smith's History," *BYU Studies Quarterly.* Provo, UT: Brigham Young University. Volume 11: Issue. 4, Article 8. Available at: https://scholarsarchive.byu.edu/byusq/vol11/iss4/8.

Johnson, Paul E. A Shopkeeper's Millennium: Society and Revivals in Rochester, *New York, 1815-1837.* New York: Hill & Wang. 1978.

Joseph Smith to Oliver Cowdery. December 1834. *Messenger and Advocate,* volume 1, number 3. Kirtland, Ohio: The Church of Jesus Christ of Latter-day Saints.

Kenney, Scott G., Editor. "Vision of John Taylor," *Wilford Woodruff Journal*, Midvale, Utah: Signature Books, 1985, volume 7.

Krott, Rob (2000) "Pre-Columbian Archaeological Evidence of Cultural Contact between Norsemen and Native Americans," *Ancient American*, 5: no. 33, pp. 20–25.

Larkin, Clarence, *The Book of Daniel*, Glenside, PA: C. Larkin Estate, 1929, 267 pages.

Laurence Richard, translator. *THE BOOK OF ENOCH* FROM THE ETHIOPIC [1 Enoch], reprinted from the 1821 and 1882 editions, Thousand Oaks, CA: Artisan Sales, 1980, 92 pages.

Latimer, E. The Three Brothers: Sketches of the Lives of Rev. Aurora Seager, Rev. Micah Seager, Rev. Schuyler Seager, D.D., New York: Phillips & Hunt, 1880, p. 12 (for Aurora's death in 1819), pp. 21-22 for quotations, including his 1818 "diary." Latourette, Kenneth S. *A History of Christianity: Volume I: Beginnings to 1500*, Revised, New York: Harper Collins, 1975, 724 pages.

Marquardt, H. Michael and Walters, Wesley P. *Inventing Mormonism: Tradition and the Historical Record.* San Francisco: Smith Research Associates, distributed by Signature Books Press, 1998. This is a revisionist and unbelieving source.

MacKay, Michael Hubbard and Frederick, Nicholas J. *Joseph Smith's Seer Stones.* Salt Lake City: Brigham Young University & Deseret Book. 2016, 243 pages.

McConkie, Bruce R "Joseph Smith---The Mighty Prophet of the Restoration," *Ensign*. Salt Lake City: The Church of Jesus Christ of Latter-day Saints. April 1976.

McConkie, Bruce R. *Mormon Doctrine*, Salt Lake City, UT: Bookcraft, 1966 Second Edition, 856 pages. This is the 1966 green hardbound 2nd Ed., 1st Printing.

Meade, George Robert Stow, Editor and Translator. *Pistis Sophia*, London: The Theosophical Publishing Society, 1896.

Midgley, Louis. "The Legend and Legacy of Fawn Brodie." *FARMS Review of Books.* Neal A. Maxwell Institute. Provo: BYU. volume 13, number 1, (2001). pp. 21–71. ISSN: 2168-3123 (online) Review of *Fawn McKay Brodie: A Biographer's Life* (1999), by Newell G. Bringhurst.

Minutes of the Annual Conferences of the Methodist Episcopal Church, For the Years 1773-1828. Volume 1. New York: Mason and Lane, Pub., 1840, 574 pages.

Morton, William A. From Plowboy To Prophet, Mother Stories from the Book of Mormon. SLC: Deseret Book Co., 1912, 1952.

Nibley, Preston, editor. *The History of Joseph Smith By His Mother Lucy Mack Smith*, Salt Lake City: Bookcraft, 1958.

Nibley, Hugh W. No Ma'am, That's Not History, A Brief Review of Mrs. Brodie's Reluctant Vindication of a Prophet She Seeks to Expose. Published in Tinkling Cymbals and Sounding Brass. Volume 11, The Collected Works of Hugh Nibley. Salt Lake City: Deseret Book and FARMS. 1991, pp. 3–52.

Nicholson, Roger. "The Cowdery Conundrum: Oliver's, Aborted Attempt to Describe Joseph Smith's First Vision in 1834 and 1835," Interpreter, *A Journal Of Mormon Scripture.* (volume 8, 2014), pp. 27-44. Accessed online by this title.

Oaks, Dallin H., Testimony Before US House of Representatives, H.R. 2797, May 13, 1992 and US Senate, S. 2969, September 18, 1992, Congressional Record, Washington, D.C. Online: https://www.justice.gov/sites/default/files/jmd/ legacy/2014/07/13/hear-99-1992.pdf; https://www.justice.gov/sites/default/files/jm d/legacy/2014/02/13/hear-j-102-82-1992.pdf.

Palmer, Grant H. *An Insider's View of Mormon Origins.* Salt Lake City: Signature Books, 2002. A former church member's attempt to prove Joseph Smith did not see God or the Savior and that he made up the Book of Mormon.

Palmyra Register, Palmyra, Wayne County, N.Y., (1817-1821). Weekly. *Palmyra Herald and Canal Advertiser.* Palmyra, Wayne County, 1822-1823. Weekly. New York State Newspapers List at http://www.nysl.nysed.gov/nysnp/.

Pamphilus, Eusebius. *Ecclesiastical History.* Written in 324 A.D., translated by the University of Pennsylvania Department of History. Circa 1897-1907.

Petersen, Mark E., *Malachi and the Great and Dreadful Day*, SLC: Utah, Deseret Book Company, 1983, 76 pages.

Porter, Larry C. "A Study of the Origins of the Church of Jesus Christ of Latter-day Saints in the States of New York and Pennsylvania, 1816–1831." PhD diss., Brigham Young University, 1971.

Pratt, Orson [an original 1835 apostle]. "A[N] INTERESTING ACCOUNT OF SEVERAL REMARKABLE VISIONS, AND OF THE LATE DISCOVERY of ANCIENT AMERICAN RECORDS.," Edinburgh, Scotland, September 1840. Church History Library, Salt Lake City, Utah. See also, "Appendix: Orson Pratt, A[n] Interesting Account of Several Remarkable Visions..., 1840," pp. 2–5, The Joseph Smith Papers, accessed July 26, 2018, http://www.josephsmithpapers.org/paper-summary/appendix-orson-pratt-an-interesting-account-of-several-remarka ble-visions-1840.

Pratt, Orson. "Two Days' Meeting at Brigham City, (June 27, 1874)," *Millennial Star*, Liverpool, England. (August 11, 1874).

"Preface" to the *Book of Mormon*, ca. August 1829 [published 1830], Documents series of *The Joseph Smith Papers*. 2013, volume 1, p. 93.

Proctor, Scot Facer and Proctor, and Maurine Jensen Proctor, editors. *The Revised and Enhanced History of Joseph Smith by his Mother*, Salt Lake City: Bookcraft. 1996, 506 pp. with editor's introduction, appendixes, family genealogical charts, and index.

Proctor, Scot and Maurine. "The 19th Century Controversy about Lucy Mack Smith's History of Her Son, Joseph" *Meridian Magazine*. Salt Lake City. (January 2, 2001).

Prothero, Stephen. American Jesus: How the Son of God Became a National Icon. New York: Farrar, Straus and Giroux. 2003.

Quinn, D. Michael. *Early Mormonism and the Magic World View*, Salt Lake City: Signature Books, 1987.

Quinn, D. Michael. "JOSEPH SMITH'S EXPERIENCE OF A METHODIST "CAMP-MEETING" IN 1820," *Dialogue* Internet E-Paper #3, July 12, 2006. Enlarged December 20, 2006. Accessed online at https://www.dialogue journal.com/wpcontent/uploads/2010/04/QuinnPaperless.Pdf.

Ratzinger, Joseph Cardinal. *Catechism Of The Catholic Church*. New York: Doubleday, 1994, 1997, 826 pages.

Reeve, Rex C. "Joseph Smith, the Chosen Instrument," *Ensign*, October 1985.

Salamander Society Interviews of Fawn M. Brodie, California State University at Fullerton, Center for Oral and Public History, n. d. http://www.salamandersociety. com/interviews/fawnbrodie/. Accessed internet version on March 20, 2018.

Schmuhl, Albert F. *The Royal Line*: chart prepared for the New York Stake Genealogical Board, Church of Jesus Christ of Latter-day Saints centennial exhibition, LDS Family History Library, SLC, Utah. March, 1936. Summary: Pedigree chart showing the Biblical and royal ancestry of various families of American leaders such as Washington and church leaders including the Smith, Richards, Hanks, Grant, Lyman, Whitney families of the Church of Jesus Christ of Latter-day Saints.

Shipps, Jan. *Sojourner in the Promised Land: Forty Years among the Mormons.* University of Illinois Press. 2000.

Smith, George Albert. "History of George Albert Smith." MS, Church History Library. Salt Lake City, Utah and BYU Special Collections. Provo, Utah.

Smith, Joseph Fielding, author. McConkie, Bruce R., compiler. *Doctrines of Salvation*, Salt Lake City, UT: Bookcraft, 3 volumes, 1954, 1955, 1956.

Smith, Joseph Fielding. *TEACHINGS of the PROPHET JOSEPH SMITH*, Salt Lake City: Deseret Book Company, 1977, 437 pages.

Smith, Joseph, et. al. Manuscript History of the Church, 1838–1856, six large volumes, in the handwriting of George Robinson, James Mulholland, Willard Richards, Brigham Young, Heber C. Kimball, George A. Smith, Wilford Woodruff, and at least ten clerks or scribes, LDS Archives, Church History Library, S.L.C., Utah.

Smith, Joseph Jr. [First Vision account of 1832 in his own handwriting], "History, circa Summer 1832," p. 1-3 (manuscript); Davidson, Karen L., Whittaker, David J., Ashhurst-McGee, Mark and Jenson, Richard L., Editors, *The Joseph Smith Papers, Histories, volume 1.* Salt Lake City: The Church Historians Press. 2012. pp. 2-23 (printed volume); "History, circa Summer 1832," p. 1-3. *The Joseph Smith Papers* accessed January 2, 2018. Online at: http://www.josephsmithpapers. org/paper-summary/history-circa-summer-1832/3.

Smith, Joseph. *Joseph Smith---History* 1:1-75, *The Pearl of Great Price.* Salt Lake City: The Church Of Jesus Christ Of Latter Day Saints. 1979, 1988.

Smith, Joseph. "Church History," in *Times and Seasons*. Nauvoo, IL. 1 Mar. 1842, vol. 3, no. 9, whole no. 45, pp. 706–710; edited by Joseph Smith Jr.; includes typeset signature. The copy used for transcription is currently part of a bound volume held at Church History Library. Source for 1838 account of Joseph Smith's First Vision in 1820 at Palmyra, New York.

Smith, Joseph, et al. Authors, Roberts, B. H., Intro & Notes, *Documentary History of the Church of Jesus Christ of Latter-day Saints (DHC)*, Salt Lake City, Utah: Deseret News Press. 1902-1912, 1966-1970. 7 volumes.

Smith, Joseph. Dean C. Jessee, Ronald K. Esplin, Richard Lyman Bushman, General Editors, *The Joseph Smith Papers, Documents, Journals, Revelations and Translations, Histories*, multiple volumes. Salt Lake City: The Church Historians Press. 2008–2020.

Smith, Lucy Mack. *History, 1844–1845*; handwriting of Martha Jane Knowlton Coray and Howard Coray; 240 pages, with miscellaneous inserted pages; Church History Library, SLC, Utah. Because this manuscript is a "rough draft," most citations to Lucy Mack Smith's History in this book are taken from the "fair copy" or "revised manuscript" of 1845, the 1902 corrected edition by George A. Smith and Elias Smith, the 1948 Preston Nibley edition, and the 1996 Proctor edition, which respective bibliographies are included in this bibliography.

Professor Glen M. Leonard of BYU wrote, "Though the aging Lucy Smith stayed behind in the removal from Nauvoo, her family story remained of great interest to the saints. Many times before that final public commentary, Lucy had responded to invitations to speak of her son Joseph's early religious experiences. To save her lungs, she said, and at the invitation of the Twelve, she invited Martha Jane Knowlton Coray to record her memoirs. Lucy's dictations during the winter of 1844–45 resulted in what is now called the *preliminary manuscript* of her history.

From this 214-page manuscript, Coray and her husband, Howard, one of the Prophet's former scribes, trimmed perhaps 10 percent and added material from Joseph's own history, published not long before in the *Times and Seasons*. The product was a *revised manuscript*, "History of Mother Smith by Herself." In securing a copyright on the work, Lucy identified it as 'The History of Lucy Smith…'" (Glen M. Leonard, Reviewer, Scot and Maurine Proctor, "The Revised and Enhanced History of Joseph Smith by His Mother," *Brigham Young University Studies Journal*, volume 38, number 1 (1996): n.p., italics added). Smith,

Lucy Mack, *History, 1845*; handwriting of Howard Coray and Martha Jane Knowlton Coray; 337 pages; Church History Library, SLC, Utah. This *History* is also known as the "fair copy" or "revised manuscript" of 1845.

Author's Note 1: "Lucy Mack Smith, the mother of Joseph Smith, dictated a rough draft version of her history to Martha Jane Knowlton Coray (with some additional scribal help from Martha's husband, Howard) beginning in 1844 and concluding in 1845. In 1845, the Corays inscribed this fair copy [a revised manuscript from the "rough draft"] of the history under Lucy's direction." Online source note: http://www.Josephsmithpapers.org/paper-summary/lucy-mack-smith-history-1845/1#ft-source-note.

Author's Note 2: The Corays created two copies of the "revised manuscript" or "fair copy" of Lucy's history which were completed in late 1845. One copy was given to Mother Smith, the other went west with the Brethren and Saints when they left Nauvoo, Illinois. Years before Lucy Mack Smith died in 1855, her copy of the revised manuscript went to her son William Smith, and from William to Arthur Milliken, Lucy's son-in-law, then to A.W. Babbitt, Esq., and from Babbitt to Isaac Sheen a member living in Michigan who sold it to Elder Orson Pratt as he went East to his mission in Liverpool, England.

Elder Pratt then independently published Lucy's history of her family and Joseph Smith in 1853 without the consent of the Church or of President Brigham Young (Scot Facer Proctor and Maurine Jensen Proctor, editors. *The Revised and Enhanced History of Joseph Smith By His Mother*, SLC: Bookcraft. 1996, p. xxiii).

Smith, Lucy Mack. Biographical Sketches of Joseph Smith the Prophet, and His Progenitors for Many Generations, Liverpool: S.W. Richards, 1853.

Smith, Lucy Mack. George A. Smith and Elias Smith, editors. *HISTORY OF THE Prophet Joseph BY HIS MOTHER LUCY SMITH AS REVISED BY George A. Smith and Elias Smith.* Salt Lake City: Improvement Era: Salt Lake City, 1902.

Smith, Lucy Mack. *Hist. of Joseph Smith by His Mother.* SLC: Stevens and Wallis. 1945.

Smith, William B., "William Smith on Mormonism," Lamoni, IA: Herald Steam Book and Job Office, [1883]. Published in Dan Vogel, editor, *Early Mormon Documents,* Salt Lake City: Signature Books. 1996–2003, 5 volumes. 1:494–495.

Stark,Rodney. *The Rise of Christianity*. Princeton University Press. 1996.

Shellnutt, Kate, "Get Ready, Youth Group Leaders: Teens Twice as Likely to Identify as Atheist or LGBT—Barna findings on Generation Z pose new challenges for the church.," *Christianity Today*, January 23, 2018. Internet article accessed on April 22, 2018. https://www.christianitytoday.com/news/2018/january/youth-group-leaders-generation-z-atheist-lgbt-teens-barna.html.

Stephenson, Shirley E., "Fawn Mckay Brodie: An Oral History Interview." *Dialogue A Journal of Mormon Thought*. Arlington: Virginia, Summer 1981. volume 14, no. 2, p. 106. Center for Oral and Public History, California State University at Fullerton, Shirley E. Stephenson's interview with Fawn M. Brodie, Nov. 30, 1975. pp. 99–116.

Stowell, Josiah Jr. Letter to John S. Fullmer. 17 February 1843. Ashurst-McGee, Mark (1999) "The Josiah Stowell Jr.–John S. Fullmer Correspondence," *BYU Studies Quarterly*. Provo, UT: Brigham Young University. Volume 38: Issue. 3, Article 10. Available at: https://scholarsarchive.byu.edu/byusq/vol38/iss3/10.

Taylor, John. 1844. "Ancient Ruins," *Times and Seasons*, vol. 5, no. 23. Dec. 15.

Taylor, John, Author, G. Homer Durham, Editor, *The Gospel Kingdom*, SLC: Deseret Book Co., (1st Edition 1887), 2002, 448 pages.

The Ante-Nicene Fathers, Translations of the Writings of the Fathers Down to AD 325. Edited by Alexander Roberts and James Donaldson. 10 vols. 1885–1887. Repr., 1968, New York: Christian Literature Publishing Co., 1885.

Tucker, Pomeroy. *Origin, Rise, and Progress of Mormonism* New York: D. Appleton and Co., 1867.

Turley, Richard E. Jr., Jensen, Robin S. and Ashurst-McGee, Mark. "Joseph the Seer." *Ensign*. SLC: The Church of Jesus Christ of Latter-day Saints. Oct., 2015.

Underwood, Grant. *The Millenarian World of Early Mormonism*. Urbana: The University of Illinois Press. 1993.

Vogel, Dan, *Early Mormon Documents, Volume 1*, S.L.C., UT: Signature Books, 1996, 724 pages.

Walker, Steven C. "Seer," Ludlow, Daniel, H., Editor. *Encyclopedia of Mormonism*, New York: Macmillan Publishing Company, 1992.

Walters, Ronald G. *American Reformers, 1815-1860*, American Century Series. New York: Hill and Wang, 1978.

Walters Wesley P. 1969. "New Light on Mormon Origins, From the Palmyra Revival," Dialogue: A Journal of Mormon Thought, Volume 4, Number 2.

Walters, Wesley P. *New Light on Mormon Origins*. El Cajon, CA: Mormonism Research Ministry, 1967.

Walters, Wesley P. "Joseph Smith's Bainbridge. N.Y. Court Trials." *The Westminster Theological Journal*, (1974. volume 36, number 2), pp. 123–155.

Walters, Wesley P. "From Occult to Cult With Joseph Smith, Jr." *The Journal of Pastoral Practice*, 1977. 1 (2), pp. 121–137.

Welch, John W. Editor. Opening the Heavens, Accounts of Divine Manifestations, *1820-1844*. Provo and Salt Lake City: Brigham Young University Press and Deseret Book. 2005. 500 pages.

Widtsoe, John A., compiler, *Discourses of Brigham Young*, Provo, Utah: Deseret Book Company. 1954. 498 pages.

Wilden, Steven A. (2014) "The Gnostic Presence in Ancient Michigan," *Ancient American*. Volume 18, number 105, pp. 35–39.

Index

A

B

C

D

E

F

G

H

K

L

M

P

Q

R

S

T

U

V

About the Author

Steven Anthony Wilden received a bachelor's degree in History from Brigham Young University in 1980. He later took courses from California State University and earned a master's degree in History from George Wythe College in 1999. The following year he passed the California Architect's Examination and in 2001 became a registered architect. Steve's articles on the history of archaeology and the Smithsonian Institute, ancient American artifacts, and Gnosticism related to cultural diffusion have been published in *Ancient American* magazine. The Gnosticism article was published also in the book, *The Lost History of Ancient America*. Steve is married to the former Evelyne Cattin of Lausanne, Switzerland.

For comments or more information about the book and author:

stevenwilden@gmail.com
theseerofpalmyra.com